1990/1991 Edition

By the staff of Berlitz Guides
A Macmillan Company

How to use our guide

These 256 pages cover the **highlights of Algeria,** grouped by region. Although not exhaustive, our selection of sights will enable you to make the best of your trip.

Places of interest are described between pages 45 and 194. Those most highly recommended are flagged by the Berlitz traveller symbol.

The **Where to Go** section on page 38 will help you plan your visit according to the time available.

For **general background information** see sections Algeria and the Algerians (p. 8), Facts and Figures (p. 18), History (p. 20), and Historical Landmarks (p. 36).

Sports, shopping, entertainment and **eating out** are found on pages 198 to 215.

The **practical information,** hints and tips that will come in handy for your trip begin on page 218. This section is arranged alphabetically for easy reference.

The **map section** at the back of the book (pp. 242–251) will help you find your way around and locate the principal sights.

Sketch maps of specific sites or itineraries can be found in the relevant sections.

Finally, if there is anything you cannot find, look in the complete index (pp. 252–256).

CONTENTS

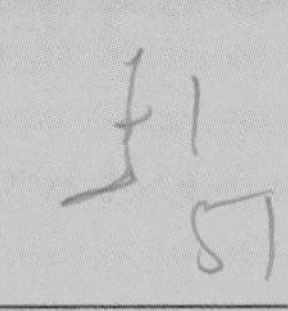

CONTENTS

Cover photo: Beni Abbès (Pierre Kunz)

Text:	Martin Gostelow
Staff Editors:	Eileen Harr-Kyburz and Earleen Brunner
Layout:	Veronique Pasche
Photography:	Bernard Joliat
	Ian Hamel (p. 125)
	Martin Gostelow (p. 167)
Sketch maps:	Max Thommen
Cartography:	Falk-Verlag, Hamburg

Acknowledgements
We would like to thank Anne-Karin Ratna, Gerard Chaillon, and the Entreprise Nationale du Livre in Algeria for their invaluable help in the preparation of this book.

Found an error or an omission in this Berlitz Guide? Or a change or new feature we should know about? Our editor would be happy to hear from you, and a postcard would do. Be sure to include your name and address, since in appreciation for a useful suggestion, we'd like to send you a free travel guide.

Although we make every effort to ensure the accuracy of all the information in this book, changes occur incessantly. We cannot therefore take responsibility for facts, prices, addresses and circumstances in general that are constantly subject to alteration.

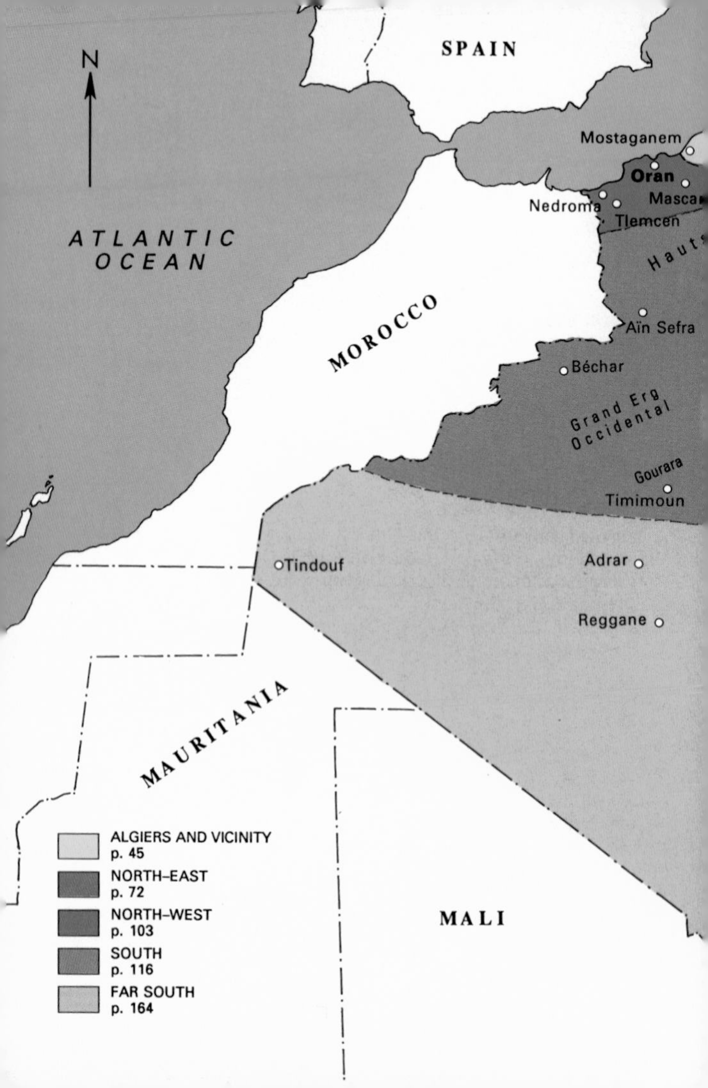
SPAIN
N
ATLANTIC
OCEAN
MOROCCO
Mostaganem
Oran
Masca
Nedroma
Tlemcen
Hauts
Aïn Sefra
Béchar
Grand Erg
Occidental
Gourara
Timimoun
Tindouf
Adrar
Reggane
MAURITANIA
MALI
ALGIERS AND VICINITY
p. 45
NORTH–EAST
p. 72
NORTH–WEST
p. 103
SOUTH
p. 116
FAR SOUTH
p. 164

Tipasa
ALGIERS
Bejaïa
Jijel
Annaba
Djemila
Tizi Ouzou
Djurdjura
Constantine
Sétif
Bou Saada
Aurès
Tebessa
Plateaux
Biskra
Djebel Amour
Touggourt
El Oued
M'zab
Ghardaïa
Grand Erg Oriental
El Goléa
SICILY
MEDITERRANEAN SEA
TUNISIA
LIBYA
In Aménas
In Salah
Tassili N'Ajjer
Djanet
Tefedest
Assekrem
Tazrouk
Tamanrasset
Hoggar
NIGER
0 100 200 300 400 500 km
0 100 200 300 miles

ALGERIA AND THE ALGERIANS

A universe within one nation, Algeria is so full of variety that whole continents cannot match it. The landscapes have few rivals on earth—or on the moon.

An area roughly equal to that of Western Europe seems to contain more than its fair share of the wonders of the world. Some days you could be forgiven for feeling that five extraordinary things before lunchtime are enough and you need to pause and recover.

Above all it's the extreme

contrasts that never fail to impress. The Algiers Kasbah and some of the newer suburbs have so many people crammed into them, but the Sahara has one of the lowest population densities anywhere, at about two people per square mile (fewer than one person per square kilometre). More surprisingly, in the high plains between the Atlas mountain ranges you can drive for hours without seeing a soul. Then,

Beauties of this land—from a radiant Taghit oasis to the soft smile of a Ghardaïan.

perhaps, a lone shepherd wrapped in his hooded woollen cloak will wave you down just to exchange greetings. City dwellers can be impatient: nomads have all the time in the world.

In Algeria, the most ancient and the most modern stand side by side: solar-powered electric pumps draw water from the depths of the desert only a spear throw away from Stone Age engravings in a rock face. The past is all around them, but Algerians don't much concern themselves with it. They take a vaguely possessive pride in the famous sights that foreigners come so far to see, but you don't get the impression that Roman cities, still less Neolithic paintings, are of consuming interest. The demands of daily life are just too great for most people.

Two explosive events in the past *are* of supreme importance to Algerians, and they're separated by 13 centuries. The first was conversion to Islam following the arrival of the Arabs in the 680s, and the second, the revolt against French domination which climaxed with independence in 1962.

The speed with which the new religion of Islam spread from Arabia to the Atlantic never ceases to amaze. The Berber people of these parts withstood invasion, as they always have, but soon embraced the faith and helped to spread it. Indeed it was a succession of leaders and ascetics from the mountains and deserts of North Africa who launched movements and dynasties that ruled from Egypt to Spain for long stretches over the next thousand years. There was a consistent refusal to compromise. Whole sects marched off into the desert rather than do so, and this ingrained stubbornness still shows up as a national characteristic. On the other hand, it was Islam with its lack of racial prejudice that unified all the varied peoples of the region.

Islam and the duties of a believer are all-important factors in everyday life: the profession of faith in one God, and Mohammed his prophet; prayer five times a day when the muezzin is heard (although, sadly, his call has long since been committed to cassette tape); charity towards the less fortunate; and observance of the lunar month of Ramadan by fasting and self-denial during daylight hours.

For those who took part, the struggle for liberation from France seems like only yesterday. But the majority are too young to remember anything of it at all, and they won't be satisfied with living on past glories. In the heady early years after 1962, Algeria's revolution was a model for others. Then the oil and gas boom allowed rapid industrialization. Algeria's good offices were sought by great powers trying to solve international disputes. Today's world of lower oil prices is much harsher and less optimistic. What is remarkable is the extent to which reconciliation has been achieved with France: there is little public or private bitterness. "That page is turned", the Algerians say.

Concentrating after independence on industry, housing for a burgeoning population (which has almost trebled since 1962) and education, Algeria paid little attention to tourism. While neighbouring countries of the Mediterranean encouraged millions of foreigners annually, and inevitably changed in character as a result, Algeria was the exception. A few imaginatively designed hotels were built—and not very well maintained thereafter. Several modern coastal resorts set out to satisfy seekers after sun and sports, but they have mostly attracted local people who find it difficult to travel abroad because their currency is not convertible. So although you'll meet many Algerians, especially students eager for a conversation, you will only rarely see groups of foreign visitors. So much the better, because it means that Algeria is still an adventure.

Should frontier officials seem rather on their dignity or a little distant, be patient. You will find that ordinary people in general are among the most helpful, friendly and polite that you could hope to meet anywhere. Once they come to know and like you, Algerians are firm friends, and hospitality is a way of life such that you will find it hard to return it in equal measure. Your efforts to do so will only be immediately outmatched.

If you can use a few words of Arabic, even if only the polite phrases of greeting, "please" and "thank you", by all means do so. But it may not be worth the trouble to learn Arabic. This is not only because of the difficulty of the language (remember the old joke: Every word in Arabic has three meanings: the basic meaning, the exact opposite, and some part of a camel's anatomy). Nor the fact that the local dialect will doubtless be unlike the one you learned. It's because nine times out of ten the reply will come in French, which is very widely spoken and understood. More Algerians still read a French-language daily newspaper than an Arabic one. And you should remember that for many people, their first language is Kabyle or another of the Berber dialects.

Most street names are in Arabic script alone, however, so you will need maps and frequent help. Aid may come from one of the many younger men who have worked for some time in London, Frankfurt, Rome or Paris. Connections with Europe are still strong, and the Mediterranean remains a link, not a barrier. It was always so; the southern land frontier was the impregnable one. Macho motor rallies only serve to point up the fact that the desert crossing is still a challenge.

Behind the coast, flat and fertile in places, steep and rocky in others, the parallel ranges of the Atlas are cut through by deep gorges and tumbling streams fed from the snows of mountain peaks (yes, there is skiing). Cedar, cork and chestnut trees share the foothills with springtime wildflowers in a profusion now forgotten in lands ruled by herbicides. Orange groves of scented blossom, apricot orchards and vineyards fill the sheltered valleys. Ambitious reafforestation schemes using drought-resistant pines are to be seen everywhere in the mountains. The High Plateaux that separate the two ranges are a green sea of esparto grass rippling like silk in the wind.

Then, south of the Atlas, the land descends again to another "sea", that greatest of all deserts, the Sahara. As the heat haze generates mirages at noon, so your imagination conjures visions of remote forts inhabited by the ghosts of lost armies, of sudden oases and their groves of palm trees, of camel caravans led by the mysterious Tuareg, the "blue men" whose heavy indigo-dyed headcloths stained their faces. And the dreams are all true, though only bats occupy most of the forts nowadays, and indigo is scarce.

Oasis towns look like perfect cubist paintings, blocks of pale blue and ochre, white and rust red, apparently piled one upon the other. Rising over them are tall, clay-plastered minarets, some topped with a whole ostrich egg. Architecture seems to have grown organically from the landscape, using whatever materials were available on the spot. Building styles

The contemporary face of Algeria, in this sweeping view over Oran.

are perfectly adapted to the climate. Labyrinthine earth-walled *ksour* (villages) are a maze of sandy alleyways shaded by roofs of mud-brick vaulting supported by palm trunks. The width of the alleys was actually determined by the length of trunk which didn't sag, and in places the roofing is so effective that people have to call out to avoid bumping into each other in the darkness. Front doors of private houses are set right in the alleys, just

Mirages

Across the burning sands a thirsty explorer is crawling towards... a lake, a grove of palm trees, a shimmering white city. Just a mirage, no doubt, but what exactly is this phenomenon, or to be more precise, what causes it?

A mirage is an optical illusion caused by refraction of light as it passes through atmosphere of varying density. Objects in the distance may be distorted or raised above their normal position. Besides the desert, any hot road in summer will produce the same results, when the intensely hot air near the surface of the ground bends the light upward. The most usual mirage is that of a sheet of water, which in fact is an image of the sky. Occasionally, light from a tree, for example, produces an inverted image of a tree, as if reflected in a pool.

The other kind of mirage occurs when light is bent the opposite way in layers of colder air—this is normally seen only over cold seas!

as they are in the traditional *kasbah*, or citadel quarter, but even when the doors are open, you can see nothing of the interior of the house. The passageway is invariably bent at right angles at least once. This need for privacy, even secrecy, is often said—by Algerians as well—to be reflected in the temperament of the people. Whether that is so or not, it is seldom that strangers are invited to private houses. If you are, of course, the rules of generous hospitality prevail.

Oases mean date palms by the ten thousand, some planted

The solution to carrying both babies and baskets, far south in Djanet.

in deeply dug craters so that their roots can reach subterranean water courses because, surprisingly, they need plenty of moisture. Sand excavated from the craters forms another paradox—man-made dunes, as if there weren't enough of the natural variety. And if you thought "a date is a date is a date", think again: there are over 50 varieties, led by the *deglet nour* (finger of light). Exported in flat, round-ended boxes, they have given generations of Western children their first hazy ideas of the Sahara—and they taste even better on their home ground. In autumn, Algeria even has its own pyramids: massive piles of dates in the markets of oasis towns.

The desert has ensnared many travellers. You are most likely to join them if you experience these vast, open spaces at dawn and especially dusk, for then the scents are stronger, the air seems lighter and the colours glow in shades of gold, peach and violet. People here have adapted to the extremes of their environment and so must the visitor, seeking shade from the fiercest sun but being

FACTS AND FIGURES

Geography: Algeria is as big as the whole of Western Europe, with a land mass of about 2,380,000 sq. km. (c. 920,000 sq. mi.). Bordered by the other two nations of the Maghreb—Morocco to the west and Tunisia to the east—it is much larger than either, taking the lion's share of the Sahara Desert. Except where great "seas" of sand dunes *(erg)* have covered it up, the land is veined by the beds of countless ancient rivers. Some must once have been rivals of the Nile itself. Although water rarely flows on the surface now, it can lie just underneath—plentiful enough to sustain lush oases of palms. In the far south-east, near the border with Libya, the land rises to the Tassili N'Ajjer, a 1,700-m. (5,500-ft.)-high rocky plateau cut by erosion into a criss-cross pattern of chasms. Further south still, the convoluted mountains and volcanic stumps of the Hoggar massif reach up to about 3,000 m. (9,800 ft.). Bounded by 1,200 km. (745 mi.) of Mediterranean coastline, Algeria stretches some 2,000 km. (1,200 mi.) south to the borders of Mali and Niger. The ranges of the Atlas Tellien (Tell Atlas) and the Atlas Saharien (Saharan Atlas) run parallel to the coast, rising to peaks of over 2,300 m. (7,500 ft.). Between lies a fertile region, the Hauts (High) Plateaux.

Population: c. 26 million. About half are under age 16.

Capital: Algiers *(El Djezaïr)* c. 3 million

Major Cities: Oran c. 1 million; Constantine 750,000; Annaba 450,000; Tizi Ouzou 350,000; Sétif 200,000; Tlemcen 200,000.

Government: The Democratic Popular Republic of Algeria was declared on September 25, 1962. The Front of National Liberation (FLN), heir to the victorious movement that led the struggle for independence, had been the sole political party for more than 25 years. Following the events of October 1988, a third constitution was adopted in February 1989, which set up a multi-party system. The president is elected for 5 years and presides over a council of ministers. He is assisted by the head of the National Assembly.

At the regional level the country is divided into provinces *(wilaya),* with an elected assembly which has considerable powers of decision over matters of agriculture, education, health and so on.

Religion: Islam is the state religion, followed by well over 90% of the population. Of these, most are of the Sunni persuasion. There is a very small Christian minority.

prepared for crystal-cold winter nights, too, with ten times more stars than a city dweller has ever seen and meteor showers like spent rockets. Weird, flickering flames on the horizon signal the burning off of waste from oil and gas wells that keep Algeria in the major league of producers. In part, it was the decline of oil prices in the early 1980s that concentrated government minds on other sources of revenue, including thinking again about tourism.

In the far south, 2½ hours' flying time from Algiers in one of Air Algérie's jets, you can take a four-wheel-drive vehicle from Tamanrasset to the magical Hoggar massif, a land of the strangest volcanic upthrusts of contorted rock rearing to some 3,000 metres (about 10,000 ft.). This is no empty land: tracks of lizards and snakes, small rodents, delicate, huge-eared little fennec foxes and gazelles mark the harshest terrain. The evidence is all around of a time when there was enough rainfall to fill the rivers and support prolific vegetation and animal life. Early man was here and left stone axes and flint arrowheads that can still be found scattered about. From a much earlier geological period, ammonite fossils suggest that part of the area was once under the sea.

Visit the proud but friendly Tuareg people and you may be lucky enough to see a camel race, a hilarious melee of flailing legs and yelling riders. These dromedaries seem able to race in only one gear, a rolling gangling gait that all the efforts of jockeys and supporters fail to affect. Wheeled safaris, trekking and camping, sleeping in tents or under the stars in the extraordinary Hoggar will run you out of adjectives but leave you with memories, and probably photographs, of sights that are "out of this world". Because of the altitude and the dry air, the climate is not unbearably hot, and winter days can be idyllic. Perhaps the southern Sahara may be the health resort of the next century.

As if the Hoggar were not the last word, away to the east more mountain heights mark another unique treasure, the Tassili N'Ajjer. Deep ravines and sandstone pinnacles conceal rocky overhangs where, more than 6,000 years ago, Neolithic men painted the scenes that filled their lives. Giraffes, antelopes and ostriches, fish from the rivers, domestic cattle and beautifully sinuous dancers adorn rock walls. Tens of thousands of these pictures decorate an amazing 13,000 square kilometres (5,000 sq. mi.) that are recognized as "the greatest open-air art gallery in the world". You can only reach the area by walking, with a guide to prevent you from enlisting in the legion of the lost, and with donkeys to carry your load.

"Algeria goes to your head", they say. All those contrasts, all that variety. One of Air Algérie's internal flights may provide a metaphor: hard to get a seat, absolutely full, take-off time not certain, but pretty reliable. One day's flight might be postponed because of sand-storms, but it'll get there in the end. Look at your fellow passengers. They're a microcosm of the wonderful national mixture: keen students going back to college, businessmen in smooth suits, swaggering soldiers, veiled woman in a *haïk* with only one eye showing, young lady in the latest fashion, ancient granny from Constantine with a white embroidered handkerchief over her mouth, venerable sage in a brown burnous, haughty Tuareg and stocky, black-robed M'Zabite trader. Plus, because this is Algeria, plenty of children. And you, a rare outsider but politely accepted by them all.

HISTORY

Algeria's complex history has an extraordinary physical presence. In the oases, you'll find some shopkeepers offering you a basketful of stone axes to rummage through, pieces made by Palaeolithic hunters; or a small boy will show you the matchbox full of flint arrowheads, razor sharp, that he has collected from the desert, dating from between 6000 and 1500 B.C., broadly the Neolithic period.

It seems that in those days the climate was much wetter south of the Atlas mountain ranges than it is now. Although the drying-out process had already begun, the scenery was probably like the savanna of East Africa is today, with similar though more abundant wildlife. Rock engravings in the mountains and, in the far south-east, the famous rock paintings in the Tassili N'Ajjer, deep in the desert, include scenes of hunting in lively detail. Giraffes, antelopes, elephants and rivers full of fish, as well as archers and dancers, show how different everyday life was then.

Later Tassili paintings, those dating from about 4000 to 1500 B.C., depict the domestication

Rock paintings of Neolithic cattle-herders have withstood the passage of centuries.

of cattle. Towards the end of that phase, a remarkable overlap of prehistory and recorded history occurs. Many paintings and engravings across a wide geographical area show horses and chariots, in a vivid documentation of the arrival of a new people from Egypt and Libya. As "Berber" tribes (the name comes from one given them later by the Romans, who called all those who couldn't speak Latin "Barbari"), they spread over much of North

Africa. Most Algerians today are at least partly of Berber descent.

Phoenicians and Carthaginians

While this was happening on land, Phoenician sailors from the Eastern Mediterranean were venturing further and further west on their voyages. By around 1000 B.C. they had established a number of trading settlements on the Algerian coast, coexisting more or less peaceably with the Berbers. Legend has it that the Phoenician Queen Dido of Tyre founded the colony of Carthage, in what is now Tunisia, in the year 814 B.C. Whatever the

exact truth of the matter, Carthage eventually grew in influence to eclipse the other Phoenician cities of the east.

By about 500 B.C. Carthage was the centre of a great trading republic that had gradually absorbed the ports along the Algerian and Moroccan coasts, including those on the sites of today's cities of Annaba, Skikda, Algiers, Cherchell and Ténès. The olive, the vine and large-scale wheat-growing were introduced. The Berber kingdoms of the interior assimilated those Punic (Carthaginian) customs that most appealed to them, as well as adopting the Punic language. In a pattern that was to be continually repeated over the centuries, they resisted any attempt at political domination.

When a dynamic new power across the sea, Rome, began to throw its weight about, a clash with Carthage became inevitable. First the Carthaginians were forced out of Sicily. Then Rome invaded North Africa, and the Punic Wars were on. They took place between 264 and 146 B.C., and although the Carthaginians won several rounds, they were in the end utterly defeated. During the wars, the Numidian Berbers under King Masinissa (c. 238–148 B.C.), whose capital was at Cirta (now Constantine), allied themselves to Rome, though Masinissa himself died before the fall of Carthage. The Ro-

The superb ruins of Djemila the Beautiful, founded by the Romans in AD 1.

mans divided his kingdom of Numidia, but his grandson, Jugurtha, seeing what he considered to be Rome's expansionary designs, cunningly reunited it. He conducted a long and skilful resistance against a succession of Roman armies (the Jugurthine War, c. 112–105 B.C.). Jugurtha's fight to remain independent has made him one of Algeria's national heroes to this day.

Roman Province

For another century and a half, Rome avoided a full-scale takeover of North Africa, though an expedition led by Lucius Balbus penetrated far into the Sahara in 19 B.C. Influence was exerted through allies and vassals, most notably the enthusiastic Romanizer Juba II and his wife Cleopatra Selene, intriguingly the daughter of Mark Antony and Cleopatra. (They had both been brought up in Rome after being taken there as children to be shown off in triumphal processions celebrating Roman victories.)

Juba was installed by Rome on the throne of Numidia in 29 B.C. Four years later the Emperor Augustus rewarded him with Mauretania, which he ruled until his death (c. A.D. 24). The kingdom of Mauretania comprised most of present-day Morocco and northwestern Algeria. What Rome required of this client state was a steady supply of wheat, olive oil and other agricultural products.

About A.D. 42, after the infamous Caligula had ordered the murder of Mauretania's then ruler, Juba II's son Ptolemy (reigned 24–40), the country was divided into Roman provinces. There was a western and an eastern province, the former with its capital at Tingis (Tangiers in Morocco), and the latter with its capital at Caesarea (Cherchell in Algeria). Rome began to recruit among the Berbers for a North African army, the Third Legion Augusta. Many Berbers were made Roman citizens and one, Septimius Severus, became emperor (193–211).

Roman citizenship was later conferred on all free people of the provinces by Caracalla, son and successor of Septimius. Triumphal arches dedicated to these two, and to the wife of Septimius, Julia Domna, are among the most impressive monuments that you'll see in Algeria. In the standard Roman manner, veterans of military service were settled in special new towns and given good agricultural land to farm. Long periods of peace and prosperity ensued, interrupted by revolts among the always fiercely intractable mountain tribes and by attacks from beyond the frontiers.

Some of the most magnificent Roman ruins to be found anywhere are in Algeria. Timgad is all four-square efficiency as befits its founder, that most military of emperors, Trajan. Djemila seems almost ready for reoccupation, so perfect are many of its old Roman buildings. Breathtaking mosaics are on a vast scale and of a fluidity that seems specially characteristic of North Africa. Many of them feature sea creatures, ships and sailing. Perhaps they were commissioned by merchants who had done well out of the seaborne export trade with Rome. The quantities of artwork in general attest to the riches of the province and the cultured life that its leaders could afford.

For almost 400 years the empire ruled. During the 4th century, Christianity spread and basilicas were built in every city. (Sometimes more than one, as different sects vied for supremacy.) St. Augustine, one of the greatest early Christian thinkers, was born in what is now the town of Souk Ahras and became bishop of Hippo (now Annaba).

Vandalism

The end of Roman power in Africa was long in coming, yet stunningly sudden. Vandal tribesmen, of Germanic origin, had been rampaging around Europe for some years, leaving a trail of destruction. Then in 429 all 80,000 of them abandoned Spain and crossed the Strait of Gibraltar into Numidia. In just one year they plundered their way along the entire coast as far as Carthage. They made the city their capital and settled down to live off the fat of the land.

Despite the Vandals' success as a sea power, their rule was comparatively short-lived. By the early 6th century, the Emperor Justinian, claiming the succession to Rome, sought to re-establish imperial control over North Africa. He invited the Vandals to return to the fold without bloodshed, but their new (and last) king, Gelimer, responded with a rude letter suggesting he "mind his own business". When his bishops promised the help of the Almighty in a holy war to recover the lost provinces, Justinian needed no further encouragement. In the year 533, he despatched his best general, Belisarius, with 5,000 cavalry and 10,000 infantry to do the job.

Schism

Christianity had not long been given official approval in the Roman Empire when there was a row over the election of the bishop of Carthage. On one side was most of the Catholic establishment in Rome supporting the original appointment. On the other side were the North African followers of a certain Donatus, who at one time replaced the appointed bishop. The argument was eventually decided by the Emperor Constantine himself, against the Donatists. When persecution from 317 to 321 A.D. failed to dissuade the Donatists and end the schism, a period of tolerance was established. A sort of competition developped between them and the Catholics, and many cities ended up like Timgad, with two cathedrals. The Donatists were against state control in church affairs and had a programme of social revolution. They gained strength but were exiled in 347. When Julius "the Apostate" became emperor and withdrew state patronage from the Catholic church, the Donatists returned and became the principal sect in North Africa. In the end they were opposed by locally-born St. Augustine of Hippo (Annaba), and in 412 they began to have many of their civil and ecclesiastical rights taken away. Still, they did survive into the 7th century.

It was a classic case of setting a thief to catch a thief. Many of Belisarius's troops were Huns, notorious for being even more drunken and destructive than the Vandals themselves. Soon the expedition had gained possession of many cities on the coast and a few in the interior. Returning to Constantinople, Belisarius was to be awarded a triumph, coincidentally the first non-imperial recipient of the honour since Balbus for *his* expedition into the Sahara in 19 B.C. The captured Gelimer had to crawl before Justinian muttering, it is said: "Vanity of vanities, all is vanity".

Always short of reliable soldiers (the best went off to help recapture Italy), the Byzantines built new defensive walls around the towns, such as those at Tebessa, which still stand today—mute witnesses to the precarious nature of the imperial revival. Forced into intrigues and unpalatable alliances to maintain an increasingly untenable position, the Byzantine generals faced successive revolts, attacks and religious schisms. Lacking support from their distant capital, they couldn't hang on to power for ever. It must have been almost a relief when chaos was swiftly brought to an end in one of the most explosive "clean sweeps" in history. This was the Arab advance and, supremely significant in the life of Algeria ever since, the conversion of the people to Islam.

Clear New Message

It was in the year 610, in far-off Mecca, that the Prophet Mohammed, the initiator of Islam ("submission to the will of God"), received his call. The Koran, the holy book of the faith, was revealed to him over the next twenty years and written down in what is recognized as the most perfect Arabic. In 622 he moved to Medina and it is from this *hegira,* or flight, that the Islamic calender is measured. By the time of his death in 632 he had united most of the nomadic peoples of the Arabian peninsula. Arab armies had formed and were ready to launch themselves on a mission to spread the message.

Their confidence and their success were equally great. Ramshackle and discredited empires and their effete rulers fell in rapid succession. Just as quickly, whole populations turned with enthusiasm to the new religion. The Prophet had declared that converts, of whatever race, were all equal in the faith, which encouraged its ready acceptance.

By about 660, the Arabs had begun to advance into Algeria. In 683, the dynamic general Okba Ben Nafi could ride his horse into the sea on the Atlantic coast of Morocco, declaring that there were no more worlds to conquer, no more peoples to convert. Of course, it was not that simple. On his return through the northern Sahara, at the oasis of Biskra, Okba was killed in battle during a Berber rising, the first of many. But the rebellions were primarily against outside domination, not against Islam.

Many Berbers joined in the Muslim conquest of Spain, and when there was a large-scale and successful revolt in North Africa in 740, it was by the Kharidjites, in the name of a stricter version of Islam. Only in 911 were these zealots, characteristically unwilling to compromise, driven by the new Fatimid rulers into the desert. They went first to Sedrata near Ouargla, then to the M'Zab, where their descendants still live today. (The Fatimids took their name from Fatima, the daughter of the Prophet and wife of Ali, from whom their leader claimed to be descended.)

Dynasties

In truth, the Muslim territories had become far too large for any one ruler to control. That wasn't to stop some from trying. The next six centuries are a confusing picture of shifting power, family intrigues, fragmentation and reunification. First, the Fatimids decided that Egypt would be a more suitable stage for their ambitions and set off to capture it in 969. They established their capital at Cairo three years later and handed over power in Algeria to the Zirid family, who unwisely did not continue to pay lip service to their former patrons. Possibly as a result, a wave of plundering tribesmen from Upper Egypt called the Beni Hilal descended on North Africa around 1050, in a dreadful echo of the Vandal invasion. They so wrecked the settled rural economy of the Berbers that many were forced to become nomads on the fringes of the Sahara.

Then a new reforming sect swept in, spearheaded by veiled men from the deserts to the south of Morocco. Under the name of Almoravids, they were led for some 50 years by one man, the Emir Youssef Ben Tashfin. He was already an old man when he decided to take over Muslim Spain and put a stop to Christian advances there. Before his death in 1106, he brought the western half of Algeria under control as well, founding the city of Tlemcen and adorning it with the first of its beautiful mosques.

During the 40 years of comparative tranquillity that followed, the Almoravids were seduced by the soft life in their Spanish province of Andalusia. Yet another group of strict believers, feeling that Islam as it was then practised had become insufficiently ascetic, emerged from seclusion in the Atlas mountains. Known as the Almohads (unifiers), they swiftly overthrew the Almoravids, and during the 1150s brought all the Maghreb (Tunisia, Algeria and Morocco) under their sway. They left fine buildings, but the unity they had imposed did not last even until the end of the century.

More dynasties—the Hafsids from Tunisia, the Zianids based in Tlemcen and the Merinids from Morocco—rose and declined. A multiplicity of independent principalities divided the land. Weakened,

At El Eubbad, inside the kouba *of Sidi Bou Mediene, an Algerian holy man.*

the coastal cities were subject to attacks by a resurgent Spain, which only a few years previously (1492) had expelled the last Muslims from its own territory. Oran was occupied by the Spanish in 1509, and they would stay for almost 300 years, discounting a couple of decades in the early 18th century.

Alarmed, Algerian emirs in the other Mediterranean ports, who had themselves been engaging in raids on Christian shipping for years, called on Turkish corsairs for protection. In 1519, Algiers became the capital and base for these Barbary pirates, led by the brothers Barbarossa (so-called after their red beards). Rich cargoes were seized and rich captives ransomed. Those whose families couldn't raise the money were sold as slaves.

The captains of the corsairs ruled as governors, or pashas, appointed by the Turkish sultan far away in Constantinople. In fact, Turkish control did not often extend far inland, and many mountain strongholds never submitted to Ottoman rule. By the end of the 17th century, the Turkish connection was only a polite fiction, and rulers were appointed locally, often as a result of plots and assassinations.

French Connection

The navies of Britain, France and even the young United States, did their best to suppress the Barbary corsairs, and by the early 19th century their activities had been reduced to a minor nuisance. Napoleon contemplated attacking Algiers in 1808, but he was distracted by other targets. In 1827 a matter of unpaid debts led to an argument in which the Dey (Governor) of Algiers struck a French emissary with his fly whisk during a public audience. The French king, Charles X, was persuaded that this insult provided sufficient cause for invasion. A blockade of the port of Algiers was ordered in 1827, but as it was ineffective the French decided to attack. (The official reason given was the intention to put an end to the by-now-fictional Turkish presence and finish with piracy.) In 1830 the French invaded Algiers and in three weeks, the Dey's government fell.

As a result of a vague expansionary policy rather than a clearly defined plan for colonization, the French continued to occupy the entire coast. As they moved towards the interior, they met with bitter resistance—as had every invader before them. In the west, the Emir Abdelkader fought on until 1847, and the mountainous region of Kabylia in the north-east was not pacified for over 40 years.

With the consolidation of French rule, European settlers poured into Algeria. They set up businesses in the growing cities, or tried their hand at farming on confiscated land. There were frequent uprisings until the end of the 19th century, and the 20th century had begun before French control extended to the southern Sahara. As armed opposition waned, organizations with the shared aim of restoring freedom began to form.

Three different groups participated in the early independence movement, each with a particular leader: radical Muslims, led by Sheikh Ben Badis, wanted to restore the primacy of Islam. Revolutionaries, inspired by Messali Hadj, advocated the overthrow of colonial government and the confiscation of all French-owned property in Algeria. And liberals and moderates, headed by Ferhat Abbas, thought the best way ahead was to work for the evolution of democracy, so that Algerians could eventually control their own destinies again. Even the third group made little progress in the face of French intransigence and some cynical ballot rigging. Repression alternated with limited reforms, but the fundamental injustice remained: Algerians had few political rights, and if they were granted greater freedom, they would overwhelmingly reject the French connection. Attempting to escape this dilemma, the French gradually created the fiction that Algeria was not a colony, but an integral part of France. To many Algerians, this meant that there would be no hope of peaceful progress to independence.

Events during World War II further weakened France's position in Algeria. Although most of the colonies supported General de Gaulle and the Free French, the authorities in Algiers backed the Vichy regime that was collaborating with Nazi Germany. So when American and British forces landed at Sidi Fredj in 1942 and overthrew the collaborators, French prestige in Algeria was in tatters. It was only very marginally restored by the establishment of the Free French government, although in one extraordinary quirk of history Algiers was briefly the provisional capital—of France. Many Algerian troops *(spahis)* joined the Free French army, fighting in the campaigns

The soaring Memorial to the Martyr, in the background, honours Algerian independence.

across North Africa and Italy, and they gained new perspectives on freedom. It is significant that some of them later became leaders in the independence struggle, where their military experience was invaluable.

The end of the war brought restoration of French control, and colonial "business as usual". Algerian nationalists wasted no time in announcing an independent government, on May 8, 1945. (It was V.E. Day, when Europe was heaving a collective sigh of relief over the defeat of Nazism.) Demonstrations in Sétif and other towns in the Constantine region soon turned to violence, and tension escalated with the massacre of close to 100 European settlers. The uprisings were viciously and bloodily suppressed and thousands of Algerians last their lives. One of the military commanders responsible declared: "I have given you ten years of peace, but do not have any illusions". He was addressing, of course, the French politicians and settlers, and his prediction was uncannily accurate.

After 1945, the independence movement was forced underground, but planning and organizing continued. A number of the more prominent activists were arrested by the French authorities, but there were always more to take their place.

On November 1, 1954, a group of young leaders proclaimed the formation of the Front of National Liberation (FLN). Shots were fired near Biskra and in a dozen other places. Almost eight years of bitter war had begun. Many in France urged a negotiated solution, but a succession of governments, swayed by the pressures of the European settlers and military commanders, decided to use force against the nationalists.

Over the years that followed, ever more repressive measures were employed, not excluding torture and napalm bombing of non-combatants. Endlessly increasing numbers of troops were thrown into the campaigns of "pacification". To try to prevent supplies and reinforcements reaching the hard-pressed revolutionaries, the French constructed vast electrified fences and minefields along the borders with Tunisia and Morocco. Algerians were uprooted from their homes and put into guarded camps to prevent them from helping the FLN. Agriculture was in ruins, forests burned, villages destroyed: the death toll reached into the hundreds of thousands.

Independence

In 1958, the French generals and settlers, detecting a weakening in the resolve of the politicians in Paris, demanded the return to power of General de Gaulle, expecting his full support. High drama unfolded in Paris as he was indeed called, after more than 12 years in the background, to take over the government. The National Assembly was suspended: the Fourth Republic was effectively dead. Within days, de Gaulle was in Algeria amid scenes of extraordinary emotion, telling the army and settlers: "Je vous ai compris!" (I have understood you). His listeners no doubt thought they knew what he meant, but in later years they would reflect that it was as Delphic as many of his other utterances.

In the event, de Gaulle came to recognize the long-term futility of the struggle to preserve French rule. Settlers' revolts, military mutinies and attempts on his life notwithstanding, independence for Algeria was agreed at the French spa of Evian in 1962. Despite guarantees of the rights of the settlers, almost all chose, after the bitterness of the revolution, to leave the country. The victorious Algerian forces, led by Colonel Houari Boumedienne, entered Algiers on September 10, 1962. Ahmed Ben Bella, who had spent the previous six years in French prisons, became prime minister and, a year later, president of the independent nation.

Houari Boumedienne (an assumed name, taken in honour of the famous 12th-century scholar and teacher, Sidi Bou Mediene) had been a hero of the revolution. In 1965 he ousted Ben Bella—believing him to be too much addicted to the "cult of personality", and his policies wasteful and confused—and became president himself.

The war had left Algeria's economy in chaos, and in any case it had long been distorted as an appendage of France. Everything had to be built anew. Socialism and state control were to be the guiding principles. Industrial, agrarian and educational revolutions were launched, funded in part by the income from Saharan oil and natural gas exports. If mistakes were made in over-centralizing, it was understandable. Falling oil prices later encouraged a greater degree of flexibility in the planning process. In 1978, Houari Boumedienne died. Another veteran of the independence struggle, Chadli Bendjedid, became president.

Algeria's population continues to grow rapidly, with the challenges that this brings. One outlet for the surplus labour force had long been employment in France: soon after independence there were more Algerians in France than there had ever been settlers in Algeria. Now, new policies in Paris have largely closed that door. Unrest in 1988 and 1989 resulted in the promise of a greater degree of popular participation in the running of the country, and more opportunities for the younger generation.

Algeria's revolution has been a model for many who have felt themselves to be oppressed, and the progress of the country will continue to be watched by the entire world.

Heroes of the Revolution

As you travel around Algeria, you'll notice some street names appearing over and over. Many of them commemorate leaders in the long struggle for liberation. The names that most often appear are those who were killed before victory was achieved, whose reputations were not eroded by later controversy. (Some confusion can result from the Algerian custom of putting family names first: Ben M'Hidi Larbi, rather than Larbi Ben M'Hidi.)

***Colonel Amirouche** (an assumed name) was born in Tassaft, Kabylia in 1926. He took control of the FLN forces in eastern Kabylia on the death of the former leader and became a regional commander in 1957. He fought with single-minded ferocity until he was killed in an ambush near Bou-Saada in 1959.*

***Ben M'Hidi Larbi** (1923–57) was one of the prime movers in the independence struggle. A leader in the Oran region at the start, he later moved to Algiers. He is quoted as having remarked to a colleague: "I would like to die in battle, before the end". Ben M'Hidi organized the general strike of January 1957. Trapped in Algiers, he was captured in late February. He died in prison soon afterwards and is generally believed to have been murdered.*

***Ben Boulaid** (1917–56), a miller from the Aurès, led FLN forces in his region from the very first day. Captured in February 1955, he made an amazing escape nine months later from the condemned cell. He resumed active command in his region, but was killed in March 1956 by a booby-trapped radio set.*

***Didouche Mourad** (1927–55) was the youngest of the senior commanders at the outbreak of fighting. In charge of his own Constantine region, he was killed in battle in January 1955.*

***Colonel Lotfi** (an assumed name) was born in 1934 in Tlemcen. He became commander of the Tlemcen sector from 1955 and later took over the whole of western Algeria. He was killed in battle near Béchar in 1958.*

***Abane Ramdane** (1920–57). Several years in French prisons and long hunger strikes damaged Abane's health. One of the chief policy-makers of the FLN inside Algeria in the early years of the war, he was killed in Morocco in 1957 after a leadership split.*

***Zighout Youcef** (1921–56), a wheelwright in the town near Constantine that now bears his name, joined the FLN early on. He took over when his young chief Didouche Mourad was killed. Zighout initiated the policy of "total war" in 1955. He died in battle in September 1956.*

HISTORICAL LANDMARKS

Prehistory

c. 200 000 B.C.	Palaeolithic hunters in Algeria.
c. 6000–1500 B.C.	Neolithic man creates rock engravings and paintings in the Atlas and Sahara. Domestication of cattle.
1500 B.C.	Ancestors of the Berbers arrive from Egypt and Libya.

Early Civilizations

1100 B.C.	Phoenicians establish trading settlements along the coast.
800–500 B.C.	Phoenician settlements are gradually absorbed into a Carthaginian trading republic.
148 B.C.	Death of Masinissa. His kingdom of Numidia divided by the Romans but reunited by his grandson, Jugurtha.
146 B.C.	Punic Wars end with the fall of Carthage.
105 B.C.	Berber kings and princes rule as allies or vassals of Rome.

Roman Empire and Aftermath

A.D. 40	Algeria is integrated into the Roman empire. Berber strongholds in the mountains refuse to be assimilated.
193–211	North African-born Septimius Severus becomes emperor. Caracalla confers Roman citizenship on all freemen of the empire.
4th C.	Spread of Christianity.
429	Vandal invasion.
533	Belisarius defeats Vandals. Interior ruled by Berber confederations. Period of confusion, uprisings and heresies follows.

Arab Advance and Dynasties

660	Arab advance and advent of Islam.
740	Berbers revolt in support of the Kharidjite version of Islam.
911	Fatimids drive Kharidjites into the desert.
935	Algiers *(El Djezaïr)* founded on ancient Phoenician site.
972	Fatimids take over Egypt and establish a capital at Cairo.

c. 1050	Invasion of the Beni Hilal from Upper Egypt.
c. 1060	Almoravids reunite North Africa and Muslim Spain. Tlemcen founded.
c. 1150	Almohad rulers supplant Almoravids.
13th–15th centuries	Rise and fall of Hafsids, Zianids and Merinids. Independent principalities divide the land.

Ottoman Empire

1509	Spanish occupy Oran. Emirs appeal to the Barbary corsairs for help. Algeria comes under Ottoman rule, though much of the interior remains independent.
1671	Local rulers take over. Nominal sovereignty of the Turkish sultan recognized until 1710.
1792	Spanish forced out of Oran.

French Connection

1830	French land at Sidi Fredj *(Sidi Ferruch),* capture Algiers.
1834	French control the coast.
1839–47	Fierce resistance in the west under Emir Abdelkader.
1857	French occupy Kabylia. Large-scale colonization begins.
1902	French defeat Tuareg and control southern Sahara.
1940	Fall of France. Authorities in Algiers back Vichy government.
1942	U.S. and British forces defeat Vichy collaborators in Algeria.
1945	Revolt against French in Constantine region suppressed.
1954	Algerian revolution begins.
1958	General de Gaulle comes to accept Algerian cause.

Liberation and Independence

1962	Algerian independence declared. Liberation forces under Colonel Houari Boumedienne enter Algiers. Most European settlers leave. Ahmed Ben Bella becomes prime minister.
1963	Ben Bella named president.
1965	Houari Boumedienne ousts Ben Bella, takes over as president.
1978	Death of Boumedienne. Chadli Bendjedid becomes president.

WHERE TO GO

Beaches, mountains and desert; big cities and remote villages; prehistory, ancient history, Islamic history and modern development—this huge land has them all. It would be a pity, while you're here, not to experience a wide sample. Despite the vast size of Algeria, there are some factors in your favour. Except for the far south, good roads allow rapid progress around the country. The national airline, Air Algérie, has frequent flights to all the main centres and most of the larger Saharan oases. And there is also a system of long-distance buses. It can be less than a day's journey from crowded Algiers to a magical oasis.

The national tourism organization, ONAT, runs a series of tours concentrating on different aspects and regions: Roman Algeria, the mountains, the coast, the northern oases, the far south. Other travel agencies in conjuction with ONAT offer packages of their own. Even when travelling under your own steam, you could take a leaf out of their book.

There's plenty to see in the city of Algiers, but it can be frenetic and difficult to get around. Travelling in and out of the city centre is time-consuming, too, so it's not an ideal base for seeing much of the country. Bear in mind that hotel rooms are hard to find in the capital. If you are arranging your own programme, be sure to make reservations well in advance, confirm them when you can and don't arrive late in the day.

There isn't yet a wide choice of places to stay anywhere in the country. About 50 towns, including oases, spas and resorts, have satisfactory accommodation. Distances between hotels can be great, so planning your itinerary needs special care.

For the impressive Roman cities of the east, above all Timgad and Djemila, you could stay in Constantine, Sétif and Batna. If you seek mountain scenery and wildflowers in the springtime, choose the Aurès, basing yourself on Batna again, or Biskra. There's also the Djurdjura range in Great Kabylia and the Djebel Babor in Lesser Kabylia. Should you be looking for somewhere very unusual to ski, Tikjda in the Djurdjura and

A faience archway beckons the passerby to the hushed interior of a shrine in El Eubbad.

Chrea near Algiers have developed the basic facilities.

The coast has a scattering of resorts to choose from: Sidi Fredj, Zeralda and Tipasa near Algiers, Les Andalouses near Oran, Tichi near Bejaïa and Seraïdi near Annaba. They can be good bases for exploring inland, too. Those with an interest in Islamic history and architecture should stay for at least a couple of nights in Tlemcen. Of the oases, take your pick; everyone comes to have favourites. High on your list should be El Oued, Touggourt, Taghit, Beni Abbès, Timimoun and the five towns of the M'Zab. (Ghardaïa is the main town in the M'Zab where you stay.)

Finally, there's the unique south, where four-wheel-drive vehicles and trekking are the mode of travel. From Tamanrasset you can journey—on foot if you have plenty of time—to the unearthly scenery of the Hoggar and sleep out

The Hoggar Rally draws the hardiest, but you may prefer another means of transport!

under the stars. Djanet in the far south-east is the starting point for treks to the Tassili N'Ajjer, famed for thousands of prehistoric rock paintings. Walking is the only way to reach the "lost world" plateau of the Tassili, but donkeys can carry your baggage. To cater to travellers who want to explore places even more remote, agencies are constantly coming up with new itineraries in the south. It's an adventurer's dream world.

Getting Around

If you have your own car, you'll find the standard of driving in the main to be quite good. The possible exception is on the heavily travelled east-west arteries between the main cities—the Oran-Algiers-Constantine routes—where drivers are pushing to keep up to demanding schedules. Always be on your guard and drive defensively.

With your own means of transport, you can reach even the remoter sites in the northern half of the country, and all the main oases of the northern Sahara, by surfaced roads. Some are excellent, some only adequate. Tamanrasset in the far south can also be reached by a surfaced road, but a visit to the rest of that extraordinary region entails a lot of planning and extra equipment.

Although Sonatrach, the national oil and gas company, does publish a road map of Algeria, it is hard to find one on sale. Better to take your own. Street maps are virtually non-existent, even of Algiers. Unless you are a reader of Arabic, you won't be able to understand street names, except in

Helpful vocabulary

Abou (bou)	*father (of)*
Aid (Id)	*holy day*
Aïn	*spring*
Ait	*children of (tribe)*
Adrar	*mountain*
Akba	*pass*
Akbar	*great, high, elder*
Alfa	*esparto grass*
Bab	*gate*
Bahri	*north*
Barkhan	*moon-shaped sand dunes*
Behar	*sea*
Ben (Ibn)	*son of*
Beni	*sons of (or tribe)*
Bled	*countryside*
Bordj	*tower or small fort*
Burnous	*hooded robe*
Caid	*chief, high official*
Chaouia	*Berbers of the Aurès*
Cheche	*Tuareg headcloth*
Chott	*salt marsh or dry lake*
Dar	*large house*
Daira	*government building*
Djebel	*mountain*
Djedid	*new*
Djemaa	*mosque*
Djemal	*camel*
Djemil	*fine, beautiful*
Douar	*village, encampment*
Erg	*desert of dunes*
Feche feche	*soft, deep sand*
Foggara	*underground water channel*
Gerba	*goatskin*
Guelta	*pond in rocks*
Hadj, hadji	*one who's made the pilgrimage to Mecca*
Haïk	*white enveloping woman's garment*
Halou	*sweet*
Hammada	*rocky or stony plain or upland*
Hammam	*bath, spa*
Hassi	*well*
Imam	*Moslem leader*
Kabyle	*Berber people and language of Kabylia*
Kebir	*great*
Kef, kiffan	*cliff(s)*
Khalifa	*officer*
Koubba	*whitewashed tomb of a holy man*
Ksar, ksour	*walled village(s)*
Lalla	*lady, holy woman (polite)*
Ma (meh)	*water*
Maghreb	*west, esp. north-west Africa (Morocco, Tunisia, Algeria)*
Marabout	*wise and holy man*
Medersa	*Moslem college*
Medina	*town, old part of city*
Mehari	*riding camel*
Mers	*port*
Mihrab	*alcove in mosque indicating Mecca*
Minaret	*tower of mosque*
Muezzin	*one who calls the people to prayer*
Nakhla	*palm grove*
Nour (nur)	*light*

Oued (wadi)	*river, or dry river bed*
Ouled	*children of*
Oum (um)	*mother*
Rai	*popular music*
Reg	*desert of pebbles and sand*
Riadh	*large garden*
Rmel	*sand*
Sahel	*coast, or dry region of thorn bushes and grass*
Sahra	*desert*
Sahraoui	*desert dweller*
Sebkha	*salt lake or lake bed*
Segia	*irrigation channel*
Seif	*sand dune shaped by prevailing wind*
Sharia	*road or avenue, also Islamic law*
Sidi	*master or holy man*
Souk, suk	*market*
Sour	*wall, fortification*
Srir	*flat plain of fine sand*
Targui (Tuareg)	*desert nomad(s)*
Tamahak, Tamashek	*Tuareg language*
Tassili	*high plateau cut by chasms*
Tizi	*mountain pass*
Zaouia	*place of a religious community*
Zeriba	*reed hut*

and some expressions

Allah	*God*
Balek	*attention! watch out!*
Baraka	*God-given fortune*
Insh'allah	*if God wills it*
La (leh)	*no*
Naam	*yes*
Labass	*greetings*
Salaam aleikum	*greetings*
Saha	*thank you, agreed*
Shoukran	*thank you*
Si	*Mr., sir*
Wallah	*exclamation (Good heavens!)*

When providing information on a country such as Algeria, one finds not only a mix of French and Arabic, but various transliterations of Arabic as well. With regard to maps, information brochures, street signs, or even official usage, there exists an inevitable confusion between the English, French and Arabic names and spellings. Although every attempt has been made to be consistent, certain discrepancies are bound to occur.

Oran where they still survive in both scripts. So you will find yourself constantly asking the way. Fortunately the road direction signs are still given in French as well as Arabic. Refer to the maps of Algeria and the major cities at the back of the book, beginning on page 242.

ONAT offices exist in most cities and towns, but they serve mainly as travel agencies for Algerians and will rarely be of much practical help to you.

If you are relying on public transport, remember that buses tend to start very early, even before dawn. You'll need to get your ticket the previous day at the bus station *(gare routière).* Turn up early to get a good seat.

Slightly more expensive, but certainly an option, and not requiring so much forward planning, shared taxis *(taxis collectifs)* run in a well-developed network all over the country, linking each centre to its neighbours. Anyone can tell you where to get a shared taxi: in small towns it's usually the main square. In principle, drivers wait until they have a full load and then take off, but it can depend somewhat on whim. Taxis, shared and ordinary, are painted bright yellow. Conveniently, they bear the name of their home province on the doors, and often the name of the town they come from on the back, so you can guess where one is likely to be going.

You'll see plenty of local hitch-hikers, and if you have the time to wait, you might choose to join them. Some drivers will expect you to contribute to their costs. In the desert, the long, hot delays make it less enjoyable. In any case most vehicles do not have spare seats (and scarcely ever more than one). Women, even in pairs or accompanied by men, should not hitch-hike in Algeria. It simply would not be understood.

One railway line runs from east to west, and others link some of the more northerly oases with the coast. Services are slow and infrequent, so it would be difficult to schedule a whole itinerary, but one or two trips by rail could add variety to your travels. Second class is usually jam-packed, so the small premium for first-class tickets is probably worth paying.

Distances to the far south are so great that unless you have lots of time and stamina, flying is the only sensible way to reach the region. Once there, you can undertake whatever physical challenges you feel fit for!

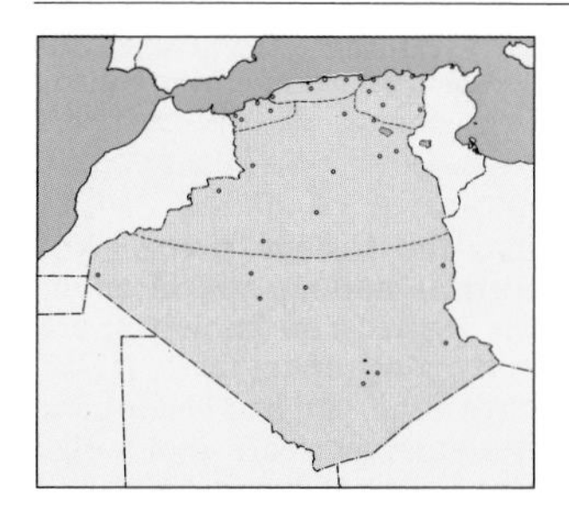

ALGIERS AND VICINITY

Many organized tours to Algeria don't bring their participants to Algiers at all. Those going trekking in the far south, for example, may only encounter the airport and a hotel at the airport or at Sidi Fredj, both before their exertions and on their way home. This is a pity: for one thing, the museums in the capital could put their experiences in the Sahara into context. If you have the choice, the great dilemma is whether to visit them at the beginning or at the end of the trip. You'll certainly get much more out of the museums if you have seen some of the country first. Although the reverse is also true, on balance it is the museums that need the spice of extra interest that comes with recognition. Ideally, therefore, see if you can put in a museum day—or two—at the end of your itinerary.

Several points of interest lie within excursion distance of the capital: the classical sites of Tipasa and Cherchell to the west, and the mountainous region of Great Kabylia to the east, with its national park and traditional Berber villages.

ALGIERS

The city's name in Arabic is El Djezaïr, meaning "the islands". If you wonder where the islands are today, they've long since been incorporated into the moles, or breakwaters, protecting the magnificent harbour. Although a Phoenician and Carthaginian settlement, it was still quite insignificant in Roman times compared with Cherchell along the coast. The city grew under the Arabs, and it was a brief Spanish occupation of the islands in the 16th century that triggered an appeal to the Barbary corsairs for protection. They made Algiers their base, and for almost three centuries raiding shipping in the Mediterranean was the city's chief activity and source of income. Infuriated European states sent their navies to bombard Algiers on numerous occasions, with little permanent effect. In 1830, Algiers was the first objective of the invading French forces when they landed at nearby Sidi Fredj.

"Get high", literally, should be your policy for enjoying Algiers. First, to admire the view. Even if you have arrived by sea on a clear morning and marvelled at the white terraces shimmering in steep steps up the hillsides, climb or take a taxi to one of the vantage points. It could be the Hôtel El Aurassi, or the Az Zahira balcony near the western suburb of El Biar, the Bardo Museum or the Memorial to the Martyr. Then you can orient yourself, look at your map and work out a strategy for getting where you want to go in what can be a confusing city. The best time for photographing from these high places will probably be in the early morning, or just before the sun drops behind the hills, especially if rain has recently cleared the air.

Climb, too, to keep cooler. Those who could afford to build houses in the hills have done so ever since Algiers burst the limits of the Kasbah, which *was* the city until the early 19th century. Up in the breezier parks and gardens you can relax before plunging again into the frenetic streets. No, there is nothing restful about the centre. You know you are in a major capital there. If you have a car, you had better park it somewhere safe and walk. The policy of starting high has other benefits, too: many of the tourist sights are well up the hills. After a visit, you can walk gently down. If you keep descending, you won't so easily get lost. Eventually you always end up at the harbour or the bay.

This bold splash of colour and design is one of modern Algiers' little surprises.

Why worry about getting lost? First, because Algiers led the way in painting over street names in French, leaving only the Arabic script. Next, names have been changed over the years to honour different heroes and public figures, but people may still use the old ones. Even some taxi drivers stop to ask the way, and you'll have to do the same. The maps of Algiers at the back of the book (pp. 246–248) will help.

A high point in every way is the **Bardo**, the late 18th-century villa at the top of Rue Didouche Mourad, close to where it meets the Avenue Franklin Roosevelt. The building now

houses a museum of prehistory and ethnography, but, like a vision out of the Arabian Nights, it would be worth a visit even if it were empty. For this is a palace with an elegant courtyard, gorgeously embellished with fountains and multicoloured tiles by the thousand. Some individual tiles, Dutch or Italian faience, are museum pieces in themselves.

The Bardo's comprehensive collections of fossils and Palaeolithic and Neolithic tools and weapons can give an idea of North Africa's distant past in just a short visit. If you have been, or plan to go, to the Tassili N'Ajjer, look for the

The Hôtel El Djezaïr—posed like a palace from a Thousand and One Nights.

meticulous copies of the Tassili rock paintings made by Henri Lhote's expedition in the 1950s. It is quite uncanny to see the bones and horns of extinct animals alongside Stone Age paintings and carvings showing the same species.

The ethnographic exhibits in upper rooms of the palace are reached through the courtyard. Dress styles of different regions—Constantine, the Aurès, Tlemcen, Ghardaïa—and their lavish embroideries and ornaments compete with decorated weapons. Don't miss the Kabyle jewellery in blue, yellow and green enamel with amber, and old silver coins, though it may spoil you for the modern versions in the state craft shops. Displays of traditional life in the central and southern Sahara compel

admiration for the durability of a precarious existence. In contrast, the pampered harem long vanished is illustrated by a re-creation of the Delacroix painting, *Women of Algiers.*

It's a short walk uphill to another museum, **Musée National des Antiquités Classiques et Musulmanes**, entered through imposing gates. Look out here for Roman glass of such delicacy that its survival seems a miracle, and for mosaics including a huge head and a *trompe l'œil* key pattern. A bronze head of a beautiful girl comes from Timgad, and there is just a hand left of what must have been a double life-size bronze figure. The Islamic section has an 11th-century *minbar* (preacher's chair) from the Great Mosque of Algiers and wonderful embroideries from the Turkish period and from Morocco.

While you are in the **Mustapha** area, it is worth walking south across Place Addis Abeba to the **Hôtel El Djezaïr**. Anyone will tell you the way. Formerly the St. George, this was the favourite hotel of British people who liked to winter in Algiers in the 19th century. Getting away to the sunshine is nothing new. In fact there was quite a British colony of those who came and stayed. The neo-Moresque style Anglican church of the Holy Trinity is nearby, and the British Embassy not far away. The El Djezaïr has been extended in recent years, with a new wing by the architect Fernand Pouillon, blending traditional Islamic and modern styles.

Diar El Mahçoul

You won't have missed the most dominant sight of the Algiers skyline, the **Memorial to the Martyr** *(Makkam Ech*

Chahid), on top of a steep hill some 3 kilometres (2 mi.) south-east of the city centre in the suburb of Diar El Mahçoul. Three stylized palm leaves cast in concrete form a tripod that soars 92 metres (302 ft.) and supports a TV tower at the apex. Built in 1982, it commemorates the 20th anniversary of Algeria's independence from France.

Beneath the memorial's terrace, where soldiers stand guard around the clock, is the **Museum of the Djihad**. The word *djihad,* or Holy War, in this context refers to the whole struggle against French colonialism from the invasion of 1830 to independence 132 years later. Documents, drawings, photographs, maps, relics and models are laid out in the circular hall with moving simplicity and dignity. Most of the labelling is in Arabic only. This is more a place of pilgrimage than a conventional museum. Papers from 1808 show that Napoleon himself thought about attacking Algiers. Others make it clear that when the Dey of Algiers struck the French emissary with his fly whisk, this merely created a pretext for a premeditated expedition (see p. 30).

You may be in for several surprises here. First, the long years that it took the invaders to suppress the resistance of Bey Ahmed of Constantine, the indomitable people of Kabylia and the Aurès and the national hero, Emir Abdelkader. Then, the numerous uprisings that occurred during the rest of the 19th century and into the early 20th as France pushed south into the Sahara. These were of course the inevitable consequences of the twisted logic that said people defending their land should be punished for doing so by being turned off it.

From the 1954–62 war, see the sinister-looking cross-section of the multiple fences, mined and electrified, which the French completed with the use of conscripted labour in 1957 and kept augmenting right up to the end. These barriers ran along the borders with Tunisia and later with Morocco. Traces of them in the form of rolls of barbed wire and stakes can be seen to this day, for example near Aïn Sefra. They were designed to cut off the FLN forces in the country from external supplies and reinforcements. So daunt-

Full moon setting on this evocative Night of the Ramadan, *a miniature by Racim.*

حومة سيدي محمد الشريف
Mohammed Racim

ing and near-impregnable were they that it took superhuman self-sacrifice and the acceptance of appalling losses to break through. Near the exit of the museum, notice the photographs recording the joy in the faces of people realizing that the war was over, and independence had come at last. The museum **shop**, incidentally, is one of the best of its kind in the country with books and cards not available elsewhere.

Beneath the museum, the circular marble-lined **sanctuary** commemorates those who died in the struggle against foreign domination. The silence, semi-darkness and austerity are deeply moving.

Outside again, around the memorial and in **Victory Park** *(Riadh El Fath)* is where the city's teenagers like to meet, especially at weekends. The whole area is well supplied with cafés and shops, places of entertainment and gardens to walk in. Look down towards

the bay and you'll see another large green space, the **Jardin d'Essai**, or Experimental Garden, and nearer than that, at the very base of the slope, the Fine Arts Museum. A cable car runs down there from the Memorial to the Martyr, but it is often full and entails a wait. The walk is easy enough: the cable car is more useful on the upward journey.

You haven't come to Algeria to see European paintings and sculpture? A fair point, but there are good reasons for visiting the **Fine Arts Museum** *(Musée des Beaux-Arts)* nonetheless. The most obvious attraction is the work of the "Orientalists", the 19th-century artists who travelled from Morocco to Central Asia in search of exotic subjects. Some, like Delacroix, followed on the heels of the French army. The copy of Delacroix's *Women of Algiers* that hangs here was painted by none other than Renoir. Then there are Fromentin and Dehodencq and later, Maufra *(A Street in Tolga)* and Dinet, who became a Muslim and settled in Bou-Saada, where you can see his tomb. The Mosque of Sidi Bou Mediene at Tlemcen is recorded here by Chartaud. Still later, in the 1920s, Albert Marquet painted what is now Martyrs' Square below the Kasbah, and it hasn't changed much since.

Nothing to do with Algeria, but there are good things here by Millet, Daumier, Berthe Morisot *(Girl at the Piano)*, Derain, Bonnard and Dufy. It is all rather a surprise. Hidden in a side gallery, Room XXIV,

A lively pedestrian zone lined with boutiques awaits you in the Rue Larbi Ben M'Hidi.

and not to be missed, is the collection of miniatures of Algerian scenes by Mohamed Racim (1896–1975). Look at the unbelievable detail of his *Barbary Pirates,* for example. Has there been anything like it since the Persian miniaturists, whose tradition Racim follows?

Down on the first floor, the sculpture gallery houses mainly French bronzes. There's a replica of Rodin's *The Age of Bronze,* of compelling realism, and a variation of *The Kiss,* of equally startling eroticism. A cool *Venus* by Maillol and *Hercules the Archer* by Bourdelle also stand out.

City Centre

From the Bardo, it's a long but downhill walk to the centre along **Rue Didouche Mourad**, which at the lower end alternates airline offices and some of the better shops. It can be a long drive, too, for the street is usually choked with traffic. If you are driving, you'll note that it is one way: the reverse journey can be quite confusing to strangers, even by the standards of Algiers.

As a visitor you need landmarks, and at the crossing of Boulevard Khemisti and Rue Larbi Ben M'Hidi you have one in the "Moorish palace" of cream and gold which is the main **post office** *(Grande Poste).* Downhill lies the port. Uphill along **Boulevard Mohamed Khemisti** stands the imposing rectangular block of the Palais du Gouvernement (1930) and further up the hillside behind it, the equally colossal Hôtel El Aurassi.

Now head past the post office into **Rue Larbi Ben M'Hidi**. (If you're in a car, you'll be in trouble, for this soon becomes a pedestrian zone.) Stroll along here, with thousands of others, to find department stores, craft and book shops and street cafés. After the tree-lined Place Emir Abdelkader with a fine equestrian statue of that 19th-century hero, you'll quickly reach the lower end of the Kasbah if you keep walking through the less impressive streets.

Kasbah

The Kasbah, subject of a hundred clichés! The word simply means "citadel", or old walled town, and every North African city has, or used to have, one. The Algiers Kasbah is a tangled maze, with its high houses clustered so closely together that they exclude the sun from the network of alleys. In places, the rooftops are connected in a second spider's web of walkways. Population density is probably greater now than ever, thanks to a high birth rate and years of migration to the cities. So the whole area is crowded, though mainly with little boys, or so it seems. Not even the most rose-coloured spectacles could make it look very clean. But being so historic it really shouldn't be missed.

The best technique for a quick survey is again to start from the top, near the 16th-century fort, and walk down, past the vegetable, the spice and the butchers' shops, all spilling out into the narrow twisting passageways and steps. There are plenty of modest little restaurants here, too, where you can experience the everyday food of the average Algerian. A guide is not strictly necessary, but he might be able to take you into one of the houses and out on a terrace or roof for a view. (Agree on a fee for the guide in advance.)

Most of the important buildings are in the lower part of the Kasbah, near the port and Martyrs' Square. From the 1500s to the early 19th century, much of this area was the site of a complex of palaces used by the Dey of Algiers and his government. Now little is left, apart from the Palace of the Princesses *(Dar Aziza),* facing Place Ben Badis. Though faded, the tiled and stuccoed courtyard still gives some idea of its 16th-century elegance. Across the square, the **Djemaa Ketchaoua** of 1794 has had a chequered career, including conversion to a cathedral and back to a mosque again. Reconstructed in the 1840s, the mosque helped to set the fashion for the neo-Moresque style of architecture of so many 19th-century buildings in Algiers. A short walk to the north leads to the **Museum of Popular Arts and Traditions** *(Musée des Arts Populaires),* housed in the Khadoudja Palace (1570). The collections of old carpets and jewellery allow you to put in perspective the examples that are made today.

Emerging from the Kasbah's narrow streets into the vastness of **Martyrs' Square** *(Place des Martyrs)* itself, you'll see on the south side a dazzling white mass, crouching like a lion. This is the **Djemaa El Djedid**, a mosque of Turkish design, sometimes called the Fishermen's Mosque because it's right near the fish market, overlooking the port. Very much in the tradition of the mosques of Istanbul, it was built by the Turks in 1660. The minaret in white and ochre is one of the landmarks of

Algiers. Across the square, beyond the not very appropriate Neoclassical Chamber of Commerce, stands the **Great Mosque** *(Djemaa El Kebir)*. Credited to the 11th-century Almoravid founder of Tlemcen, Youssef Ben Tashfin, it is a simple rectangular hall, the aisles separated by arched colonnades in white, adding to the feeling of dignity and restraint.

Port

If you walk back from the Great Mosque past the fish market and Fishermen's Mosque, and continue south along the waterfront, you'll reach the main railway station and then the Gare Maritime, the terminal for trans-Mediterranean ferries. Unfortunately the roads parallel to the sea have been sacrificed to commerce and traffic rather than pedestrians, but the view back towards the Kasbah is still fine, dominated by colonnades that seem to float in a mirage of shimmering white when seen from an arriving ship.

WEST FROM ALGIERS

Starting below the Kasbah, the coast road heads north-west past Bab El Oued (River Gate), an unprepossessing suburb that grew up in the colonial period. It was the edge of the city then, populated by poorer European settlers, mainly Spanish. Since independence, expansion has pushed the limits further out. You have to fight through heavy traffic to reach open country and a string of little resorts and fishing villages. After 20 kilometres (12 mi.) the main road carries you away

Shades of Marseilles, as you approach the waterfront of Algiers from the sea.

from the sea, but signs off it point to Nadi Snawbar (and to the old name of Club des Pins). Here begins the stretch of coastline the promoters of tourism have dubbed the Turquoise Coast. How they do love a label, though this is accurate enough. Sandy beaches dominate the next 60 kilometres (37 mi.). Club des Pins (for once an old name seems to have stuck) doesn't only have the sea: it has that modern manifestation, a huge conference centre, the **Palais des**

An Algiers landmark—the minaret of "Fishermen's Mosque", by the fish market, naturally.

Nations, ideal for hosting everything from OPEC to UN and Palestine National Council meetings.

Now coming in quick succession, the holiday resorts and hotel complexes: **Moretti, Sidi Fredj, Zeralda**, all in white. You can choose from hotels, apartments, bungalows and campsites. There's tennis and sailing (Sidi Fredj has the best yacht harbour). Windsurfing is in its infancy, as yet. You could try out the benefits of the rediscovered ancient arts of thalassotherapy (sea-water treatments). Again, facilities are best at Sidi Fredj, where the hotel complex is the largest. When deciding to site it just where the French had landed in 1830, the Alge-

rians joked: "Now they can land again, but this time with their traveller's cheques!" If you are using one of the resort hotels as a base, by choice or because Algiers hotels are full, ask about shuttle buses to the city or to the airport. If you have your own transport, the quicker way is not by the coast road but the one inland through Cheraga.

As cliffs and beaches alternate along the route westward, there's a change in the face of the landscape. A sea of plastic greenhouses, wherever they can be squeezed in, caters to the local and export demand for winter salad crops. "They don't taste the same", grumble Algerians, just like anyone else, "but better than nothing". After the Mazafran, a real river, stretches remarkably undeveloped countryside of sheltered valleys. Beyond Aïn Tagourirt, a sign points to the **Royal Mauretanian Tomb** *(Tombeau Royal de Maurétanie),* 3 kilometres (2 mi.) away on a hilltop. Close up, you see that it is a huge mass of fine stonework—a cylinder 61 metres (200 ft.) across, topped by a stepped cone. Sixty Ionic columns decorate the lower part, which has four fake doors oriented towards north, east, south and west. The crosses on the stone doors account in part for an old name, Tomb of the Christian Girl, that some still give it. But the monument dates from before the time of Christ. What was it? Some have guessed that it was the tomb of the wife of Juba II, King of Mauretania and Rome's friend, but mostly it's thought to be older, from around 100 B.C. Like the pyramids long before, it may have been designed to protect some royal remains from grave robbers. If so, like them, it was a failure. The tiny entrance below ground level near the eastern door was rediscovered in modern times, but there was no treasure left, nor any bones.

If you suffer from claustrophobia, skip the next bit. If not, duck through the low opening and look in the vestibule for the carved lions. Then make the long curving walk inside. Notice the false ends of the passageways and other devices to put off fortune hunters. You're guaranteed to be disoriented. After about 180 paces you might expect to be back where you started, but in fact you are near the centre and, appropriately enough for a tomb, it's a dead end. Pashas from Algiers, frustrated at not finding the legendary treasure inside, tried to blow the monument apart. It says a lot for the ancient builders that the resulting damage was limited to a partial collapse of the eastern wall.

Tipasa

Or rather, the four Tipasas. Back on the main road after the diversion to the mysterious tomb, a few more kilometres bring you to a view of a pretty little cluster of all-white cottages on a promontory. It's not an old fishing village, but the specially built resort of **Tipasa-Village**, with riding, tennis, pools and the rest. Pay a visit, even if you don't stay the night.

Just west begins modern Tipasa, with its parks and gardens, little fishing port and small restaurants. Try one for variety and economy if you're booked into a hotel.

Next comes old Tipasa and its **Roman ruins**, which are so much vaster than the present-day town. Founded by the Phoenicians in the 5th century B.C., Tipasa became a colony of Rome in the 1st and 2nd centuries A.D. Rivalry between the Catholics and heretical Donatists eventually led to the destruction of the ancient town towards the end of the 5th century.

The largest remains—an amphitheatre and temples—stand in public gardens, the "archaeological park". Though it may not be very good for the ruins to have trees growing on the site, it's nonetheless delightful, and more shaded than usual.

On the south-eastern perimeter lie the remains of huge **baths** *(thermes)* and a **museum** *(musée)* with fine pre-Christian sarcophagi and mosaics. Look especially for the mosaic panel of African heads and slaves which was found here in 1917. Afterwards, walk out into the park, through the ruins of the amphitheatre and north past the well-preserved **forum**, still with most of its flagstones.

Private villas and more baths line the clifftop as far as the great Christian **basilica** on the highest point of the next headland to the west. The old city wall runs alongside the basilica. Cross it to find the **necropolis**, where Bishop Alexander gathered the remains of saints in the 5th century. Walk back along the wall and you come to the **theatre**. But it really doesn't matter where you wander: this is a tranquil and evocative place. Note that the ruins close at 5 p.m.

West again lies the "fourth Tipasa", the resort complex of Tipasa-Matares or **Tipasa Plage** (beach). Like the village, this is the work of the architect

An ancient mosaic of three enchained slaves, a forceful reminder of Tipasa's Roman past.

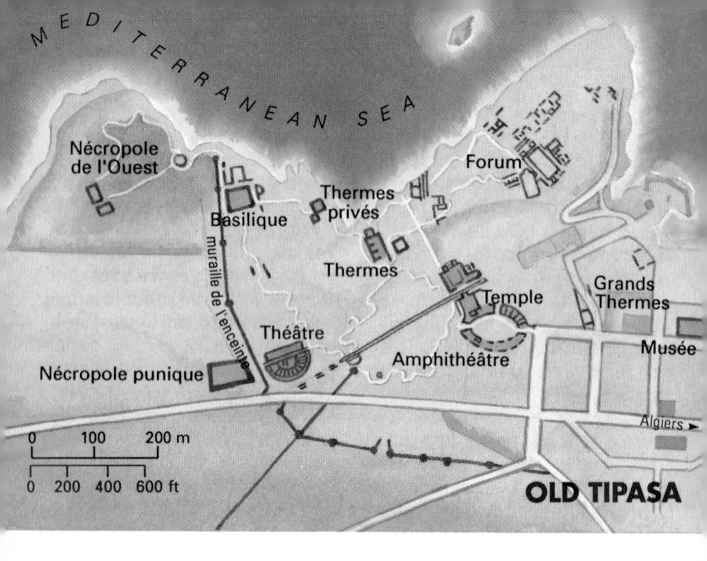

Fernand Pouillon, who almost single-handedly changed the hotel scene in Algeria in the 1970s, with his imaginative designs. Tipasa Beach resembles a D.W. Griffith film set of a walled Arab city. As in all holiday centres on Algeria's coast, it's packed in summer, cavernously empty in winter.

Cherchell

Head west from Tipasa for 30 kilometres (18 mi.). The main road takes a bend inland through rich farmland and orange groves before hitting the sea again at Cherchell, once the Phoenician port of Iol. Later the Romans themselves moved in. Disappointingly little of any size survives, much less than at Tipasa, despite Cherchell's greater importance. You may see evidence of the earthquake that shook northern Algeria in October 1989. Most of the damage was in rural areas in the Tipasa-Cherchell region.

Martyrs' Square *(Place des Martyrs)* in the centre of town has some relics dotted about, but the real treasures are in the **museum**, facing the square. It's arranged around an open courtyard like part of a Roman villa, so the light is natural and lovely. Here as elsewhere in museums, photography is not allowed, alas. Juba II is recorded as having copies made of some of the greatest Greek sculptures, so it's likely that the divine Apollo, after Phidias, is one of these. You can't miss the vast Hercules or the uniformed Augustus. One of the finest mosaics you will ever see, surely, is the brilliantly coloured, utterly lifelike set of *Scenes of Working in the Fields.* Those North African mosaic artists had some secrets that set them apart. After these, the mosaic garden along the road, with rather inferior examples, is an anticlimax. Go there first, if you have time to spare.

On the eastern edge of town, opposite the mosaic garden and overlooking the sea, a 17th-century shrine *(koubba)* includes the tomb of the religious teacher Sidi Brahim El Ghobrini. The setting is fine, but the fragile old buildings are neglected.

To continue west on the winding, narrow coast road you need plenty of time and, preferably, your own transport. If you have both, the

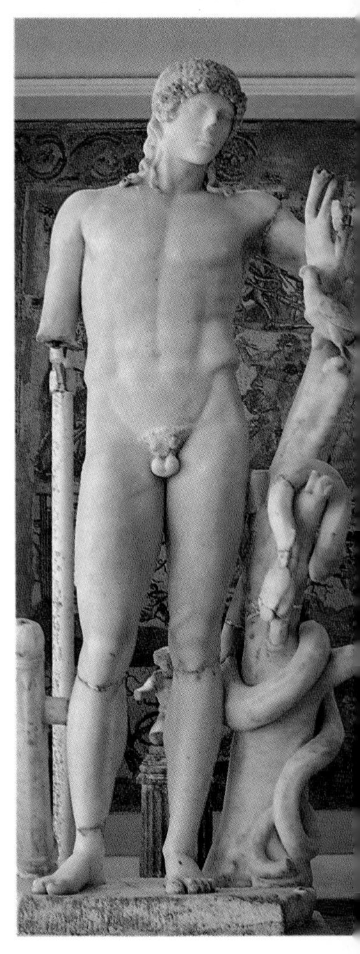

Gracing Cherchell's museum, this Apollo is a fine Roman copy of the great Greek hero.

scenery all the way to **Ténès**, 108 kilometres (68 mi.) from Cherchell, and to a lesser degree, **Mostaganem**, a further 160 kilometres (100 mi.), is worth the trip. There are countless beaches and bays, and some marvellous views.

The Main Road West

This route from Algiers ignores the coast entirely, first heading inland across the Mitidja plain to **Boufarik**, a market town with an orange festival in spring. This is now surrounded by such productive land that it is hard to imagine the area as the malarial swamp it once was. The town of **Blida** bursts with the overspill from the capital. If you have time, take the zig-zagging road to **Chrea**, 1,500 metres (4,900 ft.) up but a mere 20 kilometres (12 mi.) away. Spring here is idyllic, summers are cool and in winter it's a ski centre.

Just west of Blida, instead of the direct road to Khemis Miliana, the alternative along the deep **Gorges de la Chiffa** leads through a favourite holiday area for the people of Algiers, with waterfalls, forest walks, serious rock climbing and a lot of Barbary apes. But watch out: they may help themselves to your picnic. Khemis Miliana (literally Thursday Market) has grown up on a road, rail and river junction, but apart from communications hasn't much to interest the visitor. **Miliana**, now by-passed by the main road, is much more appealing. The town is ringed by orchards and hosts a cherry festival in May.

Further west, and about 200 kilometres (125 mi.) from Algiers, **Ech Chlef** has the strange look of a town without a centre, the result of a double tragedy. In 1954, when it was known as Orléansville, the town was shaken by a massive earthquake and largely razed, with heavy loss of life. Reconstruction was in full progress in 1980 when, by this time re-named El Asnam, the unfortunate place was hit by an even more violent series of shocks, the most extreme ever recorded in North Africa. This time 25,000 were killed, and hardly a building survived. You can still see some abandoned ruins left as monuments, while the town under its latest name is being rebuilt in a ring around the old centre.

EAST FROM ALGIERS

Coast road or main road further inland? That is the question. Anyone heading east in a hurry takes the highway to Tizi Ouzou. If you have more time, it's worth following the coast for a while. How far depends on your mode of travel: the road eventually becomes rough, tortuous and devoid of public transport.

The former, quiet little beach resorts around the bay of Algiers have been gobbled up by the capital's expansion and industry. **Bordj El Kiffan** (16 km./10 mi.) can be lively: a lot of students lodge here and commute to their colleges. Not until you reach **Aïn Taya**, twice as far from the city, does the beach become pleasant. Huge stretches of sand eastwards past **Boumerdes** absorb Algiers holidaymakers in summer, but there are almost no facilities to compare with the leisure complexes at Sidi Fredj and Tipasa. This may well be good news to you. If so, push on east, to one of the least developed coastlines on the Mediterranean.

Dellys, 105 kilometres (65 mi.) from Algiers, is a sleepy port that now hints but little at its long history. A few fishing boats bring in their catches early in the day, so look out for something fresh for lunch in one of the cafés. Further east along the rocky coast, **Tigzirt** is lively and growing fast. Just like its hordes of children, in fact. As the nearest place on the sea to teeming Tizi Ouzou, the Kabyle capital, it is bursting at holiday times. Ruins are always made more romantic by the sound of waves on a beach, and so it is with the remains of a **basilica** near the harbour. Look for the Christian symbols among the striking bas-reliefs.

Coastal traffic this far mostly goes inland from Tigzirt over the steep and twisting pass to Tizi Ouzou, while the corniche continues past ever more remote beaches. You probably won't see more than a handful of vehicles in an hour. From **Azeffoun**, the next fishing village, a rough track leads inland for a few kilometres to the mainly undug remains of Roman Rusuzus. The coast road then deteriorates, though scheduled for eventual improvement. It is impassable after heavy rain, but with a tough vehicle and in the dry season you might explore it and find a lonely paradise beach or the clear water of a rocky cove.

GREAT KABYLIA

The mountainous region of Great Kabylia *(Grande Kabylie)* extends to the east and south-east of Algiers as far as Bejaïa and the Djurdjura range. It's a mere 80 kilometres (50 mi.) from the sea to the Djurdjura's 2,300-metre

(7,500-ft.) peaks. The range is cut up by scores of gorges. Much of it is thick forest, and the few roads are narrow and sinuous. It's hard work to get around, but doubly worth the effort.

Kabyle people take life on their own terms. Sharp and argumentative, they make good lawyers and politicians. Having been here long before anyone else, they don't like outsiders telling them what to do. Over the millennia, their homeland was such a bone in the throat of past invaders that most learned to leave it alone.

The Kabyle language is a branch of Berber: even if you don't speak Arabic, you'll be able to tell that this language is different, though there have been many borrowings—in both directions. So when you come across local people who speak English, remember they are using their fourth language.

Women especially dress differently in Kabylia. They don't veil by tradition, and they wear very bright and disparate fabrics. You can still get quite good modern versions of their silver filigree and enamel jewellery. But the chunky antique bracelets and pectorals, heavy with coral and semi-precious stones, are beyond most pockets now. Men almost always used to wear a light-coloured wool burnous, but that's now limited to some in the mountain villages, where you can buy wonderful examples.

A Kabylian girl lends colour to villages that tumble along ridges of the Djurdjura range.

Tizi Ouzou, capital of the province, stands at the junction of the major roads, so you'll probably travel through town or even stay here. *Tizi* is the Berber word for "pass": this is the pass into the mountains from the west. Tizi Ouzou is ballooning visibly, with some of the most impressive public buildings in the country— hospitals, university departments, sports complexes. The Hotel and Tourism Institute has its headquarters here, and certainly has work in plenty to do. Despite all this modernity, the Thursday **market**, west of the city, retains the flavour of Kabyle life.

Into the Djurdjura

By way of contrast, go to the Djurdjura and its national park. The ideal is to make a loop, heading south-east into the heart of the massif on one route and returning by another. Don't forget, though, that the roads are likely to be blocked by a snowfall any time from early winter to late spring.

Make first for **Larbaa-Nath-Iraten**. The French had suffered so many setbacks in 27 years of attempting to subjugate Kabylia that in 1857, on the orders of an impatient Napoleon III, they built a new fort, right in the heart of the area that was giving them the most trouble. This is it, and the view is commanding, as it was meant to be. Today, there's something more peaceful: a craft centre specializing in embroideries.

Aïn El Hammam, 1,080 metres (3,500 ft.) up, offers another panorama of gorges and needle-like pinnacles. You can actually stay here, too, in a pleasant hotel which makes a good base for hiking and climbing expeditions.

From Aïn El Hammam, the road climbs to the **Tirourda pass** (1,760 m./5,780 ft.) and new prospects to the south. Continuing right down into the deep valley of the Oued Sahel, you can link up to a more westerly road across the Djurdjura that will take you back to Tizi Ouzou by way of the pass of Tizi-N'Kouilal and through cedar forests and barren peaks.

The Djurdjura National Park takes in a tract of the highest land. **Tikjda**, within the park, is a ski resort in winter (there's a lift, a ski school and a few chalets) and a centre for walking in summer. Sadly, in many parts of Kabylia, devastating forest fires have stripped and blackened the mountainsides. Wild orchids, fragile and scented narcissi and cyclamen bravely push through the ash after the first rains, but the loss of ancient stands of oak may be irreparable. All over Algeria, reafforestation schemes are under way, but it's a mammoth task.

Notice how villages cling to the hilltops, often with the houses pressed close together, blind walls on the outside, all designed for defence. The minarets of their mosques used to double as lookout posts, and the houses usually had as much room for the livestock as for the family. Villagers still like to keep a few sheep, a cow and maybe some goats. They also cultivate cereals and, where the climate and altitude permit, some olive and fig trees. Fresh green, red and black figs—luscious. Dried on flat baskets, they are a staple food for the rest of the year.

Don't miss a famous cluster of five mountain villages, the **Beni Yenni**. Again, there is a chance to stay in a small hotel. To get the flavour of each village, and to see its particular crafts, much the best way around is to walk. You can watch silversmiths, enamellers, potters and woodworkers in their workshops—but don't expect prices to be any less than they would be in Algiers. (Roadside vendors on the way down to Tizi Ouzou just occasionally undercut them.) While walking about, you may be lucky enough to be invited into a house. However, this is more likely to happen if you spend some time in the village, so that people can get to know you a little (despite the language barrier).

East from Tizi Ouzou

The road sometimes follows the heights, sometimes the valleys. Watch out for Barbary apes in the woods. The males might be sitting by the road, because they've been fed from passing cars. If you can stop, you may catch a glimpse of the females, babies clinging to their fur, taking refuge in the trees. In the more open land around small villages, prickly pear cactus is grown as a highly effective fence as well as for the fruit. (Never tried one? As soon as you touch it, the myriad tiny hairs stick into your skin and irritate it for hours. Slice the fruit open while holding it in newspaper, and scoop out the flesh with a spoon. Don't get the hairs in your mouth or on your lips, or you will be sorry you ever tangled with the thing.)

El Kseur, on the main route south-west of Bejaïa, has some colourful craft shops and busy

In the port of Bejaïa, fishermen still head out to sea each morning.

markets. Just before reaching Bejaïa itself, at **La Réunion**, there's a sign by the side of the road, put there by the Commonwealth War Graves Commission. If you go the short distance down a track, you'll come to a beautifully tended green garden, with about 250 graves of British, Australian, Canadian and other Allied servicemen killed in the campaigns in this part of North Africa in 1942–43. They were all so young, so far from home. It is very moving.

Bejaïa

This town seems to have had more names and more ups and downs than most of the good harbours on the Algerian coast. As the Hammadite capital in the 12th century, it was said to have had 100,000 inhabitants. Even allowing for the cavalier way the old writers threw numbers around, it must have been impressive. A story is told of how the Hammadite sultan was showing the holy man Sidi El Touati the marvels of his city, when the sage held up the sleeve of his ragged robe, and said "Look!". And lo!, when he looked through it the sultan could see nothing but ruins.

Etiquette

Alcohol *is forbidden to Muslims, so don't offer it to them unless you have been given an indication that it would be welcomed. Never make a show of drinking in public.*

Alms. *One of the duties of Islam is to give to the poor. If you choose not to give something, be restrained in your mode of rejection.*

Dress *should be conservative. Shorts are not appropriate for men or women except on the beach or sports field.*

Gifts. *If you take someone a present, it will probably be opened only later.*

Help *if you can when you see a vehicle broken down in a remote area. Perhaps you can only give a little water, or the very tool that will get it going again.*

Houses *are especially private places. Never look through a crack in a door or over the wall of a courtyard.*

It is still the custom of riders in the south to dismount, and enter a town on foot. Otherwise it would be too easy to catch glimpses of the secluded women.

If you are invited to someone's home, don't admire any of the possessions too vocally: they may be given to you. Don't be in too much of a hurry and don't be embarrassed if food is produced and the hosts, especially the women of the house, don't eat with you.

Mosques. *Never just walk in. If you wait near the door, a caretaker will usually come. Find out if visiting is allowed (especially women). Take off your shoes before entering (or put on the overslippers that some mosques provide). Be discreetly dressed and quiet.*

Photography *is usually forbidden in mosques and certain other holy places. Avoid photographing without permission. It is best to get to know people first, not try to steal a picture.*

Pork *or anything containing it or cooked in pork fat should never be offered to Muslims.*

Ramadan *is a trying time. Don't make it more so by eating, drinking or smoking in front of Muslims during the daylight hours.*

Tea. *In the south, especially, the serving of tea takes a long time and follows an etiquette all its own. If you are visiting someone, you'll be offered a small glass. Drink it quite quickly, with some noisy appreciation. A fourth refill is an indication that although your presence has been more than welcome, it's really time to leave.*

Women *are esteemed in many ways in the world of Islam, but they shouldn't be assertive in public. Western frankness and openness may not be appreciated and can be misinterpreted. You may make some progress if the men in a group deal with officialdom. Don't stare at people, particularly veiled women.*

So it was to be, within a few decades. Of all that magnificence, only the outlines of two gates remain today.

Bejaïa was able to repel the first French attacks, though, before falling in 1833. Why did the French name it "Bougie" (Candle)? The answer is, they didn't. They called *candles* after Bejaïa because that was where the best beeswax candles came from centuries ago.

The port with its yards full of containers, car ferries to Europe and natural gas terminal, not forgetting the fishermen, lies at the base of a cliff. Somehow a road makes its way up to the city perched on the top, where many of the streets are linked by flights of steps. Stand in **1st of November Square** *(Place du 1er Novembre)* for a fine view of the harbour and the bay.

The **museum** *(musée)* in the same square has relics from the Roman and Hammadite past of Bejaïa. Walk from there down **Rue Si El Haoues** for some good fish restaurants. If you want even more expansive views than the ones from the city, climb to **Monkeys' Peak** (it's not far from town) or drive out to **Cap Carbon**, the extremity of the promontory 7 kilometres (4 mi.) to the north-east.

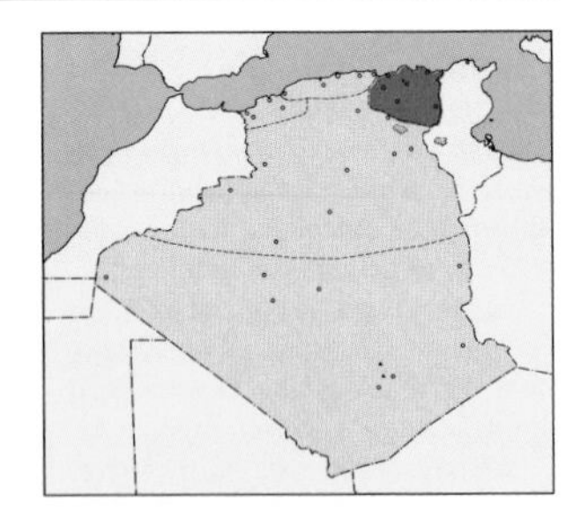

NORTH-EAST

Hot springs, orchards laden with fruit and waving wheat fields vast enough to rival the prairies—no wonder the Romans regarded this as one of their jewels. But don't think that the famous ruins of Timgad and the other Roman cities are the only reason to come here, or that the rest is for passing through on the way to somewhere else. Sudden mountains with villages like eagles' nests interrupt the vistas. The people, whose ancestors resisted every invader, provided some of the most dauntless fighters in the struggle for Algerian independence. It can't be a coincidence that so many writers and religious and political leaders, ancient and modern, were born in this land of variety.

LESSER KABYLIA

The region extends along the coast from Bejaïa to Jijel, taking in the hinterland of the Babor range, as well. Lesser Kabylia *(Petite Kabylie)* may be lesser in altitude and extent than its big sister to the west, but its spectacular shoreline is labelled the "Sapphire Coast" with good reason.

After Bejaïa's industrial outskirts, the road escapes from the smog and smells of the gas terminal and follows the sea around its sandy bay, where there's end-to-end camping along the beach in summer. Bejaïa has its own favourite resorts along the gulf, headed by **Tichi** with a Pouillon-designed hotel.

From here, you might divert up into the national park of the **Djebel Babor**, especially if it's springtime and you like to hill-walk among wildflowers, cedar and oak forests. On the road to Sétif, the 8-kilometre (5-mi.) **Gorges de Kherrata**, one of the deepest gashes in all the Atlas ranges, is called Chabet El Akra (Ravine of Death). The new main road spends a lot of time in tunnels. Be sure to take the old road where you have an alternative. Apart from its quietness, you'll enjoy views of soaring mountains instead of having to stare at the lights of a hundred heavy trucks in the darkness of the tunnels, and you may well see some Barbary apes by the roadside. People in passing cars no doubt used to feed them, but now that nearly all traffic uses the tunnels, pickings are slimmer.

Back on the coast, the road, or **Corniche Kabyle**, hangs giddily over the sea or dives through tunnels on its way to the resort and fishing village of Ziama Mansouriyah and beyond. Blasting the tunnels in places revealed natural caves full of stalactites and stalagmites. The best is the **Ghar Adim**, at Dar El Oued, 40 kilometres (25 mi.) from Tichi. Ask at the first house about visiting it.

The port of **Jijel**, remarkably, has kept almost the same name from Carthaginian times. It was so cut off by the lack of roads that it was often an independent fiefdom of pirates' lairs, or the object of invaders hoping to set up a base. You'll find the beaches not yet much exploited, and plans to do so are going to conflict with commercial expansion, Jijel being an alternative port to Skikda for the Constantine region.

Sétif makes a convenient base for visiting the Roman ruins at Djemila, provided no hotel is open at the site itself.

The altitude (1,100 m./3,600 ft.) gives the town a freshness, even in summer. Wide suburban streets and the brilliance of bougainvillea in its gardens make Sétif one of the more attractive of the expanding provincial centres. Notice how the old town has a rectangular pattern of streets, because, you've guessed, they follow those of a Roman settlement. The city walls were only pulled down in the 1920s: walk the loop of the boulevards laid out in their stead. Sétif was one of the places where the preview of revolution, the risings of May 8, 1945, took place and was bloodily put down.

While you're here, the **museum** on Boulevard de la Palestine is worth seeing for its mosaics, especially one depicting the *Triumph of Bacchus*. The other highlights, the treasures from the fortress of the Beni Hammad, are especially important to students of Islamic history.

The **fortress** (60 km./37 mi. south-west of Sétif as the crow flies, but twice as far by road) marks the site of the 11th-century capital of the Hammadites. Excavations cover an enormous area. The fortress *(kalaa)* itself is in ruins, but there were evidently many palaces and mosques. Of the Great Mosque, the outline and a section of the typical square **minaret** remains. Above, on a rocky eminence, stand the ruins of a **signal tower**, which is said to have been one of a chain by which messages could be sent all the way to the coast.

Djemila

It's less than 50 kilometres (30 mi.) from Sétif to Djemila by the Constantine road. Imagine one of the most perfectly preserved Roman cities, with a climate like permanent spring. See it up on a ridge where two deep valleys meet, surrounded by higher hills. And think of having it all to yourself, or perhaps sharing it with only a couple of little girls herding some goats along one of the stone-paved streets.

Djemila (the Beautiful) was what the Arabs called the town. To the Romans it was Cuicul, and with Thamugadi (now Timgad), one of the most important of the cities built for veterans of the imperial army in newly gained or precariously held territory. The Emperor Nerva ordered the construction of Cuicul at the end of the 1st

Rich green foothills ripple down the Djebel Babor near Djemila.

century A.D. Retired soldiers were given grants of land so they could settle down to family life. Intermarriage with local women usually followed.

You enter the site at a point near the museum. Judge whether to visit it right away or later by the time of day: the ruins look their best in the early morning or late afternoon, not at midday. A long, tree-lined path takes you near the highest, most complicated and chronologically youngest group of buildings. It will make more sense to continue on the path to the **triumphal Arch of Caracalla** dedicated to Emperor Caracalla and his African-born father, Emperor Septimius Severus, and mother, Julia Domna. The beautifully engraved inscription is still in position; the three stone pedestals on top would have carried statues of the dedicatees.

The long road downhill, continuing in the direction you have walked so far, but to the

The majestic ruins of Djemila; colourful mosaic details found in the museum.

right of the arch, is the column-lined **Cardo Maximus**. The street traverses the oldest section of the ancient city, so it's the best place to start looking at details. Passing elegant houses to the right, then a temple of Venus, you arrive at the basilica, a government administration building. On the other side, away from the Cardo, lies the **northern forum**, with a great carved altar in the middle. Next along the Cardo, and possibly more ready for occupation than any other part of the site, is the **market** *(marché)*. It was paid for by Lucius Cosinius, as an inscription proudly declares. It says how much it cost him, too: 30,000 sesterces, no less. The 18 little shops are in good shape, stone tables intact. The standard volumes used by the inspector of weights and measures, carved in another stone table, can still be seen. Right next to the market, two cavernous prison cells are waiting. Did they throw cheating merchants into them? Behind the market, facing the forum, stands the imposing temple of the **Capitol**, dedicated to Jupiter, Juno and Minerva, patron deities of the city. The first set of public baths in the town adjoins it on the "downhill" side. The last substantial building on the Cardo, the palatial **House of Europa** takes its name from a mosaic of Europa and the Bull excavated there. Look for it in the local museum.

Now retrace your steps along the Cardo. Morning and afternoon, you'll see a few small

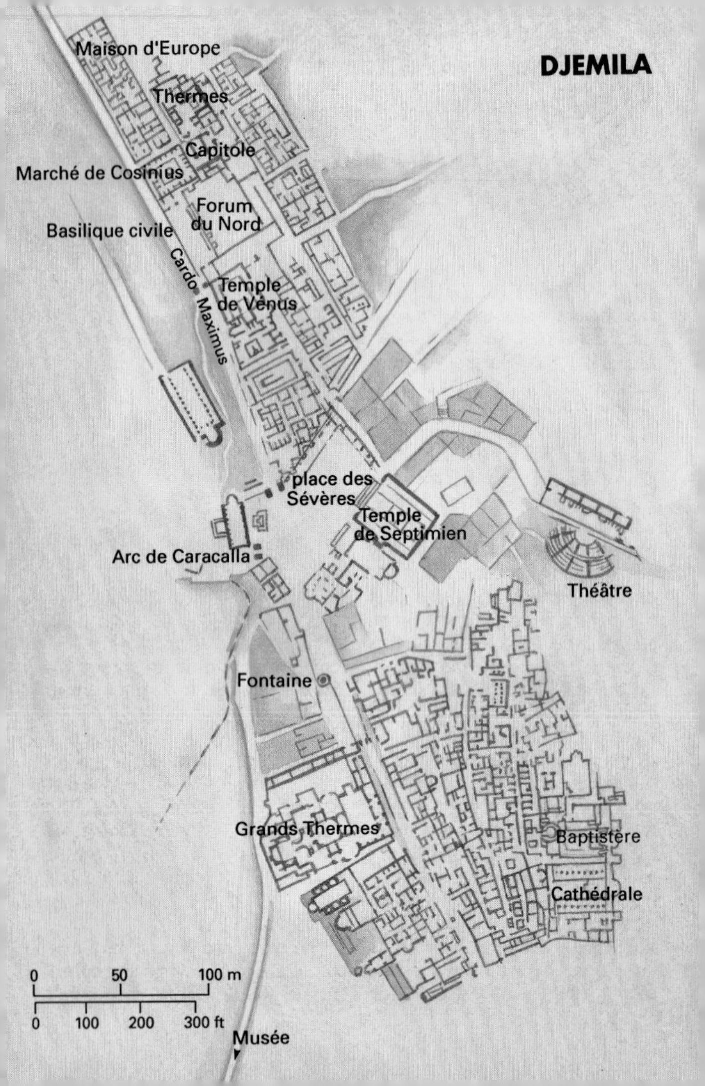
DJEMILA
Maison d'Europe
Thermes
Capitole
Marché de Cosinius
Forum du Nord
Basilique civile
Cardo Maximus
Temple de Vénus
place des Sévères
Temple de Septimien
Arc de Caracalla
Théâtre
Fontaine
Grands Thermes
Baptistère
Cathédrale
0 50 100 m
0 100 200 300 ft
Musée

children on their way to school and back: it is the shortest way across the valley from their village to the present-day town of Djemila. Stop again at the arch of Caracalla to inspect the later, larger **Severan forum** *(place de Sévères)*, finished at the beginning of the 3rd century. The monumental **temple** opposite is dedicated to Septimius Severus. Try the effect of standing at the top of the massive staircase—nothing quite like it exists anywhere else in Roman Africa. A huge marble head of the emperor, with wavy beard and curiously curled hair, now in the museum's sculpture court, used to stand in this temple.

Behind the temple and around the hill, you'll come upon the enchanting **theatre**. Set as usual into a recess in the slope, this one is different from most in the nature of its "backdrop". Sit amongst the imaginary audience of 3,000 and look beyond the stage straight across the deep valley to farm buildings just like those seen in Roman mosaics.

Now back to the areas that you skirted on the way down the path. The southward extension of the Cardo passes a charming conical public fountain still in good order. Above that, between the Cardo and your original way down, you reach the aptly named **Great Baths** *(Grands Thermes)*. Dating from the late 2nd century, they're much the biggest installation in the city. Clamber to the highest point for the best view—not only of the baths but of the whole panorama. The walls you see to the right are the site of a Christian cathedral and baptistry (the restored cupola belongs to the latter).

Pay a visit to the **museum** *(musée)* before you continue on your way. The displays of sculpture, inscriptions, pottery and above all the marvellous mosaics will round out your impressions of Djemila. Note that although the main site stays open every day, the museum itself closes on Saturdays.

CONSTANTINE

Irresistible to the ancients who were looking for an impregnable location, the setting of Constantine *(Qacentina)* is still breathtaking. You expect to see mountain villages or remote monasteries, perhaps, perched on the edge of such chasms, but not large cities like this. Throw something out of the window of some Constantine houses and it will fall 200 metres (about 600 ft.) or so.

That, it is said, is exactly what one ruler of the city, Ahmed Bey, used to do with his enemies, having had them sewn up in a sack first. He seems to have been the archetypal despot with an enormous harem, but in the end he salvaged his reputation by leading a stubborn resistance to the French

Perched imperiously on the edge of a chasm, Constantine overlooks the impressive Gorges of the Rhummel.

occupation in 1837, first in the city and then by fighting on in the Aurès mountains for a further 11 years.

Before the Romans renamed it, Constantine was called Cirta. The long-lived Numidian King Masinissa, who had helped them against Hannibal in 202 B.C. and again in the Third (and last) Punic War, had his capital here. It was the base for his grandson Jugurtha's struggle against Roman hegemony. Later, the Romans installed their vassal Juba II. Then, when they eventually absorbed Numidia into the empire, Constantine became the chief town of a confederation of colonies in the area. Falling to the Arabs early in the 8th century, it was subject to the typical ebb and flow of dynasties until a Turkish expedition installed a governor, or Bey, in the 1600s.

If anything, the centre of Constantine is even more difficult than Algiers to drive around or park in. So whether you have a vehicle or not, the best plan is to walk. The city centre, old and new, is quite concentrated. Orient yourself at **Martyrs' Square** *(Place des Martyrs),* near the imposing Air Algérie office, and not far from the elaborately neo-Moresque Hôtel Cirta—almost a national monument, with its exterior now restored to former splendour. A very short step, for the two squares almost adjoin, leads to **Place du 1er Novembre**. Its open-air cafés, thronged by day, close mysteriously early in the evenings. A lively esplanade extends to the west.

Just beyond begins the **Kasbah**. It's a maze, but perhaps you're getting used to that by now. There are some quite broad, straight streets, as well as alleys so narrow that two people can hardly pass. The mosque **Djemaa Souk El Ghezal** in Rue Didouche Mourad is a curiosity: built in the 18th century, it was used as a church in the 19th, when it was given a miniature replica of the dome of Florence cathedral. Next to the mosque, facing a little tree-lined square where old men gather to play dominoes, is the **Palais de Hadj Ahmed**. Vast and now decaying, the palace has colourful tiles and picturesque murals. The notorious Bey had little time to enjoy himself here. The palace was finished in 1835, only two years before the French took over.

The **Great Mosque** *(Djemaa El Kebir)* to the south, is much older in parts (13th Century), and the building, like many others, incorporates columns and capitals from Roman ruins. Just below it, the **medersa** (Islamic college) has students spilling out into the street. Right nearby, a little flight of stairs leads downwards to a thrilling experience—or a fright for those who suffer from vertigo. Out from the dizzying cliff springs a suspension footbridge, the **Passerelle**. It crosses over the gorges of the Rhummel hundreds of feet deep, swaying perceptibly as each pedestrian passes. The view from all Constantine's bridges *(ponts)* makes it worth walking to get to them: the **Sidi Rached**, south of the Passerelle; the **El Kantara**, north of the Passerelle, with the remains of a Roman bridge below it; and the **Sidi M'Cid**, suspended 175 metres (574 ft.) above the Rhummel where it begins to widen at the northern end of the Kasbah.

Keep a little time for one more short walk to the south of Martyrs' Square, up to the **museum** on the plateau of the **Koudiat Aty** quarter. The prize exhibits include a delicate little bronze *Winged Victory* found in the Kasbah last century, gorgeous mosaics from Djemila and what just *may* be King Masinissa's own short sword in its wooden sheath. If you are planning to visit Tiddis, look for the everyday and precious objects excavated there. Fans of the 19th-century Orientalists will find a good selection of bright, romanticized scenes of souks, sultans and dancing girls here. Who knows, with the return to fashion of these works, they may become the museum's main attraction.

Tiddis

The site of Roman Castellum Tidditanorum lies only 30 kilometres (19 mi.) north-west of Constantine but a world away from its bustling crowds. There is no regular public transport, but it's worth making an effort to get here—not just for the ruins but for the landscape and views, the wildflowers and the solitude. For it is most likely that you will be quite alone. A south-facing hillside looks at first like a dozen others in the vicinity, with rust-red stones and even redder earth, until you come closer and see how much of it is manmade.

The slope was too steep and rocky for the classical, linear town plan, and the paved main street winds its way up the hill. Carts couldn't manage the ascent, so the usual grooves in the flagstones are absent. What was the attraction to the Romans, and to the Berbers who were here before them and long afterwards? To the latter, it may have been the clay, for Tiddis, "the Red", was a prodigious producer of red pottery for a thousand years after the empire had gone. (And the **potters' quarter** accounts for a large part of the area.) To the Romans it must have been the hot springs. Were there any, in all the territories they conquered, that they didn't channel into **bath houses**? Here, it was *cold* water that was a problem. Roman engineers built vast reservoirs to hold the rainfall, and you can still work out the distribution system. It may be that ancient Tiddis enjoyed running water for more hours per day than present-day Constantine during periods of shortage. One square bath next to the main street, with its low seat, steps leading in and out and herringbone brick floor, would make a pretty good jacuzzi today.

Natural caves in the hillside were enlarged to form temples and shrines and then churches after Christianity was legalized. Possibly the most photographed feature here is a carved stone relief of male genitalia—equipped with wings and legs like a chicken—that marks the entrance to a **shrine** to Mithras, a favourite deity of the imperial soldiery.

Higher up the hill, poker heads of yucca-like flowers push through the earth. A walk to the summit past the biggest cisterns gives a stunning view to the north, where the Rhummel cuts a gorge almost as steep as it does through Constantine, but this time through wild, deserted country.

Skikda

Growing up as the port for Constantine (85 km./53 mi. inland) and now Algeria's biggest terminal for the export of oil and liquefied natural gas, Skikda probably won't appear in the plans of most visitors—unless they are concerned with the petroleum business. The origins of the town date back to Phoenician days, but the remains of a very large **Roman theatre** and the long beaches are not enough compensation for the proximity of refinery, pipelines and so much industry.

Under the French name Philippeville, the area saw some of the most horrifying events to mark the earlier phases of the war of independence. On August 20, 1955, FLN units made the first widespread attacks on colonists' houses and farms, as well as on military posts, killing 71 Europeans. In the French reprisals perhaps 100 times as many Algerians were killed, among them people who had no connection with the uprising. The hatred engendered on both sides by these events meant that any hope of compromise was effectively dead. To the FLN came many of the new recruits who were essential to its ultimate success.

THE AURÈS

Impressive even for mountainous northern Algeria, the Aurès stands up like a fortress. The contrasts within this compact massif are concentrated into extremes. Peaks rising to more than 2,300 metres (7,500 ft.) are separated by deep and winding canyons. The high ground is jagged rock, scorched in summer and blasted in winter by bitter winds. Along the river valleys stretch orchards of apricots and pomegranates and, on the south side, palm groves just like oases. The tough Chaouia people (the name means "shepherds") who live here are the greatest of individualists. The Aurès, virtually impenetrable to a succession of invaders, was their last refuge and here they kept to their own way of life, their dialect of the Berber language and their customs.

Some of the mountain-top villages, already hard to see because they are built from and into the surrounding rock, can only be reached by precipitous steps. Every village serves as a watchtower over the roads and paths below. The Romans never subjugated the Chaouia, contenting themselves instead with settling the plains, building an army base at Lambesis *(Tazoult-Lambèse)* and the veterans' colony of Thamugadi *(Timgad)*. From there they made occasional punitive expeditions into the mountains when they felt a show of force was needed. Right down to the time of the French, the Aurès was the hardest nut to crack, and there were frequent insurrections.

Imitating the Romans, the French established a garrison at Batna. The Aurès was in the forefront of the revolution. The region joined in the rising on November 1, 1954 and saw bitter fighting through that first winter under the legendary leader, Ben Boulaid, who devoted the remaining sixteen months of his life to the liberation struggle. You'll still see the abandoned remains of Aurèsian villages destroyed in retaliation for FLN attacks.

In the plains 29 kilometres (18 mi.) to the north-east of Batna, though almost in the shadow of the Aurès, stands a remote, strange and in its way perfect monument, **Le Medracen**. If you have already been to the Royal Mauretanian Tomb near Tipasa, you'll recognize the style. A colonnaded base is surmounted by a flattish stepped cone. This tomb is probably older—from about 150 B.C. and is attributed to Micipsa, son of the great King Masinissa. It could have served as a model for the larger version. Like it, Le Medracen also has 60 columns and a hidden corridor to the interior, now blocked again by collapsed stones and earth.

In fact, in architectural terms the design turned out to be a dead end. As with the pyramids, there was little space inside and, apart from tombs, such shapes, however appealing, had few uses. Still, if you like to feel "king of the castle", it's a fairly easy climb up the massive steps of curved stone blocks to the top of Le Medracen. A king without subjects, probably, for this is another place of wonderful solitude.

Batna

With its better-than-average hotels, Batna can serve as your base for combining visits to the Aurès and the great Roman and other sites in the area. It has evolved since independence into a modern industrial and university city, though it still has the appeal of a frontier town. If you'd prefer an oasis atmosphere, Biskra (see p. 118) on the south side of the massif has the better climate, and you can make trips into the mountains from there.

Between Biskra and Batna you have a choice of three routes through the Aurès, plus various diversions. The most famous view is found on the easterly route, which follows the valley of Oued El Abiod. 94 kilometres (58 mi.) south of Batna, you look down from a high point called the **Balcon de Rhoufi**, outside the village of Rhoufi, as the river snakes through barren hills, its gorge a ribbon of palm gardens.

Nearer to Batna, above the Abiod, turn up to the little town of **Arris**, home of Ben Boulaid. A **craft museum** here celebrates the strikingly heavy jewellery and dark wool car-

pets made in these mountains. At nearly 1,200 metres (3,900 ft.), Arris is one spot to start walking, above all in the flower-scented spring. This is country asking to be explored on foot, for so much is inaccessible any other way. Whether you hike or drive it, the short, steep climb to the north-

From the Balcon de Rhoufi *a remarkable blend of village and land.*

west over the 1,700-metre (5,600-ft.) **Teniet-Bahli pass** takes you by way of terrific views to the middle valley of the massif, that of the Abdi.

TIMGAD
Musée
Thermes du Nord
Porte de Lambèse
Cathédrale
Porte Nord
Cardo Nord
Thermes de l'Ouest
Bibliothèque
Thermes de l'Est
Porte de Mascula
Decumanus Maximus
Arc de Trajan
Forum
Cardo Sud
Marché de Sertius
Théâtre
Capitole
Thermes du Sud
Cathédrale Donatiste
Fort byzantin
0
100
200 m
0
200
400
600 ft

Tazoult-Lambèse

To the south-east of Batna, within sight of it's expanding suburbs and industry, these vast and confusing remains once provided Rome's North African legion, the Third Augusta, with a base. Three different installations went up here and there are monuments and ruins scattered in every direction. Of ancient Lambèse, only one substantial building survives, the fine **Praetorium**, with the Third's insignia above the door. It's only guesswork to suggest that this was the headquarters of the commanding general, but the flat area in front of it certainly looks like the parade ground. Two great main streets met near the Praetorium, the Via Principalis and the Via Decumana, with a four-way arch at the intersection. The road to the east led through another arch and then, paved all the way, to Timgad (ancient Thamugadi) and on to Tebessa. The oval **amphitheatre**, a short walk to the south, has been so quarried for its stone that no seating is left, but you can make out the underground rooms and corridors where animals were kept for the contests.

Less excavation work has been done here than at other major sites, and the present-day village probably covers a lot of remains. Ask there for the way to the small **museum** to see superb mosaics and other finds, or you will leave with an impression of just dust and tumbled stones. Unless you're an archaeologist, it's best to visit Tazoult-Lambèse on the way to somewhere more magnificent. Not on the way back, or you risk anti-climax. Which more magnificent place? The answer, resoundingly, is nearby Timgad.

Timgad

It was in the year 100 when that military martinet and arch empire-builder Trajan ordered the construction of Thamugadi, now known as Timgad. The self-confidence of the conquerors was at its peak. They didn't even feel it necessary to give the new military colony a wall, though the turbulent Aurès dominated as even today, the southern horizon. That was part of the reason for locating it here, of course, to reinforce the frontier. Soldiers need to be kept occupied in peacetime, too, so putting the Third Legion to work on this project had another advantage. But the main idea seems to have been to build a centre of Roman civilization and culture. In particular, the 20-year

veterans of imperial service and their families could be given an entitlement of land in the fertile plains around, and were expected to help defend it if the need arose.

The site lies due east of Tazoult-Lambèse. You enter today through the **north gate** *(porte nord)* of Trajan's town, to be surrounded by a forest of truncated stone columns. You soon see that you are in the grid of streets that was laid out at the very beginning. The paving stones of many streets survive: sandstone for the side streets, limestone on the main arteries, the Decumanus Maximus and the North and South Cardo. Practically every building can still be seen in outline, and some are beautifully preserved. There isn't anything quite like this in Europe.

Thamugadi was pretty well buried by the earth and sand of a thousand years when the existence of ruins here was reported by the Scottish traveller James Bruce in 1765. Excavations—begun in 1880 and still not complete—revealed more and more. The place has been compared with Pompeii. In fact, they bear little resemblance, except that both were covered up a long time ago, one slowly, the other suddenly.

A stele unearthed after a thousand years of lying buried, at Timgad.

The site shows how fine urban facilities could be mass-produced on the very frontiers of empire. Walk south along the North Cardo and in the fifth block on your left, you'll pass the **library** *(bibliothèque)*, before reaching the magnificent Decumanus, the grand avenue. Look along it to the right (the west) to the **triumphal Arch of Trajan**. You'll notice the grooves worn into the roadway by ancient carts. (Guides always say "chariots", and no doubt there were some of those, too.) Where flagstones are missing you can see the details of the efficient drainage system. It was reached through heavy, circular stone manhole covers and still looks to be in good shape.

Facing you here at the centre of the city is the **forum**. You can climb the steps up to the central square where there must have been dozens of statues. Many of their bases remain, inscribed with the names of emperors and governors. Less exalted but more entertaining inscriptions and graffiti include a cheerful Latin assertion: "Hunting, bathing, playing, laughing—that's living!"

Back in the Decumanus, turn east, and notice the **public latrines**, the side-by-side two-person stalls separated by stone dolphins. Nothing but the best public facilities would do in ancient Thamugadi. Finally, before the street reaches the Mascula gate you come to the **eastern baths** *(thermes de l'est)*. All the separate hot rooms, cold rooms and the rest can still be distinguished.

Work your way back to the forum and cross to the south side where the 2nd century **theatre** has been partially restored. Originally the building could hold over 3,000 spectators. In recent years there have been festivals of dance and drama here, and the old theatre has been used again.

Further on, just outside the chequerboard of streets, the **southern baths** *(thermes du sud)* are a mass of brick and stone, but you can make out the underground heating systems. In case you are wondering, yes, there are **western** and **northern baths** *(thermes de l'ouest* and *du nord)*, too, the last being the most important. (They lie just outside the north gate.) And that wasn't all. Thamugadi could count no fewer than 14 different establishments. "Which baths shall we go to tonight, Petronius?"

Look south from the southern end of the original city, and you'll see the substantial walls of a fortification. When the Vandals invaded Roman Africa in 429, local Berbers took advantage of the weakened state of Thamugadi to seize it. Then, when the expedition sent from Constantinople by the Emperor Justinian retook the area in 539, they didn't attempt to rebuild the city, but constructed this **Byzantine fort**, with barracks, a church and, of course, more baths.

Unusually, the temple of the **Capitol** stood just outside the grid of streets, on the southwest corner of the city. But not much remains now of the building, except its vast stone platform. Further off in the same quarter lie the relics of an ancient quarrel, the **Donatist cathedral**.

Walk back towards the Arch of Trajan past the **market of Sertius** *(marché de Sertius)*, paid for by a local citizen of that name. This lovely little colonnaded court, so perfectly preserved with alcoves and

You can just make out the tracks of old carts, along the way to the Arch of Trajan.

stone tables, looks as if it's all ready for boutiques to be set up tomorrow. The arch itself straddles the road that curves away downhill towards the western baths and **Lambèse gate**. If you continue past the arch to the north-west corner of the old city, the outline of another large church marks the location of what was probably the Catholic cathedral. Head back to the north gate. The great mass of masonry on the left was once the great northern baths, naturally.

The **museum** *(musée)* near the main entrance closes before the site does, so if you linger for the beauty (and photo opportunities) of sundown in the ruins, you'll miss it. This would be a pity: the mosaics are a revelation. They've been mostly displayed on the walls to give a better view. Look for the one depicting a dining table set with every kind of delicious food, and for the floral "carpet" designs.

GUELMA

Orange and olive groves, grazing cattle and fertile fields of grain and sugar cane surround this hilltop town 106 kilometres (65 mi.) east of Constantine, whose history comes straight from the textbook pattern for the region. Founded by the Numidians and conquered by the Romans, Guelma was sacked by the Vandals and fortified by the Byzantines. It fell early to the Arabs and the succession of dynasties that followed. Then came Turkish hegemony, French occupation and construction of the "new" town, with rapid growth after independence. Some of the streets with their bright, white houses are now pedestrian precincts, and there seem to be even more than the usual quota of schoolchildren and students. Right in the middle, a restored Roman **theatre** is still used for meetings, plays and concerts. The **museum** of antiquities, displaying some imposing busts and mosaics, opens off the theatre—ask the guard to unlock it for you. One wall is dominated by *The Triumph of Amphitrite,* a frequent subject of North African mosaics. She was a Nereid and a wife of Neptune, who appears very often himself.

Pleasant though the town is, the main attractions are outside. For connoisseurs of extremes, there's the almost

The children aren't petrified by the Bath of the Damned, *a waterfall turned to stone.*

boiling-hot "Bath of the Damned", **Hammam Meskoutine**, less melodramatically called Hammam Chellala on the road sign 15 kilometres (9 mi.) west of Guelma. The name apparently derives not from the hellish heat of the waters but from several rocks nearby that were said to be the rest of a wedding party that was turned to stone for breaking some taboo. What looks like a huge waterfall, steaming dramatically, is seen at second glance really to have turned to stone, because chalk, dissolved underground by the springs, has been deposited over the centuries in a great stalactitic curtain of white and yellow where the water flows over a cliff. There's still a hotel here for those taking the cure, following of course in the footsteps of the Romans.

An extraordinary sight lies 12 kilometres (8 mi.) from the boiling springs, just off the minor road to Roknia and set in another of Algeria's places of breathtaking silence and solitude. **Dolmens**, Neolithic tombs formed of massive slabs of rock, are found scattered over Europe, Asia and North Africa, but here are *3,000* of them in one place, clustered on a rocky plateau on the edge of a vertical cliff. The whole area is a sea of wildflowers, especially in spring. Gouged marks in the ground show where wild pigs have been rooting for bulbs.

Hammam Berda (Héliopolis), a pretty village with hot springs and a Roman bath restored for use today, is within sight of Guelma. It has a modern claim to fame, for it's the birthplace of Houari Boumedienne, commander of the army of liberation and president of Algeria from 1965 to 1978. This part of the country provided many of the leaders in the struggle. Guelma had been one of the points where the uprising of May 1945 broke out, and the reprisals against people of the town were among the most vicious, convincing many Algerians that only armed revolution could bring independence.

ANNABA

Closer to Tunis than Algiers, the port of Annaba (*Bône* to the French, *Hippo* to the ancient world) is rather out on a limb. But there are plenty of reasons for coming to the region, and both ferries and planes from Europe land here. That means you can make it the start or the finish of a trip and avoid backtracking. One warning: if you bring your car in through the port, be ready for a very long wait at the customs. They don't see many tourists' vehicles here: the system is tailored to the exhaustive inspection of the mountains of goods brought back by locals who have been abroad. Make sure you have reserves of food, drinks, books to read—and patience.

The Phoenicians and Carthaginians naturally did not ignore such a fine bay. The name Hippo signifies "shelter". The city centre later moved south from the port to the adjoining plain where the Roman ruins of **Hippo Regius** stand today, next to the main road. It's a site of scattered, disconnected columns, confusing in comparison with Algeria's "big two" of Timgad and Djemila. Tourists are admitted on Wednesdays, Thursdays and Fridays only at 8.30 and 10.30 in the morning and 12.30 and 2.30 in the afternoon. Be punctual: you won't be able to get in even five minutes after these times. Photography is not allowed.

Near the entrance, look for the villas with mosaics still in place and, just to the west of them, the vestiges of the **Christian basilica**. This must have been the church where St. Au-

St. Augustine of Hippo

"Give me chastity—but don't give it yet", he quoted memorably in his Confessions. *Born in 354 in Souk Ahras in north-eastern Algeria, Augustine spent a famously riotous youth, enjoying, by his own account, a promiscuous existence at the university in Carthage and for some time after. (It might seem unfair that in later life he preached that women were a temptation to be resisted, and set the church on a puritanical path.) At about the age of 29 he moved to Rome, taking his mistress and son with him.*

The beginnings of a change in his ways came when he was posted to Milan and became the protegé of Bishop Ambrose (he was to be made a saint, too), who baptized him in 387. He was joined by his mother, Monica (likewise sanctified), who seems to have influenced him to return to Africa in 388. However, she died before she herself could make the voyage.

In 395 Augustine was made bishop of Hippo. Reckoned to be the greatest Christian thinker of his age, he wrote a library of books. His energy was also spent in the struggle against the Donatist schismatics, who at times in the years after 311 were in a majority. Augustine died, possibly from malaria, as the Vandals were battering at the very walls of Hippo, in 430.

gustine preached, for he was bishop of Hippo for many years. It was built on the site of earlier villas, incorporating their mosaic floors of secular design. Some of these are among the fine selection now in the **museum** here, along with marble and bronze statues. The main east–west and north–south streets of the city, the Decumanus and the Cardo respectively, cross near the great **forum**, the most striking survival here.

The modern **Basilica of St. Augustine**, a huge white church with a dome and two towers, dominates the area from a hilltop near the ruins. Completed

The imposing white Basilica of St. Augustine towers above the ruins of ancient Hippo.

in 1900, it uses masses of Algerian marble and onyx. You'll see a giant statue of the saint in bronze. Inside, a wax effigy incorporates what is said to be his right forearm. From the square in front of the church you'll get a better idea of the layout of ancient Hippo than you do while in the ruins themselves. It is sometimes clear enough for good views of the Edough mountains west of Annaba and the stretch of bay with its beaches to the east, when there isn't too much smoke from the huge steel works south of the city.

The modern city of Annaba stands nearer the original site by the harbour. It is neatly split by the north-south **Revolution Avenue** *(Cours de la Révolution),* tree-lined and elegant. To the east stand the jumbled houses of the old town, dilapidated from age and wartime bombardments (World War II, that is). The narrow streets (often blind alleys) rise to the 11th-century mosque, **Djemaa Sidi Bou Merouan**. You'll want to have a look at the central hall, which contains many columns from old Hippo. But the climb is worthwhile more especially for the views of the port and coast that you get by walking along the line of the old city walls. West of Revolution Avenue, the newer city spreads out, and ringing it, forests of recent apartment blocks built to cope with explosive population growth.

You could stay in Annaba itself, but for something original, head out of the city for **Seraïdi**, only 10 kilometres (6 mi.) to the west. In that short distance the road zigzags up to almost 900 metres (2,900 ft.) and into pine and oak forests before reaching a cool mountain resort. One of the architect Pouillon's most "organic" creations, the white Hôtel El Montazah seems to be suspended above the steep slopes and the shining sea.

Seraïdi, despite the altitude, does have its own beaches at the end of a twisting little road. The road to the west winds downwards, through cork oak trees, their trunks black where the bark has been peeled away. Some of the little traffic you'll encounter will be tractors or trucks hauling loads of cork sheet. Look out for woodpeckers, hummingbirds and wildflowers along the way. After 40 kilometres (25 mi.), the road reaches the resort and fishing village of **Chetaïbi**. Talk to the fishermen at the port and you'll find characters among them who have sailed the world. The few tumbled Roman stones in the vicinity are hardly worth searching out. From here, a narrow, pretty road travels south through the oak forests of the Edough. It

joins the main road west of Annaba in rich farmland covered with vines and fruit trees—though before the area was drained this was all malarial swamps.

East from Annaba, the main road leaves the coast for a while, but returns to it through oak forests to **El Kala**, a dis-

tance of 87 kilometres (54 mi.). The claim to fame of this little port is that it was the first French foothold on the North African coast. In 1553 a trading and fishing company from Marseille won permission from the Dey in Algiers to set up a base here. You can continue 12 kilometres (8 mi.) more to the Tunisian border. The road passes through a land of lakes and woods. Turn down narrow lanes to the coast to find the magnificent little beaches of El Kala National Park.

An ethereal view from the hotel El Montazah in Seraïdi, by the architect Pouillon.

SOUTH TO TEBESSA

An excellent road first paved in the time of Emperor Vespasian takes you 230 kilometres (142 mi.) south to Tebessa's Roman and Byzantine ruins. You can make the trip by rail, too. On the way you pass **Souk Ahras** (ancient Tagaste), the birthplace of St. Augustine. A **museum** there named after the saint displays general Roman art and artefacts.

If you're interested in tracing Augustine's footsteps, pay a visit to **Madaura**, just off the road to the south (turn left at Drea along the track). The saint's schooling took place in the town, which also claims fame as the birthplace of Apuleius, 2nd-century author of the ribald collection of tales called *The Golden Ass.* Actually, Augustine's youthful excesses smack more of that classic of soft porn than the holy tomes he wrote later in life. There's a full range of ruins at Madaura including Byzantine walls from the brief 6th-century renaissance.

Tebessa

Before moving west to Lambesis, North Africa's own Third Legion Augusta made its headquarters in Tebessa (then called Theveste), in the foothills of the Djebel Doukkane. The legion's engineers and construction brigades enlarged the city and built paved roads to Carthage, Hippo and Constantine. By the time the bulk of the troops left, Tebessa was a thriving colony.

You approach the town today through spreading suburbs of pastel-coloured apartment blocks. This is clearly a place scheduled for major expansion, and one with civic pride, too. Park benches and flower beds everywhere relieve the stark modernity, as do the unmistakeable lines of ancient ramparts—the massive **Byzantine walls**, erected in 535. They enclose the whole of the old city, most of which is now a pedestrian zone.

The east gate leads to the market. The west gate clearly incorporates older stonework, but above all look at the remarkable **north gate**. This was adapted in 535 from a triumphal arch of 214, which, like the one in Djemila (p. 74), honours Emperor Caracalla and his father and mother, Septimius Severus and Julia Domna. On the upper east and west archways are medallions showing the imperial parents. Climb to the walkways behind the ramparts for the best view, and watch the traffic of the town—yellow taxis, donkey carts, veiled women—pass through. Inside the walls, just to the west, look for the pretty **Temple of Minerva** with its frieze of bulls' heads.

Ask near the west gate for Tebessa's **carpet factory**. You'll find the manager very welcoming. There's no pressure to buy, but you will be tempted. Several men and women work in spacious rooms on the two main traditional types. The thick-pile carpets with a simple pattern resemble a fleece and probably first developed in imitation of one. The other kind is very firm and tightly woven. Quite subdued colours are used here. However, it is often the case elsewhere that the gaudier palette of chemical dyes has been too enthusiastically adopted.

Outside the walls, about 500 paces to the north, massive ruins mark the site of a **Christian basilica** from the late 4th century. With great stairways, vast areas of mosaics and burial chambers, it's an impressive assertion of power for a time when the church was riven by feuds and schisms. Look for the monks' cells, if that is what they were, in the far left corner from the entrance. You may think them more like rooms in one of those Japanese capsule hotels.

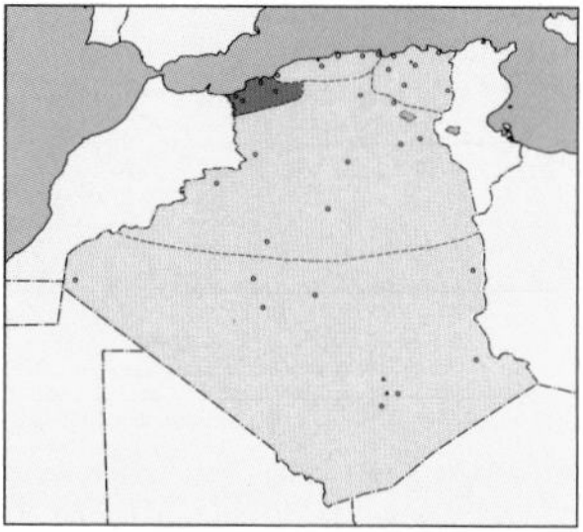

NORTH-WEST

Algeria's past has been nowhere more convoluted than here. It is tempting to call this the north-west frontier, for it was a battleground. Disputatious Islamic dynasties, Spanish invaders and Turkish pashas fought for it, attracted by the fertile land and fine harbours. Tlemcen, an architectural jewel of Islam, changed hands a dozen times. From their first landings in 1830, the French needed 17 more years to establish themselves over the whole area in the face of the resistance of the Emir Abdelkader. From then until 1962, European settlement was most concentrated in this region, and especially in its chief city and port, Oran.

Inland, enormous areas were converted to vineyards, par-

ticularly after phylloxera devastated the winegrowing regions of France. Even if you don't visit this part of the country, you'll probably try the wines. The ones from Mascara are usually rated the best, and Tlemcen's are not far behind. Land given over to vines has been much reduced since independence. This is to allow the production of food, and because domestic consumption of wine is quite small. Most of the local wine is exported to Eastern Bloc countries in barter trade deals. So much of the white wine goes abroad that it is remarkably hard to find any in Algeria at all.

The bust of an Algerian hero, Abdelkader, in front of Oran's ornate National Theatre.

ORAN

This is Algeria's second city. The official name, not much used, is Wahran. For a long time Oran considered itself at least the equal of Algiers. The growth of the capital has now left it far behind.

Oran's story is one of ups and downs. It thrived as the port for Tlemcen in that city's heyday, but almost three centuries of Spanish occupation up to 1792 cut Oran off from its natural hinterland. Spain had seen Oran as the capital of a new empire in North Africa. In fact it became no more than a fortified enclave. Only when the French pacified the interior did the city begin to grow rapidly. Interestingly, the majority of settlers were again Spanish.

The atmosphere of Europeanized, pre-independence Oran is conveyed by Nobel Prize-winning author Albert Camus in his novel *The Plague*. Although Camus was born in Algeria (at Drean, near Annaba, in 1913), he is rarely mentioned here today. Despite his early sympathy with the independence movement, his novels scarcely refer to Algerians, but concentrate on the *"pieds-noirs"*, inhabitants of European origin, born in Algeria.

You may arrive in Oran on a ferry—there are services from France and Spain—or plane. You may be passing through on the way to or from Tlemcen or the Moroccan border. The port is so important now that it's odd to discover that it was considered an unsafe anchorage in the past. Extensive modern moles and jetties have made the difference.

The heights above the harbour make a good place to start a short walking tour. The old Kasbah is small and very rundown and is gradually being demolished. The **Great Mosque** *(Djemaa El Kebir)*, near the ramparts, was built after the Spanish were expelled in 1792. In fact the victorious Turkish pasha proclaimed that he was paying for it out of the ransoms of Spanish captives. If you can find the caretaker, climb up to the top of the minaret for a spectacular view of the city.

Just to the south, **1st of November Square** *(Place du 1er Novembre)*, with its period piece of a theatre (1906), marks the beginning of **Boulevard Emir Abdelkader**. Four short streets up that, and just away to the right, you'll see the former cathedral, Sacré Cœur. Now deconsecrated and turned into an impressive **library**, it was only finished in 1943. A strange neo-Byzantine design, it has modern stained glass (you can look inside) and a great arc of mosaics depicting the *Signs of the Evangelists* over the doors.

Another short walk away on Boulevard Zabana, the **museum** deserves more visitors than it gets these days. It has a crowded collection of paintings by minor Impressionists and Post-Impressionists and, more to the point in the Algerian context, there are fine works by Orientalists. Look out for Fromentin, Dehodencq, Girardet and other artists who worked in Algeria. You'll find scenes by Etienne Dinet, here given the Muslim name of Nasr Eddin that he took when he was converted, and Brest's pictures of the Hoggar. The ethnography section features a telling comparison between traditional tent life and palace life. There are lots of flints and coins.

West of Oran

If, in the old days, Oran was a town without a good harbour, the next bay to the west was the exact opposite. It was a very good harbour indeed, as you can see from heights between the two. The Arabic name says it all, **Mers El Kebir** (the Great Port). The problem was, there was no easy way inland, and the path to Oran was so difficult that everything was moved between them by sea. Mers El

The story behind these cedar doors is just as fabulous and intricate as the fine workmanship and detail that went into its making...

Kebir was a naval base a thousand years ago and remains one to this day. In July 1940, after the fall of France, many ships of the French Mediterranean fleet took refuge here. To prevent the possibility of their falling into German hands, a

British squadron outside the harbour called them to surrender. When this was refused, the Royal Navy opened fire, sinking several French ships and causing many deaths in an episode that generated enormous bitterness. At the time of Algerian independence, France retained control of the naval base, but departed in 1968.

West of Mers El Kebir, a string of beaches and little holiday villages leads via the coast road to **Cap Falcon** and more magnificent views. **Les Andalouses**, a purpose-built resort 32 kilometres (20 mi.) from Oran, is a white city of chalets, apartments and hotels. There's even a disco. In summer it's jumping, and you probably can't get a reservation except long in advance and through ONAT. Among other sports they promote underwater fishing holidays here. In winter it's like a ghost town.

TLEMCEN

Most overseas visitors on holiday don't come to the north-west for the beaches, though. No, they are here principally to go to Tlemcen *(Tilimsen),* 170 kilometres (105 mi.) south-west of Oran. If you have an interest in Islamic history and especially architecture, this is the place. If you're not yet interested, it's the right spot to start. Be prepared for total immersion. More than anywhere else in the country, you need to plan your time carefully, because the mosques are only open for visits between 8 and 11 a.m.—and not at all on Fridays—and they are not all located near each other.

Present-day Tlemcen has a population approaching 200,000. It had almost as many in the 14th century, according to the writers of the time. But that was at the height of Tlemcen's magnificence as one of the great cities of the Arab and the wider Islamic world.

The site is ancient: you can look up at the cliffs to the south and still see the mouths of caves where early man lived. The Romans built a town north-east of the present city, but only a few stones survive, like those with inscriptions outside the museum. Almoravid empire-builder Youssef Ben Tashfin founded Tlemcen in the late 11th century. The name derives from a Berber word meaning "water source". Later dynastic contention came in the special form of a long struggle between the Zianids, established here around 1236 by the Berber chief Yaghmoracen, and their bitter rivals the Merinids, rulers of Morocco and southern Spain.

Heart of the city is the citadel, the Mechouar, with its massive patterned walls, but they are mainly a 19th-century reconstruction. The buildings inside aren't of as much interest as others in the city. Across the street in Avenue du Commandant Feradj, you will find a helpful Information Office *(Syndicat d'Initiative)* with an excellent city map and a lot of other useful advice as well.

Head now for the adjoining squares at the city centre, **Place Mohamed Khemisti** and **Place Emir Abdelkader**. On the north side of Place Abdelkader stands the **Great Mosque** *(Djemaa El Kebir)*, begun by Youssef Ben Tashfin. What you see today dates from the remodelling ordered by his son Ali in 1136, plus enlargements from the time of Yaghmoracen, when the minaret was added. Inspired by the Great Mosque at Cordoba, it is simple in concept. Size was achieved by multiplying the naves and transverse galleries, to 13 and six respectively. There's no great vaulted roof or soaring dome here, but a forest of columns, monumental in their effect. Look at the exaggerated horseshoe arches, and the multi-lobed arches around the *mihrab*. Ornamentation is given its head in the cupolas over the central nave. One is intricately ribbed and pierced and the other, over the *mihrab*, shows just a suggestion of a "stalactite" design. This involves filling a large arch or dome with lots of little arched recesses, so that there are projections where they meet. In its most developed form, the projections really do hang like stalactites.

You don't need to get to the next mosque before 11 a.m., because it has been deconsecrated. In fact it has served as a **museum** for the last hundred years. It's the Sidi Bel Hassen, facing the Khemisti end of the double square. This one is a little gem dating from 1297, the time of the second Zianid sultan, who ordered it to be built in honour of his father, Yaghmoracen. The onyx columns, the sculpted plasterwork, the pierced stucco, all give an impression of great delicacy. It is almost a shock to realize that most plaster tracery like this was originally a riot of bright colours and gilding. (Rather like finding out the truth about all those now-so-austere Gothic cathedral interiors. They were painted, too.)

The museum building may

upstage its contents, but that's no reason to overlook some worthy exhibits: mosaics made of semi-precious stones and 12th- to 14th-century wood-carvings. The massive stone balls on display are supposed to have been catapulted into the city during one of the Merinid sieges. In an upper room, the huge collection of minerals and remarkable fossils donated by a certain Abbé Brevet seems not to have been touched since the museum opened.

If you emerge into Place Khemisti in the late afternoon, prepare to be bowled over. Maybe it was asleep when you went in. Now it will be jammed with most of the young male population, overflowing from the teahouses. It seems to be a ritual to have tea after work, or school, or any other time.

North of the square, just outside the old city walls, the Merinid mosque, **Djemaa Sidi Haloui** (literally, St. Sweets) commemorates a law professor from Seville who settled here and changed his occupation to sweet-seller. Someone accused him of plotting against the sultan, and he was executed in 1337. Justice quickly reversed itself, because this tomb and mosque were already completed by 1353. The minaret is typically Merinid, and the interior is notable for its carved cedar roof.

Tlemcen doesn't only mean mosques, of course. In the narrowest and some of the poorest-looking streets you can find embroiderers and leather workers, jewellers and cabinet-makers. Boxes inlaid with mother-of-pearl are a traditional product, and carpets are still made here as well as imported from all over Algeria and the Middle East. Tlemcen once controlled the trade between the coast, the Sahara and beyond. The instinct lives on. So it does for music-making. The city is the centre for the study of classical Andalusian music, which developed in Spain during the Muslim occupation and thereby combined Arab and European music of the time. In many ways it is believed to preserve medieval European styles more purely than any other surviving form. Surely not coincidentally, some of the stars of Algeria's very own favourite popular music, *rai*, come from Tlemcen.

El Eubbad

The countryside around may remind you of southern Spain—Andalusia, in fact. This similarity was not lost on those who, forced to leave their Iberian homes, came here as the tide of Muslim conquest turned. Tlemcen's greatest shrine is the tomb of a wandering teacher and holy man born in Seville in about 1126, who became known as Sidi Bou Mediene. (The spelling varies, but if the name seems familiar, that is, of course, because it was adopted by the revolutionary leader who became president in 1965, Colonel Houari Boumedienne.) Sidi Bou Mediene came here on his travels and announced that it would be a fine place to be buried. Later, as it happened, he died nearby. Remembering his wish, his followers brought his body to the hillside village of El Eubbard, overlooking Tlemcen's cupolas and minarets.

It's only a short walk from Tlemcen, and shorter still if you are starting from the Hôtel Les Zianides. Happily, though, the city has not quite grown out to engulf the village. On the way up the hill, you'll pass olive groves and orchards, a vast Muslim cemetery and ruined shrines before you arrive at El Eubbad. The **shrine** *(kouba),* of Sidi Bou Mediene is reached through a courtyard with marble and onyx columns. Water from the shrine's well is said to be highly beneficial, and the marble rim has been cut in deep grooves by the iron chain used for hauling it up. The room containing the tomb itself is one of those places that instantly compels silence and contemplation—all dark and mysterious with candles and embroidered hangings. Over the centuries it has been ever more richly decorated with amazingly coloured tiles and suspended shells of ostrich eggs.

The **mosque** is just as remarkable as the shrine, but whereas the architecture of the latter evolved naturally, the mosque was more carefully planned. It dates from 1339, during one of the periods when the Merinids were in control. If the style—the horseshoe arches and extravagant arabesques in coloured tiles and carved plaster—reminds you of the Palace of the Alhambra it is no coincidence. The Merinids also ruled Granada at the time. The cedar door covered in bronze actually came from Spain: according to legend it was constructed as ransom for a prisoner and then ceremoniously "committed to the deep". Miraculously, it washed up on the shores of North Africa.

Inside, see how the carved plaster decoration of inscriptions, floral and geometric designs wraps around and over the massive white arches. The

mihrab has a delicate stalactite cupola and subtly carved capitals to top its marble columns.

The minaret, from the same period, is one of the more attractive examples of patterned relief brickwork and ceramic decoration. If you ask the caretaker, he may allow you to climb it for the view. A few steps from the mosque you will see the **medersa**, Islamic college, built soon afterwards. The Arab statesman and great historian Ibn Khaldoun studied here in the 14th century, until he found himself on the wrong side of the Sultan of Tlemcen and wisely moved away.

Mansourah

Besieging forces had to live somewhere, but few in history went to the lengths that the Merinids did in their continual campaigns against the Zianids. They built a rival city, El Mansourah (the Victorious), only 3 kilometres (less than 2 mi.) from the walls of Tlemcen, surrounding it with massive ramparts of its own. From this base they mounted a great siege between 1299 and 1307, followed by a successful second effort in 1337. Not until the end of the century did the Zianids recapture Tlemcen and Mansourah.

The Merinids were quartered at Mansourah while they laid siege to Tlemcen for years on end.

The many towers in the walls still stand, amidst olive groves now, or with farm buildings leaning against them. The main road west from Tlemcen passes right through the old gateways.

Walk out to ancient Mansourah, west along Boulevard A.L.N., or make the short drive. Your main architectural objective is also the most obvious landmark: the **minaret** of the ruined Great Mosque. Here the word "great" is more than usually applicable. The area bounded by the walls of the mosque is vast. Most of the site has suffered the usual fate of abandoned cities, being used as a quarry. Many of the marble and onyx columns you've seen supporting the mosques of Tlemcen came from here, and no doubt the stone for humbler houses did, too. But a great part of the minaret survives. Was it too dangerous to try to pull it down or steal stones from it? From outside the front of the mosque it looks almost complete, and the stonework is stunningly carved in geometric relief. But like a film set, there's no back to it. You can see the remains of the interior spiral ramp that the muezzin used to climb to the top.

Towards the Border

The road bisecting the ruins of old Mansourah winds on out through olive and fruit trees and vines for 50 kilometres (30 mi.) to the market town of **Maghnia**. From there, it's only a short drive to the Moroccan border, but you will probably have noticed increasing numbers of security checks long before that. Relations between Algeria and Morocco have been through some frosty spells, due first to territorial disputes in the Sahara and then to Morocco's annexation of the Western, formerly Spanish, Sahara. Formalities at the frontier can take time, and there have been periods when it was actually closed.

About 25 kilometres (15 mi.) north of Maghnia, the picturesque little town of **Nedroma** saw the beginnings of the Almohad dynasty (the Almohads supplanted the Almoravids in the 12th century). The **Great Mosque** here, like the ones in Tlemcen and Algiers, was built by the Almoravids. You can still see traces of Nedroma's battlemented walls and walk the narrow streets, looking into weavers' workshops. Some of the finest woollen bedcovers are made here, and perhaps you will be able to afford a soft, beige-coloured burnous.

Sidi Bel Abbès

The most direct route to Algiers from Tlemcen, but not the main road, sets off through 90 kilometres (56 mi.) of gently rolling hills and well-watered farmland to Sidi Bel Abbès. Does this name ring a bell? It was the headquarters and training base of the French Foreign Legion for over a century. There was little else but the legion and its supporting facilities here during all that time. Sidi Bel Abbès is now one of the fastest-growing towns in the country, and the seat of a new university. The old legion barracks house a police college.

Again not the main highway, but more attractive and quieter, the road north-east leads for 94 kilometres (58 mi.) to **Mascara** *(Mouaskar)*, headquarters of Emir Abdelkader from 1832. The town is surrounded by the acknowledged best of the country's vineyards. Should you fancy water instead, divert off the direct route to **Bou Hanifia**, a spa since Roman times and well-equipped with hotels to this day. Even the river is called El Hammam (the Bath).

From Mascara to Algiers the major highway is very hectic, but if you have the time and freedom, consider a swing east for 150 kilometres (93 mi.)

La Légion

The legion and the legend have always been hard to separate, especially for a generation brought up on Beau Geste *and* Our Only Country is the Legion. *From its formation in 1831, when the French were still pacifying North Africa, there was hardly a time when legionnaires were not fighting somewhere—in the Crimea, Mexico, Indochina. Their white* kepi *headgear was celebrated around the world.*

Some 350,000 men passed through the harsh discipline of Sidi Bel Abbès, parading under a great bronze globe that bore the motto "Honneur et Fidelité", and 35,000 died in combat. After every European war there would be a wave of new recruits—those who had no other trade but fighting, and those who just loved the life. The French Foreign Legion was famous as a hiding place, and not only for jewel thieves and disappointed lovers.

The officers were nearly all French; up to half of the men, in later years especially, were German. The rest came from all over Europe. Just as soldiers in the Roman legions eventually qualified for citizenship, so veterans of the Foreign Legion had the chance of French nationality. These élite troops were given the toughest jobs, but the best food and equipment; and their official brothels went with them, too. Of course, the Legion still exists, but when it had to leave Algeria in 1962 for a new base in France, much of the magic was gone for good.

across the mountains to **Tiaret** *(Tihert),* on the edge of the High Plateaux. Except during the annual horse fair in September, the town holds less interest now than in its history, but the scenic route is a bonus. Not far from today's Tiaret, Ibn Rostem and the Kharidjites built their city of Tiharet in the 8th century. The sect was strict and ascetic, and dedicated to trade. Not for the first or last time, the prosperity that resulted from this combination brought the envy and hatred of others less dedicated and successful. The Kharidjites (confusingly called Ibadites as well) were chased out. Some ended up in the M'Zab and some on the Tunisian island of Djerba, two tourist destinations where they flourish to this day.

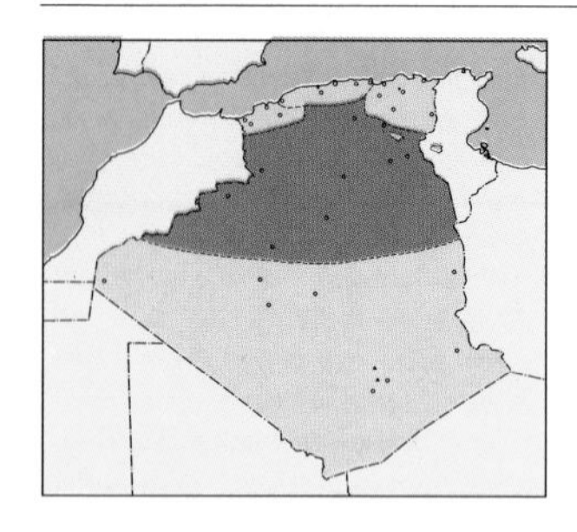

SOUTH

Plenty of innocent expectations about the desert are blown away in the reality of the Sahara. First, the landscape takes so many different forms that one word is absurdly inadequate to describe them all. That's why Arabic has so many. "Sahara" is derived from one of them, *sahra,* which means empty land. Second, there's a wonderful variety of living things, both plants and animals, to watch out for. They cope with the extreme conditions in a bewildering number of ways: so do the humans who have made this unlikely region their home.

Larger than the whole of Australia, the Sahara is by far the world's greatest desert, and Algeria takes the biggest bite. Not so long ago you could only venture here in convoys with escorts. Modern roads, reliable vehicles and tough tyres have changed all that, though the land and climate still demand the utmost respect. Fly over it, and you'll see that green oases which seem so substantial on the ground are no more than pinpricks on a huge map.

BOU-SAADA

If you only have time for a brief experience of an oasis, this could be the one, for it is nearest to Algiers. Although technically not in the Sahara, it is often the first stop on a circuit of Saharan highlights. Either way it can serve as a good introduction. Coming by road, after the last of the mountain passes you find the land levelling out into thorny scrub and rough pasture. You soon see sand dunes—not many, it must be admitted—and probably some camels, too. Flat-topped mountains around the horizon look like the mesas of Arizona. Signs warn drivers not to be lulled to sleep by the "monotonous road", although truth to tell there will be much more unvarying landscape fur-

A refreshing spot in the oasis of Bou-Saada, set amongst the dunes.

ther south. You need to acquire the frame of mind that finds these endless spaces paradoxically exciting in themselves.

Bou-Saada doesn't have massive palm groves; for those you will have to travel on. At 250 kilometres (155 mi.) from Algiers, it can even attract weekend visitors escaping from the pace and humidity, so it does possess that rarity in untouristic Algeria: a choice of souvenir shops. Never fear, the proprietors are so polite, they will hesitate to draw your attention to their carpets, desert roses and long "bou-saadi" knives in bone sheaths, which you can see being made if you walk the narrow lanes of the old walled village, the **ksar**.

For a view of the whole oasis, climb one of the hills nearby in the early morning or at sundown. Mornings are the best times, too, for seeing the markets and the streets at their most lively. In the cool of the late afternoon you may come across men playing board games on the pavement, throwing a couple of knucklebones as dice. The women tend to be heavily veiled, folding a shawl around their heads to leave just one eye showing.

Artists in search of the exotic came to Bou-Saada in the last century, and one, Etienne Dinet, made it his home for the rest of his life. He converted to Islam and in 1929, at nearly 70 years of age and only months before his death, made the pilgrimage to Mecca accompanied by his friend and adopted son, Slimane Ben Brahim and the latter's wife. All three have their tombs in a quiet spot just across the river, the Oued Bou-Saada, from the *ksar*. Dinet painted Bou-Saada's dancers, graceful women of the local Ouled Naïl tribe, in long tunics and scarves, their arms weighed down by silver bracelets. You might still see the same scene today at one of the occasional festivals. More often, men put on a colourful show in one of the hotels, with realistic stick fighting and sinuous dancing to the insistent rhythms of tambourines and wailing flutes. Some of Dinet's topographical scenes are on display in the museum in Oran and in the Fine Arts Museum in Algiers.

BISKRA

It's easy to see from a relief map why Biskra has been garrisoned by everyone from the Romans on, and why so many armies marched this way. It is the true gateway to the Sahara, but plentifully watered by rivers flowing off the southern slopes of the Aurès mountains. Strange to think of the Romans this far south, keeping an eye on the fierce mountaineers and the equally intractable desert tribes. They must have enjoyed the glorious winter climate and the hot **medicinal springs** at neighbouring Hammam Salahine. When it became fashionable in the 19th century to get away from northern Europe's cold, Biskra developed as one of the first oasis resorts. The same attractions it had then bring visitors today, whether they're seeking relief of their rheumatism or respiratory complaints, or just wanting to relax.

This is the perfect place for lotus eating, strolling in the shade of the miles of palm groves and orchards—or riding through them. Every oasis seems to have at least one special feature of its own, and Biskra's is a fleet of colourful **horsedrawn carriages** with tops that can be raised to keep the sun off, and soft rubber tyres for a comfortable ride: you'll find one waiting somewhere in the shade near the hotels. (Agree with the driver on the time or destination and the cost in advance.)

For the more energetic, there are tennis courts at the Pouillon-designed **Hôtel Les Zibans**. Here the architect has adapted traditional forms of Saharan and Islamic architecture to create fluid, organic lines that complement the landscape. Take in the view from the hotel terrace over the palm groves and the wide expanse of the *oued*. Periods of heavy rains in recent years have sometimes overfilled the river course, inundating parts of the town and washing away many of the old mud-walled buildings.

The morning **markets** here are as much of a draw as in any other major oasis: it seems to be *de rigueur* for every man within miles to attend, and the quality of produce justifies the vendors' obvious pride. It seems as though practically anything will grow here. In the new town centre, walk through the **park**, 10 hectares (25 acres) of tropical colour, scents and shade. Oleanders *(lauriers roses)*, which have now been planted in all the hot, dry regions of the world, originally came from the fringes of the Sahara, and they are stars in this garden show.

It was near Biskra in the year 684 that the all-conquering Arab general Okba Ben Nafi (he who had reached the Atlantic and ridden into the sea) was killed in battle with the still-resisting Berbers of the Aurès.

His tomb is now part of the mosque in the town named after him, **Sidi Okba**, 17 kilometres (11 mi.) south-east of Biskra. It was to become a place of pilgrimage soon after his death. Parts of the mosque date from the 10th century, but they are hard to distinguish among the effects of frequent restorations, especially those needed after extraordinary floods in 1969 undermined the walls. Non-Muslims may not be allowed inside, but they can ask permission to see the view from the minaret.

In autumn, wherever you are in Algeria, you may be offered a special treat, the newly arrived dates from **Tolga** (36 km./22 mi. west of Biskra). If you've only had "ordinary" dates before, these smooth, plump, pale gold *deglet nour* will instantly change your idea of what a date can be. The secret lies in copious supplies of water from deep wells—the sound of motor-driven pumps pervades Tolga's palm groves—and careful programmes of replanting, so that there are always plenty of younger trees whose massive bunches of dates hang conveniently at about head height.

Mud walls surround the groves, but if a grower sees you taking an interest he may invite you in for an inspection and some samples, to convince you that his dates are the best of the best. In the lightly shaded and moist ground around the trees he is probably growing crops of melons, aubergines (eggplants) and grapes as well.

An oasis is forever evolving: the remains of centuries of

*The wonder of El Oued—
a panorama of domed roofs floating
above the marketplace.*

abandoned mud buildings are returning to the soil. Newcomers to the oases are often deceived by the numbers of derelict mud houses into thinking that the population is shrinking. This is rarely the case. It is simply easier to build a new house than repair an old one. (Of course, more and more people are moving into concrete houses. They may not be as cool in summer or warm in winter, but at least they won't wash away in the rain.)

By the same token, you will see whole groves of trees neglected after they have reached a stage where it is not worth watering them, while not far away a new plantation is growing up on ground never before planted.

EL OUED

When you've seen one oasis, you certainly have not seen them all—and you'll never see another like this. Imagine turning someone loose with gigantic ice-cream scoops, with instructions to put a dome on any building they find. Imagine, under these innumerable cupolas, walls of pale yellow ochre, doors and shutters of sky blue. Ring this vision with massive, high sand dunes that threaten to engulf it. Hide the gardens of date palms in deep craters. Finally call it El Oued (the River), where there is no river within two days' march, and you have one of the unlikeliest places on earth, and one of the most enchanting.

Like other major oases, El Oued (650 km./400 mi. southeast of Algiers) has expanded in recent years. It's practically a border town—Tunisia lies a short distance away—and it is the chief of a cluster of oases, rather like an archipelago of islands in a sea of sand. The region is called the **Souf**, a Berber word implying a dry watercourse. What made the original inhabitants choose to live in such an apparently inhospitable place, where—because it is so near to sea level, though so far from the sea—temperatures can reach over 55 °C (130 °F)? It seems they were nomads from the east who dug down to reach the underground water and elected to stay, away from established settlements and unwanted rulers. One bonus was that without any surface pools, there were no mosquitoes and no malaria. (Now there are, so keep on taking the pills.) Still, it was back-breaking work to dig the huge craters that enable palms, planted in the bottom, to reach adequate supplies of moisture. It remains a colossal labour to keep the sand from engulfing the trees, and it is the excavated sand that forms some of the dunes that ring the oases of the Souf.

To get your bearings, climb the "minaret" of the Hôtel Le Souf, or better still, the real minaret of the mosque, **Djemaa Sidi Salem**, near the market, preferably in the golden light of early morning or evening. Any of the shopkeepers can show you the way. (A comical gang of little boys may bar the steps up until you pay a small

Significant Dates

A staple food, dates were the traditional survival rations of caravans or besieged forts, for humans and animals can live on dates and water alone, if necessary. The date palm was important enough to be the symbol of ancient Carthage and appeared on its coins. As a cash crop, dates are still all-important to the desert economy.

Of all the different palm trees, Phoenix dactylifera *is the date-bearing species, but there are hundreds of varieties. The big, oblong, golden, translucent* déglet nour *is the main export quality. The name means "finger of light", and this type does seem to be almost luminous as it ripens from nutty astringency to melt-in-the-mouth succulence.*

Walk around a market or a palm grove in autumn and you can sample dégla-beida *("white finger"), perfectly round orange dates or little stoneless varieties. Black, sticky* ghars *can be stoned and compressed into goatskins where they'll keep for a year or two.*

Good, well-watered palms produce several bunches of up to 1,000 dates per bunch. You'll see the top quality trees protected by high walls and the best bunches shielded from dust, birds, insects and excessive drying by plastic sacks. Paradoxically, for a desert crop, the date palm needs lots of water, though it can manage on quite salty stuff, and its gentle shade means that other crops can be grown beneath its fronds.

Dates are not its only useful product, either. The ribs of the leaves can be woven into crates, the more flexible parts of the leaves into baskets. Goats and camels can eat a lot of the leafy and other parts, and when the useful life of the tree is over, the trunk makes very durable timber for building. Anything else can be burnt as fuel, with one exception: don't throw date stones into your camp fire when you're out on a trek—the Tuareg believe that to be unlucky, almost sacrilegious. After all, if you scatter your stones on the ground, they just may germinate with the next rainfall, be it next week or in ten years' time.

sum to their leader, the "caretaker"—whether official or not, it is impossible to say.) While you are up there, you'll see just as many elliptically vaulted roofs as domes.

El Oued's building style developed in a special way for the usual reason: the local materials, namely, gypsum. Chunks of it are used for walls, bound with a mortar made by baking gypsum and mixing it with sand and water. This mixture was found to set like plaster of Paris (they're chemically similar), and someone started to use it to form the domes and vaults. Soon nothing else would do. The practical limit for strength is about 2 metres (6 ft.) across for a dome, and 2 by 3 metres (6 by 9 ft.) for a vault, but clever combinations gave quite large rooms.

In the market down below, even the kiosks have domes, and the old town is as neat and clean as you'll find anywhere in the country, with scents of rosewater, coffee and mint tea. The merchants never press their wares on you but exchange polite greetings whether you buy anything or not. New public and government buildings are attractive and conform to local styles, too. The open look of the town came with the removal of the old defensive walls in 1949, to make way for a ring road. El Oued is proud of its parks and gardens and playgrounds. Stop by the helpful ONAT office, in the centre, and pick up a town map.

The **museum** opposite ONAT at the most important crossroads has small but interesting displays of the bird and animal life and the geology of the Souf. Coins, crafts and costumes round out the collection, and there are curiosities such as models of many different sorts of dates. Most striking of all are the aerial photographs, showing the pattern of the palm gardens in their craters, like so many pockmarks on the endless sands. Somehow, with a hundred here and a dozen there, there are close to half a million trees in the Souf.

To see this method of date cultivation you will have to make a short trip out of town, say to the south-east and the village of **Amiche**, or somewhat more distant but still more dramatic, to **Nakhla** (which actually means "date palm"). Planted in pits, 10 or more metres (33 ft.) deep, the palms rarely show much more than their tops above the rim. In some places the pits are so close together that they actually share rims. Only an intricate barrier of palm fronds keeps the sand back, and still it has to be continually and painstakingly cleared from around the trees and dragged to the top of the craters. A sandstorm here is a setback that can mean a month's extra work.

Bargaining over dates, the staff of life in the south.

TOUGGOURT

On the western edge of the daunting sea of dunes called the Great Eastern Erg *(Grand Erg Oriental)*, this is the largest of a north–south chain of oases strung out for about 140 kilometres (85 mi.) along Oued Rhir, a river whose waters are mostly underground.

Until as late as 1854, Touggourt was ruled by the Ben Djellab dynasty (and "nasty" seems to have been the operative word) of independent kings. Some of their **tombs** are to be found in the cemetery. Look for a group of shrines, each with its pointed dome. Tradition says that tombs with two stones indicate the grave of a man, three a woman.

Touggourt today can boast over a million date palms, as well as so much recent expansion that the old town is ringed by new, broad streets and light industry. There's plenty to entice the traveller, though. Railway romantics will thrill at the thought that they can actually get this far into the desert by train. If they have the patience to wait for one, they're not likely to complain about the gentle progress it makes to this

The Tarqui and his camel—inseparable travelling companions.

The Camel's Secret

It is said that God has a hundred names, but the Prophet told his followers only 99 of them. The hundredth he whispered one day into the ear of his pure white mehari, *or riding camel, in gratitude for being carried out of danger. Now all camels have this knowledge. They also know that man does not and that is the reason they look so supercilious.*

Communication between oases would have been impossible without the aid of camels. No other pack animal has feet so well adapted for walking in soft sand. No other can go so far without food: a camel can live on the fat stored in its hump for months and eat the thorniest of plants if it has to.

Above all, no other working animal can survive so long without water. Somehow, a camel can lose up to a quarter of its body weight in fluid without its blood thickening. Then, when it has a chance to drink, it can take in up to 130 litres (30 gallons) at a time.

As well as all this, camels give milk, their dung makes good fuel and manures the date palms, and their hair can be woven into cloth. Finally, their meat is a staple food and their skin makes strong leather. And some fool said a camel is a horse designed by a committee!

"end of the mid-Sahara line". Another oddity—part of the water supply is pumped up from deep hot wells, so it emerges from the "cold" tap still warm, which is less than refreshing in the summer. Nice on a cold January morning, though.

Plan your visit to Touggourt to include a Friday morning, and you'll be present for the famous **market** (smaller on other days of the week). In autumn or early winter, your stay will coincide with the date harvest. Be there early in the morning to see the arrival of every kind of vehicle from ramshackle shared taxi to donkey cart, all laden with produce. You'll hardly need to ask the way—just follow the crowd. The huge market will be covered with heaps of melons, pomegranates, spinach, garlic, mint and alfalfa, baskets of pigeons, hanks of goat hair and above all, dates. Boxes of dates, bunches of dates, baskets of dates, mountains of dates. Gold, black, long, round, sticky and dry dates. You will notice that this is a man's world. Even the vegetable shopping is done by men, though you may see a few unveiled women with facial tattoos in a blue pattern over their eyes and temples.

Look for hand-made tools —the designs have scarcely changed since the beginning of the Iron Age—and clever adaptations, like the use of goatskins for carrying motor oil. As the market breaks up, another anachronism: smartly uniformed traffic police try vainly to organize the flow of donkey carts, goats and the occasional camel, all mixed up with brand-new pick-up trucks and cars.

Still in the centre, you can visit an **embroidery workshop** in action. Not far from the market, on Martyrs' Square *(Place des Martyrs),* a monument commemorates the first north–south motorized crossing of the Sahara in 1922–23 by Citroën halftracks (wheels in front, caterpillar tracks behind). Drivers all dressed up in jodhpurs, riding boots and pith helmets took 20 days to make the journey from Touggourt to Timbuktu. The labyrinthine **ksar** not far away retains its narrow alleyways, some arcaded, some completely covered and perfect for keeping the sun at bay. You'll probably want to linger awhile, but if time is short, press on to see two *ksour* not far to the south.

Sloping mud-brick fortifications surround the little oasis town of **Temacine**, 12 kilometres (7 mi.) from Touggourt on the road to Ouargla. Palm trunks, practically indestructable in this climate, are placed end-on and side by side to strengthen the walls. Dive through one of the narrow gateways and you will find yourself in a magical maze of tunnel-like alleys, where a succession of arches has enabled the complete roofing of whole sections with timber and mud-brick vaulting. Unless the children are out of school, the place may seem almost deserted at first. But, as you pass closed doors, on either side you can hear life going on. You might even catch a glimpse through a crack in the woodwork of a woman weaving at a loom.

Sooner or later, a small boy will volunteer to guide you around. By all means accept: he can take you to the 17th-century mosque, **Djemaa Soudani**, topped by cupolas of green painted tiles and mud, and beneath them an arcaded and vaulted hall in cool aquamarine and sea green. Then, if he hasn't shown you already, ask your young helper to point out the way up onto the roofs, where you can walk almost from one side of the town to the other without seeing another soul. The view up there is dominated by a decorative square tower, the minaret of the **Mosquée de Si El Hadj**. The name recalls the prince of Temacine who had it built in 1431 with bricks brought, or so the story goes, from Tunisia. "Donnez-moi un stylo!" (Give me a pen!), says the small boy, as you get back to the entrance to the town. A very fair fee, too, but after you hand it over, be prepared to make a quick getaway before children appear from everywhere, wanting one as well.

Only another kilometre or two to the south, the crumbling oasis town of **Tamelhat** may not look impressive at a distance, but there are pearls hidden there. More youthful guides—sometimes an entourage—can show you the way to the great **tomb** of Sidi El Hadj Ali, the founder of the town, a teacher and holy man, who died in 1260. Over the tomb rises one of the most enchanting creations of 18th-century Islamic art, a cupola formed of geometric white plaster relief moulding, embellished with delicate paintwork and some faience tiles. The entire interior has a wonderful lightness, and the men studying within seem happy for you to come in and admire it. Outside, on tumbled walls nearby, you'll see an intricate marble **sundial** which used to tell the muezzin when to make the daytime calls to prayer. From higher still you get a view of the quiet palm groves and vegetable gardens all round. Just in time, Tamelhat is beginning to benefit from restoration of some of its lovely old houses with their ornate doors, plaster tracery, arcades and cupolas. Many of its people are the dark-skinned descendants of those who came from what is nowadays Niger, much further south, and if you get into a conversation with a crowd of them, you'll think you are in West Africa.

OUARGLA

This giant among oases boomed in the 1960s and '70s when the oil industry was in full cry. There's a chequerboard of wide avenues and ambitious public buildings, though development has slowed a bit in recent years. The need for water far outstripped the supply from traditional sources, so deep artesian wells were drilled. The water comes up so hot that some is cooled before piping to the houses, and some is used for central heating. If you come here in summer, you won't be able to imagine that such a thing could be needed: in winter, you'll understand it well.

Some 160 kilometres (100 mi.) south of Touggourt, Ouargla *(Wargla)* is the capital of a vast region. People drive

Pastel colours and shadows play upon Ghardaïa, the largest and oldest town of the M'Zab.

in from every outlying town to engage, it seems, in a little business and a lot of gossip. The old **ksar** lies several streets north of the main Touggourt–Ghardaïa road. Dozing for most of the day inside the walls, it is quite hard to locate. Just outside the walls, the **market** is busiest in the mornings. The modernity in every direction can easily make you forget where you are, until you see the signs to the ''Salon du Dromadaire''—a venue for international camel exhibitions and trading.

The **Musée Saharien** stands close to the main road, near the roundabout. The museum dis-

plays the crafts of all the different desert regions, and some of the finest collections of the prehistory of the area—rock paintings, arrowheads and stone tools. Special local features include the treasures excavated at Sedrata, a site 9 kilometres (6 mi.) south-west of Ouargla, which became the home of the fiercely ascetic Kharidjites or Ibadites, after they were expelled from Tiharet (Tiaret) in the 10th century (see p. 115). In 1072 Sedrata was destroyed and they were again forced to move on. Hardly surprising after so long, little remains at the site but a few fallen stones and unevenesses in the shifting sands.

GHARDAÏA AND THE M'ZAB

Gasps and exclamations—no matter how many photographs you have seen or how much you've been told—are the universal reaction. If you've driven across endless surrounding wastes of the stoniest and least hospitable desert imaginable, the sudden appearance of the little winding valley, with its cluster of hilltop towns within, is one you will not forget. If you fly in, be ready with your camera in case the plane passes over them. Keep it on hand, for the road from the airport brings the same stunning revelation. Whichever way you arrive, go one day in the late afternoon up the hill after the traffic circle on the road that leads south-east to the airport. Two or three places there give the most magical views, taking in all the towns of the M'Zab, each a perfect pile of pastel-coloured cubes.

First, to clear up a source of confusion: Ghardaïa is the name loosely used for a group of five towns, of which the largest and most recent is also called Ghardaïa. That is if a foundation date put at 1053 can be called recent. The others all date from the first half of the 11th century: Melika (the Queen), Beni Isguen (Sons of Those Who Keep Their Word), Bou Noura (Father of Light, the Luminous) and El Atteuf (the Turning), on a bend of the valley.

The name Ghardaïa probably derives from an old Berber word for "heights" or "cliffs". There were people living here long before the refugees from Sedrata founded the five towns, which isn't surprising: it is too desirable a property to have been left unsettled.

The **M'Zab** is the region, and the river that waters it. That's mainly underground, of course,

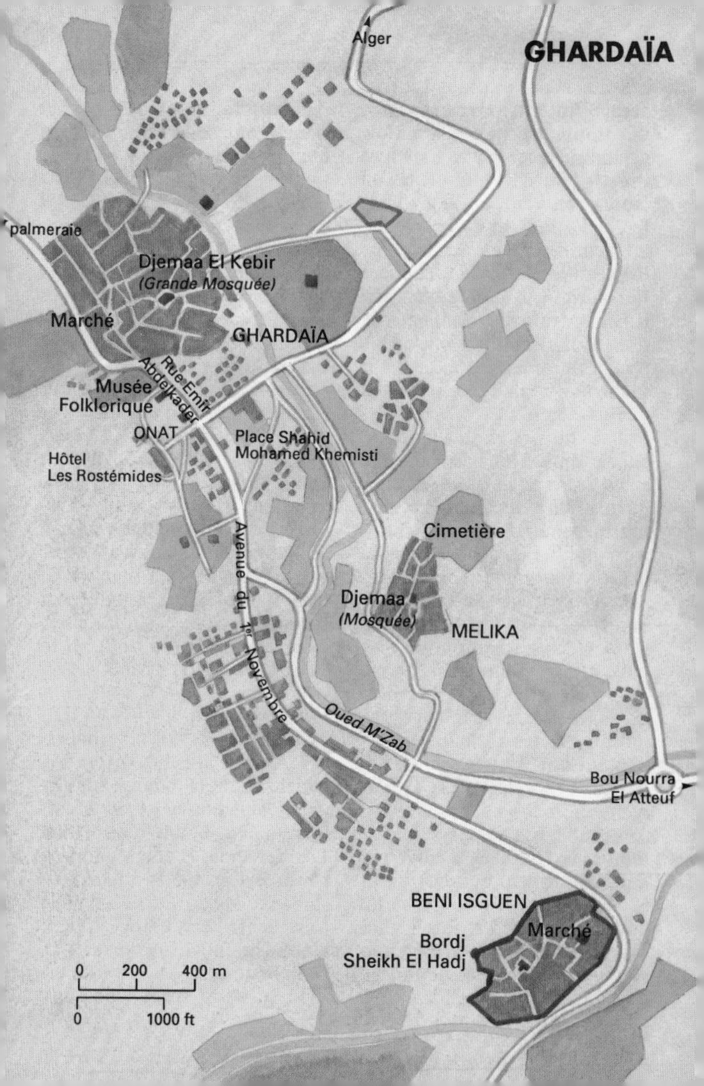
GHARDAÏA
Alger
palmeraie
Djemaa El Kebir
(Grande Mosquée)
Marché
GHARDAÏA
Rue Emir Abdelkader
Musée Folklorique
ONAT
Hôtel Les Rostémides
Place Shahid Mohamed Khemisti
Avenue du 1er Novembre
Cimetière
Djemaa
(Mosquée)
MELIKA
Oued M'Zab
Bou Nourra
El Atteuf
BENI ISGUEN
Marché
Bordj Sheikh El Hadj
0
200
400 m
0
1000 ft

but this is not a totally rainless area. Winter showers can produce quite an impressive flow on the surface. It was here that the strict Kharidjites expelled from Tahert and Sedrata fetched up. Their early leaders, incidentally, were called the Rostemides, after the eminent Persian-born commander Ibn Rostem. Ironically, considering their austere habits, Ghardaïa's opulent-looking hotel, one of the Pouillon designs, is named Les Rostémides.

The houses of each town cluster on the hills as if they've grown there. In a sense, they have. Only local stone and mortar, mud and palm trunks were used. People developed a design that suited the climate and the pattern of their lives and stuck to it. But the growth was evidently as strictly regulated as any planner could wish today. Nobody built eyesores or highrises to challenge the hilltop minarets. Space wasn't wasted: nor were precious materials or unnecessary ornament. Somehow, austerity led to beauty. Even the assaults of modernity have been diverted and controlled by the crafty M'Zabites (or Mozabites) who have adapted the ideas that suit them. Gas, electricity and running water, yes. Modern building materials and paints, too. Loss of their privacy behind their closed doors in the elegant covered courtyards and shaded terraces of their houses? Emphatically not.

Don't think of the M'Zab as a backwater. Pressure of population on the limited space and resources meant that many went to seek their fortunes elsewhere, especially as shopkeepers and traders. Most of the pastry-makers of Algiers are from here, as well as a fair fraction of those in France. Try some of the products at Ghardaïa's little pastry shops, to see what they can do. The emigrants all seem to want to return eventually, and it's easy to understand why. As a result, you'll find a good number of locals who speak English or German. Some shopkeepers even keep their radios tuned to the BBC World Service.

Ghardaïa

The main artery of Ghardaïa is the **Avenue du 1er Novembre**, which changes names to **Rue Emir Abdelkader** at the crossroads just below the Hôtel Les Rostémides. Walk along it towards the old town. Where the main road forks to skirt around it, keep going straight along the much narrower **Rue Ibn Rostem**. Lined with every kind of shop from video-hire establishments to hairdressers, this soon dives into shadow before leading directly to Ghardaïa's **marketplace** *(marché)*. Go in the morning for the most activity, when stalls are set up all over the square and under the shade of the arcades that surround it. Traditional and modern clothing, bright (mostly too bright) carpets, folk medicines, spices, copperware, antique jewellery—the tradition of trading brings a huge variety. Look for the fibrous sticks of wood that serve as toothbrushes, next door to the full spectrum of plastic junk.

The market and its access streets used to be the only parts of the old Ghardaïa open to strangers. No doubt that is why it was positioned near the edge of the original town. Now, you can walk at will through the maze of alleys, most only just wide enough for two people to pass. You'll get lost or diverted until you are back where you started, but it doesn't matter: there is something fascinating around every corner.

The **Great Mosque** *(Djemaa El Kebir)* stands at the highest point: its minaret is the mud-brown tower with inward-leaning walls and odd, finger-like protuberances on top, which is such a landmark from afar. To reach it, take the exit from the marketplace which looks most promising and climb the narrow steps and slopes. To be allowed inside (permitted for a short period in the morning) you should have a guide with you from the ONAT Office (in Avenue du 1er Novembre), but the caretaker may show you around himself. The mosque itself is dark and cool, almost subterranean inside its thick walls, and quite ageless. You may see various objects hanging in the covered passage by the doors. "Lost property" found around town is displayed here waiting to be claimed. How long would such a system last in your home town?

Back along Rue Emir Abdelkader, turn up the road towards the Hôtel Les Rostémides to find, immediately on the left, a little **folk museum** *(musée folklorique)*. Though rather a dark and dusty jumble, it's nevertheless worth a visit. One room furnished in the old M'Zabite style has a ceiling of palm beams and a collection of household goods and other artefacts.

Centre of the new town is **Place Shahid Mohamed Khemisti**, south-east of the old section. Notice the traditional arcades in the modern square and along the new streets.

There's no point in changing a winning formula.

Ghardaïa's **palm groves** *(palmeries)* lie 7 kilometres (4 mi.) north-west of town and stretch a further 7 kilometres along dry and dusty Oued M'Zab. If you have the time, it's a pleasant walk. You may want to inspect the ancient water supply system, about a kilometre from the southern end of the groves. Rain water is stored in deep wells and pumped through a comb-shaped barrage that divides the flow according to time-honoured shares. From there the water runs, after more subdivisions, into smaller channels,

Eerie tombs of Sidi Aïssa in Melika, another town of the M'Zab.

all lined to reduce leakage, to reach the separate palm gardens.

Melika

Face away from Ghardaïa on Place Khemisti and you are looking at the red-brown walls of Melika, only a kilometre to the south-east. The shortest way there is across the ancient footbridge spanning the M'Zab river bed and straight up the hill. Fork left and the rocky slope leads to a **cemetery** to the north of town. The hillside is covered with rough stone tombs, but the curious thing is the style of decoration on them. It seems that inscriptions were not permitted, so to distinguish them, broken household pots were put on top. Just a few tombs go further in special embellishment, with strange bunches of whitewashed moulded pinnacles. You may recognize one tomb, the most photographed object in the whole M'Zab and the subject of postcards and architectural dissertations. Try not to be too disappointed by the real thing. The **view** of Ghardaïa alone is worth the climb, and so is the **walk** right around Melika.

See how modernity has been tamed: up-and-over garage doors are set into the outside walls, since vehicles can't get into the town itself. But painted in traditional pale blue, they're hardly noticeable. Inside the town, you'll turn the corner of a narrow, covered street and meet women veiled in white with just one eye showing, or men on donkeys, the riders wearing such baggy pleated trousers that they can stretch right over the donkey and the load it carries, too. Through the open windows of upper rooms you can hear scores of tiny children chanting their lessons.

Beni Isguen

Only a couple of kilometres from Ghardaïa along Avenue du 1er Novembre, this strictest of the five towns allows tourists to visit, but only under controlled conditions. The consequence could have been foreseen: everyone wants to go there. You can't get in until 3.30 p.m., so dress conservatively—nothing revealing—and arrive at that time at the main gate. You will be approached by one of the distinguished gentlemen appointed by the town to act as guides. If you are only going to the **marketplace** *(marché),* which is quite near, you won't need a guide. But you'll certainly want to see more than that, so let the guide look after you. He will show you the areas of Beni Isguen that are permitted to foreigners.

You shouldn't try to photograph people: inanimate objects, views and buildings are usually allowed. As you climb the narrow streets, you'll see that most of the inhabitants are in traditional dress. Notice the fine old doors of palm wood, and how clean and beautifully kept the town is. The mosque is ringed like a fortress by thick

Light pours across the maze of roofs of the holiest city in the M'Zab, Beni Isguen.

walls and is normally out of bounds to visitors. You will have to be content with climbing the **Bordj Sheikh El Hadj**, a tower in the town's outer wall, to get another great view.

Back at the marketplace, your guide will take leave of you, and tell you the standard fee. Don't hurry away, though, because most days at this time, in late afternoon, an extraordinary sort of **auction sale** is under way. Goods, from beds to bicycles, are piled in the

Meeting a scorpion in the desert can be interesting—if you have time to see it coming!

square and a large part of the population sits or stands around. The vendors literally run around in circles calling for bids, sometimes many of them competing vocally, and athletically, at once. The cacophony as the sale nears its climax at the end of the day has to be heard to be believed. Near the marketplace, on your way back to the main gate, you'll find the best-kept and best-stocked shops in the whole of the M'Zab.

The **palm groves** south of Beni Isguen are much smaller than Ghardaïa's, but they are nearer at hand and at least as attractive. Take a stroll along the road and look over the walls at the careful cultivation. Those good-looking houses half hidden among the palms are "summer homes" occupied by their owners more than six months of the year. If you like the idea of a longer stay in the M'Zab, you may be able to rent one of them by the week.

Bou Noura and El Atteuf

If the remaining two of the five towns are not quite as celebrated or visited, it is only by comparison with the other marvels. Bou Noura, 4 kilometres (2½ mi.) to the east, is in poorer shape than the others. Possibly because the mosque is, uniquely for the M'Zab, not at the highest point, the upper part of the town is especially tumbledown and partly deserted.

El Atteuf lies 9 kilometres (about 6 mi.) east of Ghardaïa. On the main road near the town, there's a private hunter's **zoo**, with all sorts of desert fauna, from foxes to scorpions. You may wish the owner would let the specimens go, with the possible exception of the spine-chilling scorpions. Of more authentic interest are El Atteuf's two mosques. The smaller **Djemaa Sidi Brahim**, with different rooms and arcades for different seasons or times of day, has long enchanted students of architecture. Le Corbusier especially admired M'Zabite buildings and this mosque in particular. Its curved walls and niches, its asymmetrical plan and arch, and the almost organic way in which it seems to have evolved are said to have inspired his chapel at Ronchamps. The cemetery at El Atteuf, like that at Melika, contains a variety of weird tombstones with decorative pinnacles.

THE GREAT CIRCLE

You can do it in a tour bus, you can do it in a car or shared taxi, or on a motorbike. You can even hitch-hike it. Just look at the map and find the circle of roads. The names are like an incantation: Ghardaïa, Laghouat, Aïn Sefra, Béchar, Taghit, Beni Abbès, Timimoun, El Goléa. Total distance from Ghardaïa and back: about 2,200 kilometres (1,370 mi.). Time: five days minimum, but seven or eight would be better. You will never regret it.

No two of these oases, nor the smaller places on the way, are alike, and some areas are as different as could be. Only Béchar is not immediately agreeable. The rest all have somewhere acceptable, or at least picturesque, to stay. If time is at a premium, sightsee in Ghardaïa for part of a day and leave for Laghouat in the afternoon, and do the Timimoun–El Goléa–Ghardaïa stages in one day. Unless it really doesn't fit the rest of your plans, the circle is best done in the order given above. That takes you to the less remote places first.

The road north from Ghardaïa climbs out of the sinuous valley of the M'Zab and crosses rocky desolation to reach **Berriane** (44 km./27 mi.),

A palm grove of Timimoun—fragile gardens need constant protection from the sand.

which somewhat resembles the five towns. That's hardly surprising when you find that it was founded by a group that was chased out of Ghardaïa in the 17th century.

Another long stretch of dauntingly stony desert has to be crossed before sparse scrub begins to appear. About 60 kilometres (37 mi.) from Berriane, you pass a turning to the left to **Hassi R'Mel,** centre of one of the world's largest natural gas fields. Pipelines take the gas to the coast at Arzew and Skikda, and more pipes distribute it to Algeria's main cities. In a most ambitious scheme, gas is piped across the Mediterranean to Italy. In the starkest contrast with this activity are the distant low black tents of nomads, and perhaps a flock of their equally black goats. You might see the same sight anywhere from the Atlantic to the borders of Tibet, wherever the conditions of pasture and the needs of animals have imposed the nomadic life. The tents are made from strips of woven cloth, wool strengthened and waterproofed by the glossy goat hair.

By the time you reach **Laghouat** (192 km./120 mi. from Ghardaïa) you have already begun to climb into the uplands of the Saharan Atlas, an area that can get a harsh winter. The name Laghouat (pronounced "Larouat", with a throaty rolled French "r") means "the Gardens" in Arabic. It's worth a walk in the palm groves to see how shade and irrigation are used to cultivate a host of other crops.

The town grew as a military

garrison in the colonial era, when the French were trying to control the independent-minded tribes of the mountains. The French sword and the Bible arrived together and left together, so the old church known as the Cathedral of the Desert is no longer used as such. Climb up the ridge to the **Great Mosque** *(Djemaa El Kebir)* for a view over the modern town of tree-lined, arcaded streets, and the old *ksar,* all in white and pastels but fairly unremarkable. Fernand Pouillon's **Hôtel Le Marhaba** is tiled like a Turkish palace. A pity it is beginning to age like one... but it's a good base for exploring the region.

The Djebel Amour

The road continues to climb, first north and then west, into the uplands of the Djebel Amour. You begin to get a feeling of being in Central Asia. Shepherds, some on horseback, are wrapped in

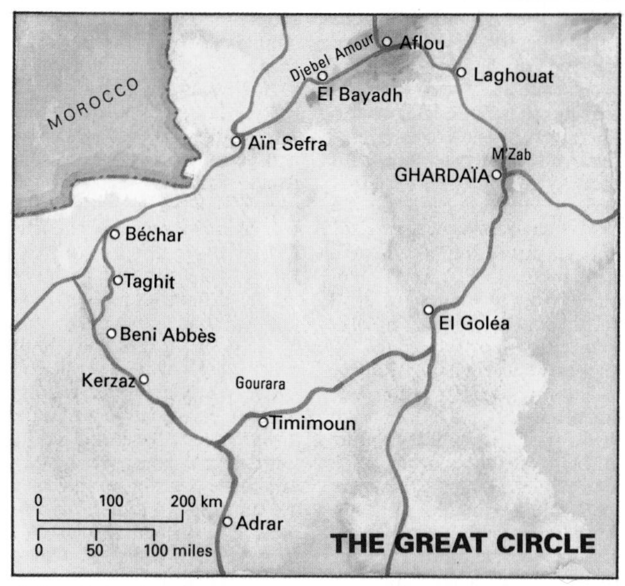

their thick, hooded woollen *cachabia* cloaks against the cold winds. It seems an almost empty land, until you spot a hamlet, sheltering for the same reason in a cliff-ringed valley quite inaccessible by road. Patches of cultivation—bright green *alfa* or esparto grass—have been squeezed in wherever sufficient soil covers the rock.

From **Aflou**, a true mountain town where they weave famous carpets, take the road towards El Bayadh, but only for 8 kilometres (5 mi.). Now for an artistic diversion. A little unmarked road turns off to the left. Follow it. After another 7 kilometres (4 mi.) there's a fork. Take the road to the right. After a further 14 kilometres (9 mi.), you'll see a hamlet nestling in the valley below you on the right among a line of poplar trees. It's called **Aïn Sfisiffa**, but there is no sign and no road to it. Stop your vehicle and look for a place to clamber down the low cliff to the right of the road. On the black, vertical rock face are some of the most dramatic and wonderfully sited **rock engravings** to be found anywhere. Though very hard to date precisely, they are probably from about 6000 B.C., the Neolithic period. Miraculously, no one has touched them or scratched them or added initials. A huge elephant protecting a baby elephant from a crouching lioness or panther forms the centrepiece, with ostriches and antelopes in attendance. Reflect for a moment on what this landscape may have been like then, when it could support that kind of fauna. A few kilometres further along the same road at **El Ghicha**, a rough road leads to the ruins of an old mill. Even more carvings cover the cliff there, this time introducing a praying man and horses which indicate a later date for some of the designs.

Back on the main road, El Bayadh stands where the Djebel Amour meets the High Plateaux. The latter tend to get a bad press from writers about Algeria. "Cold winds in winter, hot winds in summer", they say. But these plains between the two Atlas ranges have their own magic for those who like altitude and solitude, endless horizons with seas of green *alfa* (cultivated for use in animal feed or papermaking), sheep, cattle, goats and camels.

El Bayadh may be a newish town, dating from the mid-19th century, but it has become a centre for all the colourful tribes of the region. Try to get to the Thursday market, the earlier in the morning the better. If you're driving yourself, fill up here for the 230 kilometres (144 mi.) of lonely road to Aïn Sefra.

Stop just short of it at **Tiout**, a little oasis with several sites where there are rock engravings. Some near the road have unfortunately been defaced by graffiti scratchers, but at a certain angle you can see that they are not just outlines of animals. The surface within seems to have been polished. Could they have been coloured, too, originally?

Aïn Sefra

This is practically a border town, the mountains of Morocco being in sight to the west. A north-south railway line passes through the town on its way to Béchar, with a daily passenger train in each direction. In many places you'll see tangled rolls of barbed wire. They are relics of the electrified and mined lines of multiple fences that were built by the

Wild Spirit

She called herself "Si Mahmoud", a man's name, and wore men's clothes. She rode with spahis *(Algerian soldiers), drank with legionnaires and travelled alone all over Algeria. Everything about Isabelle Eberhardt was unconventional, starting with her birth.*

The illegitimate child of the wife of a Russian general and her Russian Jewish lover, she was born in Switzerland in 1877. Her education, surprisingly including the study of Arabic, came from another of her mother's lovers, an eccentric Armenian ex-priest, turned atheist. Her elder brother joined the French Foreign Legion in Algeria. When he left it, he stayed in the country, and Isabelle and her mother went to join him. Her mother soon died, and Isabelle returned to Europe. But Algeria and Islam—she had become a convert—called her back.

She reached El Oued, "town of a thousand cupolas" as she called it, in 1900, and fell in love with a young Algerian soldier, Slimene Ehni. Extraordinary adventures continued. Attacked by a fanatic, she was seriously injured. The French authorities, who distrusted her, took the opportunity to expel her. She arranged for Slimene to be posted to France, where they were married. That gave her the right to return to Algeria.

Somehow getting herself appointed as a newspaper correspondent, she covered military campaigns around Béchar, all the while adding to her notorious reputation for promiscuity and excess. On October 21, 1904, she left the Aïn Sefra hospital, where she had been having treatment for malaria. Within hours, after heavy rains, a torrent of water washed away many of the mud-built houses of the town, and Isabelle Eberhardt was among the many who were drowned. It was two days before her body was discovered, pinned beneath a beam.

French during the war of independence to try to prevent supplies and men from getting to the FLN forces from outside.

During the first years of the century, Aïn Sefra had provided the French with a base, and you can see the rather palatial army barracks that were built. The old town was the scene of a tragedy in 1904, when a flash flood in the river bed swept away many houses and their occupants. Among those drowned was the intrepid young Swiss woman, Isabelle Eberhardt. Only 27, she was already one of the most sympathetic and sensitive foreign writers about Algeria. A convert

A flash of smiles and sunlight in a ksar *near Taghit.*

to Islam, she was buried in the Muslim cemetery.

The road continues alongside the railway, passing very close to the border and the Moroccan town of Figuig. Not only a fence, still visible in places on both sides of the railway and the road, but hundreds of forts and blockhouses were built all along the track to defend it. **Béchar** is almost the end of the line, in more ways than one. It's surprisingly large and dreary, with concrete apart-

ment blocks and heavy industry. Dense traffic kicks up suffocating dust. Long ago, the railway was intended to go all the way down into West Africa, but even building it as far as this had some economic justification, for there are big coal deposits at Kenadsa, 22 kilometres (14 mi.) to the south-west. However, the discovery of oil in Algeria reduced the need to exploit the coal.

Taghit

You reach the oasis by a narrow road through sparse vegetation of thorn bushes and wiry grass tufts. A few locusts might be seen flitting about, but it's only when they join into clouds that they are a menace. Spray planes wait at many airstrips in the Sahara in case swarms should start to gather.

Taghit (say "Tareet", with a rolled r) is only 93 kilometres (58 mi.) south of Béchar. But what could be more different? It is most people's idea of an oasis, the classic oasis for those who have so far only read about them. Huge yellow sand dunes tower above it threateningly to the south-east, for this is right on the edge of the Great Western Erg *(Grand Erg Occidental)*. An old mud-walled *ksar* crowds onto a hillside and, below it, a winding *oued,* or river course, is full of lush palms, scented woodsmoke and singing birds. You can walk on the dunes at sunset and stroll in the palm groves and old town. There's even a reasonable hotel. It couldn't be more restful. It's the typical oasis at last—and there isn't another like it.

Desert Priest

The name of Charles de Foucauld keeps turning up in the Sahara. Who was he? Born in 1858 into an aristocratic family in Alsace, he became an officer in the French army and, by all accounts, a reckless, pleasure-seeking playboy inclined to be insolent to his seniors. After a row about his mistress he resigned his commission and, like a character out of Beau Geste, *set off to explore Morocco, disguised as a rabbi.*

Something about the hardships encountered on this expedition had a transforming effect on him. He became a Catholic—although he had admired the faith of the Muslims—and spent several years meditating in a Trappist monastery before entering the priesthood in 1901. Straightaway he went to Beni Abbès in the Sahara, where he did charitable work and built a hermitage and chapel that were the forerunners of those to be found there today. Then he walked *(check the journey on the map) to Tamanrasset where he built another chapel, which still stands.*

He tried to help the Tuareg of the Hoggar come to terms with their changing circumstances. (They had just suffered a traumatic defeat at the hands of a French force with overwhelming modern firepower.) He learned their language and compiled a book of Tuareg poetry, as well as Tuareg-French dictionaries. The famous hermitage at Assekrem was built to his plans in 1910. Tragically, raiders who knew nothing of his work murdered de Foucauld in 1916. His heart is buried in Tamanrasset, but the rest of his remains were later moved to El Goléa.

The church and tomb of the desert priest, Père de Foucauld near El Goléa.

South of Taghit, about 16 kilometres (10 mi.) along the river course, there's a cliff face decorated with unusually stylized Neolithic engravings of antelopes, primitive forms of cattle and an assortment of other animals, as well as outline hands.

The river at Taghit is no more than a tributary, the Zousfana. Now on the way to Beni Abbès, at **Igli**, you come to the point where Oued Guir joins the Zousfana to form the great **Saoura**, a river which you will follow for hundreds of kilometres. For the most part, however, its waters lie beneath the surface. The road winds south through seas of shiny stones, polished by blown sand, and dunes naturally stabilized by clumps of reedy grasses.

Beni Abbès

If Taghit is the quintessential oasis, Beni Abbès must be the "film set" oasis. Something about its white houses and public buildings looks artificial. And indeed, most of them are recent. But prehistoric man was certainly here and left plenty of stone tools and weapons. History records a reoccupation in the 11th century, when enough water was found below ground to establish the plantations of date palms. The French arrived in 1901 and built a fort around which the present town grew up.

Like Taghit, Beni Abbès is on the very edge of the Great Western Erg, the vast sea of dunes that this circuit of oases skirts around. It's worth the climb to the top of a high dune north of the town, towards sunset, to look out across that immensity.

On the high ground to the south stands the tiny **church** still kept up by a small group of nuns, Les Petites Sœurs de Jésus. There can't be many churches with a soft sand floor like this, and it's light and cheerful inside between the thick walls and pillars. Mass is said daily at 7 p.m. (11 a.m. on Fridays). The famous former French army officer and explorer, Charles de Foucauld, came here immediately after his ordination as a priest in 1901. He set up a hermitage but moved on to Tamanrasset and the Hoggar soon afterwards.

Near the bottom of the hill, the **museum** is unusually comprehensive. If you only go to one of the several "museums of the Sahara" at various oases, choose this one. Because it is associated with a research centre for studies on arid zones, it is better laid out and more scientifically annotated than most. Your questions about date cultivation, scorpions, those desert roses—they're crystals of gypsum (hydrated calcium sulphate) formed by slow evaporation of solutions—might find an answer here. The huge numbers

A perfect reflection of sand, sky and palms in the oasis of Beni Abbès.

of stuffed birds and animals may be dispiriting, but educational.

It is the colossal variety of living things that somehow support themselves that is so striking. You will have been getting used to the idea that the Sahara is far from empty. Now you see how all its varied faces can be habitats for the most surprising life forms. Right next to the museum, a small botanic garden and **zoo** will bring you face to face with desert foxes, fennecs and jackals and various birds of prey, all of which most people would prefer to see let go. Snakes and scorpions they may be happier to view under controlled conditions.

Towards Timimoun

The 350-kilometre (217-mi.) stretch of road to Timimoun lies ahead, with fuel available only at Kerzaz, always with the proviso that the Naftal tanker has delivered on schedule. For most of the way the route follows close to the river bed of the Saoura, whose great valley often seems to be all that is holding back the menacing orange-yellow dunes. In places it has already been smothered and overwhelmed. If the march of the sands seems inexorable, there is comfort in the fact that it is a slow advance. Signs warning of sand *(sable)* across the road usually look as if they have been there for years. The drifts are cleared, but they form again in the same places year after year.

Kerzaz has doubtless been shadowed by the same mighty dunes for centuries. Stop and walk in its green gardens and look at the deep wells, dug down to the water table. High towers of mud bricks support wooden balance poles which act as levers to allow a long lift of the buckets.

Just 90 kilometres (56 mi.) short of Timimoun, a road heads south to the string of oases called the **Touat** (Sources), now as productive of winter salad crops for the north and for Europe as they are of dates. **Adrar** with its red-mud buildings is the chief town. The surfaced road ends at **Reggane**, some 360 kilometres (225 mi.) from Timimoun. With an all-terrain four-wheel-drive vehicle you can go on, after inspections and border formalities, for the 660 kilometres (410 mi.) of difficult *piste* to the actual border with Mali beyond Bordj Mokhtar, where there is a petrol (gasoline) station. You are advised to travel in convoy. Gao, where at last you reach the river

Niger, lies another 700 kilometres (435 mi.) to the south, with a lot of soft sand between. Only the best-prepared expeditions should undertake the journey.

Back on the more beaten track, notice how the rocks take on a red-brown shade and the sand gets darker. You're approaching **Timimoun**, "the Red", set on a cliff above the expanse of a dry salt lake. Beyond that extends the sea of sand. Nearer at hand, palm groves and gardens spread across the top of the cliff, with more at the bottom.

Before reaching the town, notice the lines of mounds with openings. They're the access holes to underground water conduits, or *foggaras,* which lie from 5 to 20 metres (16 to 66 ft.) below the surface. They carry the water for considerable distances, sloping very gently down from a source. The system was formerly much more widespread, but the dangers to the tunnellers and the demands of maintenance were too great. Nevertheless, a few modern *foggaras* have been constructed, and you'll find a new system south of Timimoun.

If you put water on the sand here, you'll see it turn deep reddish-purple. So the traditional buildings of local stone or mud-brick, bound and surfaced with mortar and mud, naturally took the same colour. Everything looks the shade of oxidized burgundy, except where it's been given a white trim. Even the newest government buildings have been painted in almost—not quite—the same colour.

Nearly wide enough for a football game, the main street has been embellished with monuments old and new. It's not always easy to tell which is which. Notice the ornate **gateway** on the east side, and the **Hôtel de l'Oasis Rouge**, reconstructed after a roof collapse. Both are examples of the so-called Sudanese style of architecture, which refers, not to today's country of Sudan, but to the one-time French Soudan, a vast region south of the Sahara that incorporated what is now Mali and Niger. Sudanese buildings are typically of reddish clay with occasional white-painted outlinings and ornamental arches, pinnacles and crenellations.

Timimoun is a place where some local knowledge proves invaluable, so if a young man offers to act as guide, accept. Walk in the **ksar** and see how the side alleys are roofed over for long stretches, creating al-

Desert Life

There is such a multitude of animal life in the Sahara one cannot help but wonder how it survives. Rodents like the jerboa only come out at night: by day they stay in deep burrows. It can be 25 degrees cooler, 60 cm. (2 ft.) below a hot sandy surface. Reptiles may do the same, or even "estivate" (the counterpart of "hibernate"—they sleep the hot season away in a cool hole). But beware the horned viper: it likes to lie just below the surface with its fangs protruding, so don't run around barefoot on the sand. Insects come out mostly at night, including sometimes malaria-carrying mosquitoes. Locusts are an exception as are the dark beetles that you see marching patiently up sand dunes, but the beetles have an insulating air-gap between their wingcases and bodies, just like the double roof on some expedition vehicles. Scorpions have hard waxy skins to stop water loss, and they keep out of the sun when they can. They just might hide in your shoes or under a rock near your sleeping place. The little desert fox called a fennec doesn't just listen at night for its prey with those huge ears: they are useful for losing heat as well. Delicate gazelles don't need to drink at all—the sparse vegetation they live on somehow provides enough water. Birds and animals reduce water loss by very efficient kidney action: their urine is very concentrated or may consist only of crystals, and solid waste is excreted in a very dry form.

Many of the desert-dwelling species are able to tolerate water so salty that it would nauseate humans, and they have ways to get rid of the excess salt. Where water suddenly becomes available through rare rainfall or a flash flood, seeds, insect eggs and even the eggs of fish and frogs that have lain dormant for years can suddenly come to life. One shower is enough to trigger the entire life cycle of some plants. If you are lucky enough to see it, the profusion of flowers is unforgettable.

most complete darkness and even more chance than usual of becoming lost. The locals don't claim to see in the dark; they walk around picking their feet up at each step to avoid tripping. Where it's particularly dark, they have to resort to shouting out warnings.

Ever-cheerful washerwoman in Timimoun the Red, capital of the Gouara.

The **palm groves** and **gardens** are celebrated. Alleys just wide enough for two to pass wind their way between low mud walls. Very long and narrow open channels carry water in a network that is quite beyond a stranger to fathom. There are even channel overpasses. It looks rather like an electrical wiring diagram. Does the water seem soapy? If you follow it back towards the houses, you may come across the reason. Before distribution, a lot is used for washing clothes in a cluster of communal ponds. Groups of women and girls scrub and talk equally vigorously. They won't mind you glancing at them, but linger and stare and they'll tell you unmistakeably to get lost.

Further downstream, comb-shaped barrages divide the flow according to the rightful shares of each gardener. Ask to be shown the most complex of these subdivisions. At one small barrage, a *17-way* split of the flow takes place. (You might have noticed that one of the fountains in the main street is a stylized version of just such a device.)

The dates here are famous: there are some prized stoneless varieties among them. Mint, coriander, garlic, hot chili peppers and all sorts of vegetables are squeezed into the little gardens. (It's a shame you don't find them more often on restaurant menus.)

The Gourara

As you near the end of the great circle of oases, try to fit in a small circle, only about 80 kilometres (50 mi.) long and called by the tourism people the Circuit of the Gourara. The ONAT manager or the information office can help you find a four-wheel-drive vehicle and a guide.

The Gourara, the low-lying area to the north-east of Timimoun, skirts the edges of the salt-crusted lake bed that you can see from the town. Literally dozens of little villages, each with its *ksar*, some watered by *foggaras*, some by open channels, cluster in palm groves or on cliffs. Starting at **Massine**, almost adjoining Timimoun, you'll see the local pottery for sale. Enterprising vendors will probably also offer fabrics, flints and pieces of petrified wood from an ancient forest in the area. A little further on at a fork in the track, you can make a diversion to the left to find crystalline desert roses growing below the sand.

Back on the main circuit, the *piste* climbs to a cliff which it follows past **Tlalet**—and spec-

Desert men relax around this example of unusual Sudanese architecture in Timimoun.

tacular views to the west—to **Ighzer**. Here you have a choice of dropping down to the lake bed or continuing on high ground to the ruined cliff-edge *ksar* of **Tindjillet** and to the most northerly point on the usual route, **Semouta** (40 km./ 25 mi. from Timimoun), where the *piste* (and you) turn for home. One more diversion, to **Ouled Saïd**, is well worth making. Ask your guide to show you the village's water-rationing system, which rivals that of Timimoun for complication.

There's so much to see that you could easily spend several days in this area. The Hôtel Le

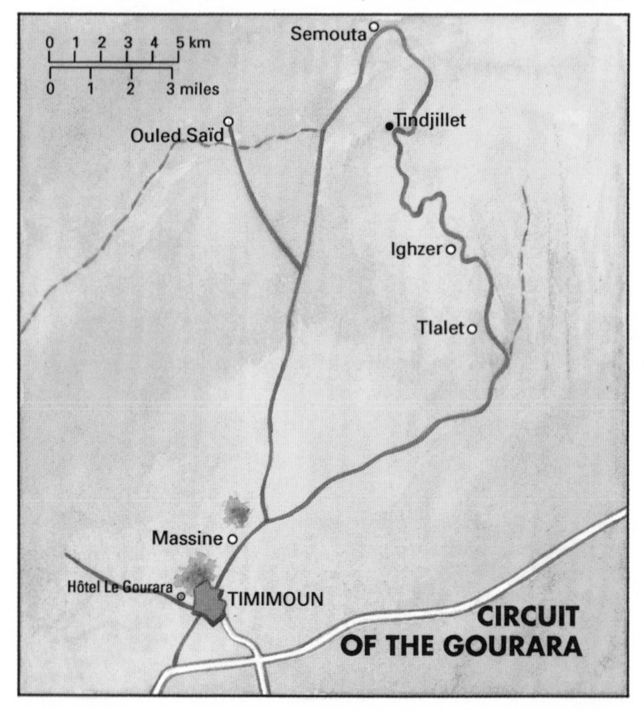

Gourara in Timimoun is not only somewhere to stay, it's a weird caricature of the *ksar* and of the gardens, with the same walled walkways outside. The view from the roof at dawn and sunset is yet another not to be missed.

El Goléa

It's 450 kilometres (280 mi.) from Timimoun to El Goléa. About halfway, at M'Guiden, stop at the petrol station, the only one on the way, and not just because it is wise to fill up wherever you can. Take a look at the glass case on the counter in the shop. Are all those huge, translucent, evil-looking scorpions and snakes dead? Oh, no. The owner blows on them and they start walking towards you. It's his party trick. Fortunately there is glass between them and you.

The flattest of flat plains takes up most of the way to El Goléa (the Citadel), a sprawling, wide-open town with a huge area of palm trees depending on artesian wells. The name refers to the rocky pinnacle to the north of the present city, with the old **ksar** on top. A Berber stronghold for a thousand years, it was taken by the French army in 1872. It's completely abandoned now, but worth the climb for the atmosphere and the view.

The remains of Father de Foucauld were brought to a church 3 kilometres (less than 2 mi.) north of El Goléa in 1929. His heart was left in Tamanrasset, where he had been killed in 1916. (The church seems almost abandoned to the encroaching sand. You may need a guide to find the way.)

Opposite the Hôtel El Boustène, Benedictine monks maintain a comprehensive museum of the geology and palaeontology of the region, which they will allow those who are specially interested to visit. The artisans' shop features locally made tapestry hangings in traditional geometric designs derived from those used in grass matting and Tuareg leatherwork. Finally, the attractive arcaded **market** in the middle of town is the place to stock up on fresh food. You may be surprised at the variety.

Now you're ready for the last lap, some 270 kilometres (170 mi.) to Ghardaïa. This section of road is notable for the army of *barkhan* sand dunes that constantly threatens it. The crescent-moon-shaped dunes slowly move with the wind, as sand blows over the sharp ridge on top and drops down the leeward side.

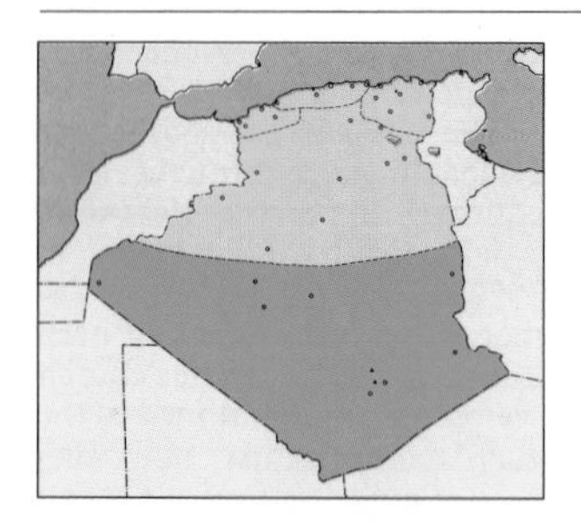

FAR SOUTH

"Alger 2,060 kms, El Goléa 1,110 kms, In Salah 710 kms", says the sign in the main street of Tamanrasset. That's 1,280, 690 and 440 miles respectively for steps on the road south. No wonder those who choose to drive look forward keenly to their arrival. And what a blessed relief it is to reach this famous outpost, whether you're coming from north or south, or returning caked with dust, from a trek or safari.

The road from the north passes through Ghardaïa (see p. 134), El Goléa (p. 161) and the last important but rather dreary staging post of **In Salah**. With an average of 55 days of sand storms annually, the town spends a lot of time simply digging itself out.

The road is surfaced all the way to Tamanrasset, but some southern sections have deteriorated seriously. However, any roadworthy car, sensibly equipped and driven with an eye to the sand drifts, crumbling shoulders and oncoming traffic, can make it. (Further south from Tamanrasset it's a different story, and plenty of small cars have come to grief.) There's a fashion among macho motorcyclists, whether groups of Italians or lone Japanese, to see how far they can go. Truckloads of Europe's youth pass through on their way to West, Central or East Africa. After all, it's not as far from here to the River Niger as it is back to Algiers. "Tam" represents adventure.

TAMANRASSET

Never mind that planes fly in every day, this still feels like the edge of the unknown. Altitude (about 1,400 m./4,600 ft.) keeps it bearable in summer, crisply cool in winter, though if you're looking for a tan, the sun blazes down reliably. Officially, the name is Tamenghest, but the pronunciation is almost the same. Most people call it "Tam", anyway, and old hands complain that it isn't what it was. Maybe so, but if by that they mean there's now

Did the Romans Really Get This Far?

The French ethnographer Henri Lhote spent years in the far south and certainly thought so. He showed that the triumph awarded to Cornelius Balbus for his Sahara expedition of 19 B.C. lists place names that can be convincingly identified with a string of oases as far as Abalessa (Balsa in the Roman records), 80 kilometres (50 mi.) west of Tamanrasset. To add to the circumstantial evidence, Roman coins and artefacts have been excavated here, though from a later period.

Lhote went further and claimed that the tireless Romans did too. He noted that the ancient historians mentioned a river Dasibari, and one local name for the Niger to this day is Da Isa Bari. But it is many hard days' march to the south, and sceptics point out that the words simply mean "the Great River".

There's no doubt, though, that trade routes joined the Mediterranean to West Africa long before the Roman era. Lhote also catalogued a chain of sites across this region with rock engravings showing chariots. Was there really a route carrying wheeled traffic so far, so long ago?

a large, comfortable hotel, the average visitor would settle for today's version. And unlike all but a handful of places in Algeria, there are quite a few tourists and trekkers in Tamanrasset.

This is the ideal headquarters for exploring the extraordinary Hoggar, or Ahaggar—the mountainous country all around—and for meeting an equally extraordinary people, the Tuareg. The first steps towards both could be a walk along the main street, here as so often elsewhere called **Avenue Emir Abdelkader**. In the offices of ONAT or a dozen private tour agencies you can compare prices and programmes for anything from a day trip in a four-wheel-drive vehicle to a three-week trek with a camel caravan. Just off the street through an imposing archway you'll find the little arcaded **marketplace** with all kinds of foods and souvenirs. Further along, there's a modest **museum**, with Tuareg weapons, leatherwork, children's toys

Proud Tuareg mounted upon their most prized possession.

and jewellery. Right next door, craftsmen are making some of the same things today, and it's good to see that in some items the quality has not seriously declined.

Red-brown mud brick, plastered with more mud of the same colour, is still the material for many buildings. Even where concrete blocks are used, they are sensibly coated with something like the traditional finish. Right on the main street stands a thick-walled red-brown fort *(bordj)* built by Father Charles de Foucauld to protect the local people from marauders. It was here that he was murdered in 1916.

Oued Tamanrasset, a wide, usually dry and dusty river bed, runs parallel to and south of the Avenue Emir Abdelkader. Try to get there soon after dawn one morning to see the **camel and goat market**, held in the wide bed of the river. You'll find plump and happy animals munching contentedly on bunches of millet while buyers and sellers argue fiercely over their qualities. On the other side of the river bed, the main **market** is much larger than the one in the town centre. The **Assihar** showground opposite, with its imposing gates, is where a great December fair takes place. That's the peak time for visiting Tamanrasset, so if you plan to be here then, make reservations long in advance. Also on this side of the river bed, and dwarfed by the modern mosque, Father de Foucauld's 1910 **hermitage** has thick insulating walls making it so narrow and corridor-like inside that you can touch both sides at once.

THE HOGGAR

It was in 1910, too, that the remarkable priest went by rough tracks to a mountaintop some 80 kilometres (50 mi.) north of Tamanrasset to establish another hermitage on the edge of the Assekrem Plateau. The journey there is still tough, but even if you make only one expedition out of town, you should follow in his footsteps. Plan to stay overnight, because above all it is the sunset and the dawn that must be seen.

Circuit of Assekrem

It makes sense to go one way to Assekrem and come back another, in a route that the tour companies call the Circuit of Assekrem. The two tracks are equally bone-shaking. Not more than many others in the far south, but hard on a vehicle. Although a conventional

Sunset on the mountains of the Hoggar—a view from the Assekrem pass that lingers…

car might make it, parts of the road get washed out by the occasional fierce rains which leave deep gullies. It's best done by four-wheel-drive vehicle, unless you have the time for a trek with donkeys or camels, or carrying your own backpack.

The eastern half of the circuit passes the huge volcanic stump of **Iharene** (or Laperrine) and the "cascades" of **Imlaoulaouene**. Don't be too disappointed if they don't live up to their impressive name. If there hasn't been much rain—the usual condition—the flow is only a dribble. Better falls are to come.

Now the road begins to climb through landscapes resembling a mad giant's quarry. A local guide or driver, and that means a Targui (the singular of Tuareg), can take you to the Neolithic tomb below the **Ahounahamt** mountains, and to rock engravings in a dozen places along the route, most involving a short trek. The animals they depict, antelopes, "big game" and ancestors of the domestic cow, have largely disappeared—with one exception, the gazelle. Keep a sharp watch on the distant hillsides almost anywhere in the Hoggar and you may be lucky enough to see them. They're almost always

A timeless glimpse across the desert—from days gone by or those to come.

in pairs, male and female or mother and offspring, and on hearing any sound they head for the horizon, seeming to fly over the rocks.

Your objective should be to reach the **Assekrem pass** (2,600 m./8,500 ft.) in time to see the setting sun light up the most tortured, weird skyline of peaks imaginable. You could climb to the hermitage just above, but that is as well left until just before dawn. The energetic, who only have to see a hilltop to want to get to the top of it, can use the one to the south of the pass as a grandstand for viewing the golden sunset.

You can stay in one of the rooms of the stone-built **refuge** at the pass where the caretaker can even provide a hot meal. (It is as well to reserve space—you can buy vouchers in Tamanrasset—and ask about food on arrival, unless you have a cook and supplies with you.) Set the alarm clock for well before sunrise, because to oversleep would be a disaster. Give yourself enough time to get ready and half an hour to get to the top. You'll need a torch (flashlight) when going up. The fiery dawn first outlines jagged pinnacles and volcanic stumps and then suffuses a sea of them with glowing light. Just as quickly, the colour drains away to leave a grey and forbidding landscape, and you can turn to

A Hoggar Day

Tuareg drivers—whether of camels or four-wheel-drives—love a sheltered dry river bed as a spot for lunch or for the night, and of course they know best. Expedition days in the Hoggar settle into a pattern, built around basic needs.

Wood has to be gathered for a fire, and it is amazing how easy it is to find some along the river bed, where it may have been lying for years. The aromatic blaze isn't to keep warm by, though it may be welcome in the early morning. It is to make Tuareg tea, a liquid of mouth-puckering astringency produced by the prolonged boiling of green tea leaves in a metal pot over glowing charcoal embers. The idea, apparently, is to extract the last dregs of tannin and then try vainly to counteract it with plenty of sugar. Following a time-honoured ritual, your driver will boil the tea up and offer you some three times. It's polite to savour a couple of tiny cups with all the lip-smacking appreciation you can muster. It isn't compulsory to accept the third time.

If you have a local cook with you, he (always a "he") may surprise you with his ingenuity, producing better food than many hotels. That is not something astonishing, you may say, but the best safari chefs rapidly whip up ambitious salads and freshly made soups, ringing the changes between crisp fried potatoes, pasta and couscous. The usual weak point is the decidedly chewy meat. Dates and mandarin oranges make the standard safari dessert. A midday siesta while it's warm will be high on the driver's agenda, and not a bad idea either.

At night you need shelter from the wind. It's up to you to find a spot to set up your bed, perhaps behind boulders or under a rocky overhang. Chances are that you'll never encounter a scorpion or viper in the wild, but be careful about putting a hand into nooks and crannies, just in case. Most agency-organized tours carry foam mattresses and blankets. You have to provide a sleeping bag, but in winter it alone won't be enough.

One of the greatest joys of sleeping in the open is to snuggle into a warm cocoon, with just your eyes showing, and watch the stars roll around the heavens. You tend to wake up often, when jackals yelp in the distance, or a confused jerboa hops right over your sleeping bag, or just because of the unaccustomed silence. You'll soon reacquire the ancient skill of guessing the time from how far Orion has moved in its nightly arc from horizon to horizon. If you've underestimated your bedding requirements, the hours before dawn will seem the longest you've ever spent.

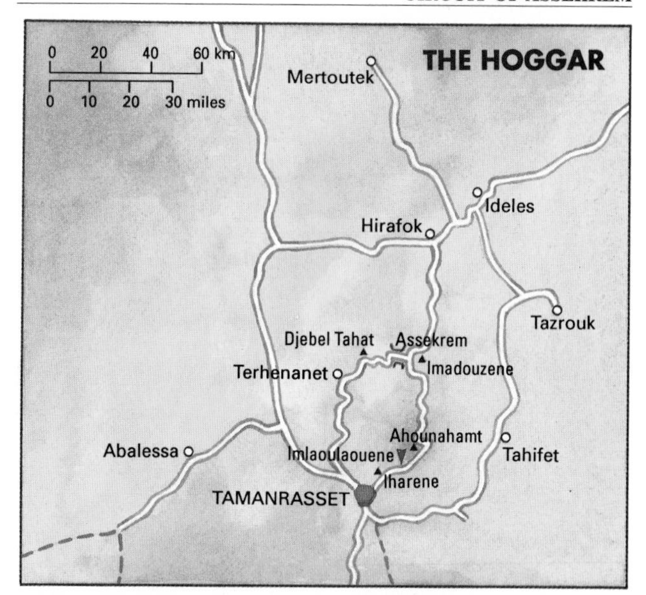

look at the hermitage with its relics of Father de Foucauld. Mass is said in the tiny **chapel** every day at 7 a.m., and you may wish to attend. If so, try to contact one of the resident brothers the previous evening to make sure that there will be room for you.

The western half of the Assekrem circuit returns to Tamanrasset by way of the conical bunch of skyward-pointing pillars that is **Djebel Ilamane**, (2,739 m./8,986 ft.). It's not a difficult climb: the road itself is almost as high. The highest peak of Algeria, **Djebel Tahat**, (2,918 m./9,573 ft.) can be seen to the north, but in fact there is majestic scenery all the way. Pinnacles, domes and towers have such deep vertical striations they seem to have been clawed by some giant cat.

(overleaf) *Crouched among the camels, Tuareg exchange daily gossip and news from afar.*

What to Take on an Organized Trek

1. *A soft, strong bag for the donkeys or camels to carry. Not a suitcase—that would be too hard to strap onto the pack animals—and nothing too precious. It will take a bashing as the donkeys push through narrow gaps in rocks.*
2. *A small marching backpack for essential supplies during the day. The pack animals often take a different route from you. Even if they don't, you can't expect to get to your bag during the day.*
3. *To put in the small pack: water bottle, water purifying tablets, suncream (a moisturizing type), chapstick for lips, snacks, camera and films (stored in a lightweight, insulated bag), guidebook and notebook, pen or pencil, tissues. Sunglasses and a hat.*
4. *Sleeping bag. In winter, a warm one. You may well be sleeping out in freezing conditions. Organized treks usually provide extra blankets and foam mattresses.*
5. *Old clothes. Whatever you take will turn brown with dust. You need basically light clothing, naturally, and in cotton rather than synthetics, but take a sweater and anorak/parka too. Slacks for women.*
6. *Your favourite walking boots or shoes. Many people prefer running shoes to hiking boots. Whatever you take should have a grippy tread. Several pairs of socks.*
7. *Torch/flashlight and batteries.*
8. *Your regular toilet and medical needs. Towel. Moist tissues are invaluable. Anti-diarrhoea pills. Anti -malaria pills. Toilet paper. Battery-powered razor if you intend to shave daily.*
9. *Detergent powder to wash filthy clothes on your return from the trek. (They'll dry in no time in this dessicated air.)*
10. *A bottle of your choice of pre-dinner drink (preferably one that doesn't need a mixer other than water).*

How fit should you be? *There's no need to be a super athlete. Plenty of older people who don't usually take a lot of vigorous exercise go on treks. The guides set a steady pace and take frequent breaks. But you need a certain amount of stamina, strong ankles (you'll be scrambling over rocks) and a degree of surefootedness. Take some long hearty walks at home before you go, use stairs instead of elevators, and you'll be able to keep up.*

At **Terhenanet**, formerly nomadic Tuareg have established a village where, despite the altitude and climate, they can grow feed for their animals. Easier than the desperate search for unpredictable wild plants, no doubt, but it is a wrench for them to abandon nomadism and engage in the despised life of a cultivator.

Circuit of the Hoggar

Just going to Assekrem and back is the minimum. Having come this far you'll probably want to explore more widely, and the Circuit of the Hoggar is one way to do it. It begins with either the eastern or western approach to Assekrem and a night at the refuge there. Just to the east (6 km./3½ mi.) the track branches northwards towards the village of Hirafok, occasionally making extravagant detours where sudden floods have washed it out. It passes the crater of **Imadouzene**, where the rim has been eroded and fissured into "dead men's fingers"—near-vertical columns of rock like a circular stockade. It's fairly easy to scramble to the edge and look into the extinct volcano itself. Vehicles take quite a pounding as they cross a sea of stones, lava, basalt, multi-coloured granites and quartzes. The little rock enclosures by the side of the track are shelters built by the workers who made it, to give them some protection against the bitter wind. Just when you are falling again into the habit of thinking this a lifeless land, squirrel-like gundi scurry among the boulders, and birds of prey circle in the distance.

Hidden in a miniature gorge to the west of the Assekrem–Hirafok track, the **Oued Zerzaoua** rises to the surface, making one of its occasional appearances as flowing water. Linking a succession of clear pools, some even with tiny, nervous fish in them, it supports a ribbon of bright green reeds before disappearing again beneath bare rock. Walk along it for a bit, seeing how many different plants, birds and insects this fragile environmental capsule supports.

Back on the circuit, the road descends to a sandy plain strewn with boulders. The isolated village of **Hirafok**, mostly of reed houses called *zeribas*, has surprising green gardens of vegetables and fruit. The secret is not hard to find: great solar panels of photoelectric cells provide the power for an electric pump to lift all the water the villagers need. You'll have an unusual chance to see the women of a rural community; it is they who come to fill the family jerry cans and buckets. The solar-powered system is spreading rapidly over remoter parts of rural Algeria, away from electrification and where underground water supplies can meet the demand.

Six kilometres (3½ mi.) to the north-east, a rocky outcrop bears some fine shallow-engraved **Neolithic pictures** of giraffes, cows and something resembling wildebeest. As usual, it is a mystery why these rocks were chosen from so many similar groups. As usual, too, you'll be glad to have a local driver to locate them.

The circuit continues to **Ideles**, a self-important little town with a central square and a police post where you check in to have your name, vehicle number and destination recorded.

You can watch while simple jewellery is made in a **smithy**. Local children observe the craftsmen, too, and learn the trade by trying to imitate them. A tiny pre-school boy pumps merrily away on goatskin bellows to keep the charcoal fire glowing cherry red.

The Hoggar circuit continues, mainly on wheels, south-east to the high but fertile settlement of **Tazrouk**. It can offer a rare chance in this area to refuel vehicles, assuming that the tanker has delivered and that the electricity is on to operate the pumps. The village straggles out along a river bed, with huge old fig trees, tall poplars turning to shining gold in autumn, apricot orchards and greenhouses for growing salad crops even in the winter.

Not far down Oued Terberber at **Touaken**, a pyramid-shaped rocky pile displays ancient engravings of giraffes, ostriches and waterbuck, as well as cows and some crude, more modern, pictures of camels. It is never easy to date these things, but some idea of the relative age of images, one to another, is possible because the surface of the rock darkens very slowly when exposed to light and air. Freshly cut surfaces are yellow and gradually turn black over the centuries. The outlines of the oldest carvings here are just as black as the rest of the rock.

Nearby at **Tibaridin**—a guide can take you there on foot—was found a Neolithic shrine with several polished rock statues, almost cylindrical but with the tops carved into simple faces. Not much remains at the site. The statues themselves can be seen at the Bardo Museum in Algiers.

A stony track, hard on any vehicle (aren't they all?), crosses the high Azrou pass through a series of lunar landscapes. Then it drops down into the next valley at **Tahifet** (105 km./65 mi. from Tamanrasset), where the wide, flat river bed supports a long string of gardens shielded by reed and thorn fences from hungry goats. You'll see ingenious goat cages, too, made of sticks and designed to protect the kids from predators as well as to keep them inside.

The last main stop on the Hoggar circuit, only 55 kilometres (34 mi.) from Tamanrasset, is at the **falls** of Tamekrest. A real waterfall, this, with enough flowing to take a shower under. Sloping sides of pink and green granite, polished and scalloped by cascades much greater than now, lead up to an idyllic little world at the top. There, lush reed beds give cover to a pair of ducks, and wagtails and swallows weave and jink overhead. The water is scarcely visible on the surface, but you can see where donkeys have made pools by scraping shallow holes in the sand. The sheltered valley below the falls makes a superb campsite for the last night on this journey. There's even the shade of trees if you need it.

Other Hoggar Expeditions

It's not that you will meet many other visitors anywhere in the Hoggar, but there is always a demand to break fresh ground. To answer it, expedition organizers have been looking south to the **Tassili N'Ahaggar.** (The word "tassili" stands for a plateau cut by gorges.) The area between Tamanrasset and the borders with Mali and Niger presents new challenges, among them more driving on sand and the need for new superlatives to describe the scenery: the red "castle" of **Abalema**, Neolithic remains at **Igharghar**, the sandstone columns of **Tagrera** and the caves of **Djebel Amaraka** with their prehistoric paintings. These are linked up in a variety of itineraries, particularly by the more adventure-orientated agencies in Europe. You'll be on the road ten to 15 days, always sleeping in the open air and alternating between trekking and driving. One thing is certain—you will never forget the Hoggar, whichever trip you take.

Equally memorable and just as remote, the mountainous **Tefedest** region is rich in rock engravings and paintings. Dating from anywhere between 2,000 to 8,000 years ago, they depict ostriches, giraffes, ele-

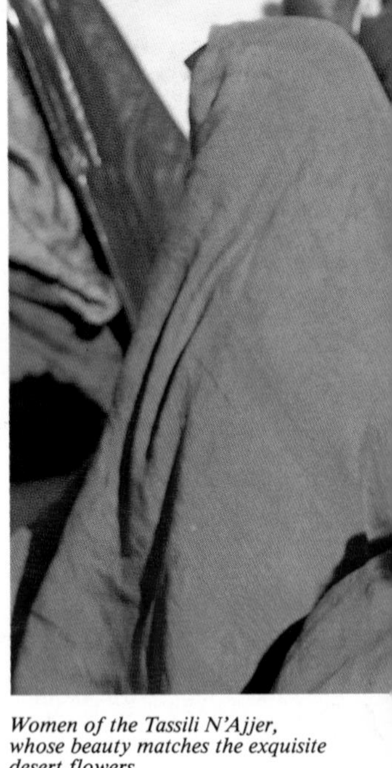

Women of the Tassili N'Ajjer, whose beauty matches the exquisite desert flowers.

phants and leopards, as well as the domestication of cattle and later, of horses. Then in the final period, the last few centuries B.C., camels appear. This is also the home of Garet El Djenoun, or Oudane, the infamous mountain of demons.

Like the comparable sites of the Tassili N'Ajjer, those of the Tefedest can only be reached on foot, but they are less often visited. The Tefedest is truly "off piste". Treks start from **Mertoutek**, an isolated Tuareg village some 230 kilometres (145 mi.) north of Tamanrasset. You will need at least a week out of "Tam", a guide and donkey driver. The rewards of undiscovered country and magnificent prehistoric art await you.

TASSILI N'AJJER

Probably no region on earth can boast such a concentration and variety of prehistoric art. Tens of thousands of rock paintings from around 6000 to 500 B.C. are certainly a great attraction in themselves. But also consider that they are found in one of the most extraordinary landscapes imaginable, which alone would be worth the journey. The combination of the two is surely irresistible.

Why doesn't everyone go? Quite a number do. This is one of the handful of destinations in Algeria where you will meet more than a couple of dozen foreign visitors at a time. But it's a long way—over 1,600 kilometres (1,000 mi.) from Algiers by air—and there are only a few flights a week. By road it is much further, and long stretches in the south are unsurfaced and difficult to cross. Most of the paintings are up on a plateau which, like Conan

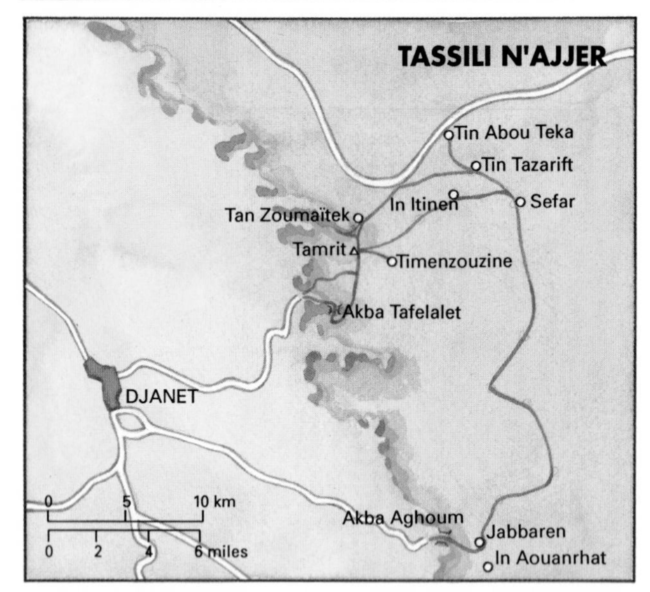

Doyle's "Lost World", can *only* be reached by walking and at times scrambling over rocks. When you get there, some facilities are rudimentary, the rest don't exist. All of which sorts out people into Type A and Type B: those who are put off for all kinds of good reasons, and those who are turned on by the challenge.

There's more that Type Bs need to know. The area is a national park, and you cannot go wandering around on your own. You can arrive independently in Djanet, the oasis from which the treks start, but when you apply for a permit to enter the park, you will be assigned to a group. Unless, that is, you join a trek planned by one of the local agencies. In that case, cooks, food, a guide, donkeys and their drivers are all provided. If you want to take your own food along and prepare it yourself, you'll reduce the cost, but don't expect to find plentiful or economically priced supplies in Djanet.

Most visitors come to the Tassili N'Ajjer with a tour group on an inclusive package. If you are looking for one to join, whether in your home country, Algiers or Djanet, try to find out fairly precise details of the itinerary, the conditions and what is provided. After all, you will have come a long way, and prices are high. There are no low cost "deals". It would be a shame if you missed some sights that you were particularly hoping to see.

For the same reasons, don't try to compress the Tassili N'Ajjer into three or four days. Merely to arrive in Djanet, get organized and trek up to the plateau takes two days. Coming down and leaving takes another. So three days would scarcely allow you time to see any of the prehistoric art at all. Five days is the sensible minimum, seven would allow a longer trek or a variety of additional short forays.

Djanet is not one but a cluster of villages, all within easy walking distance. Their *ksour* cling like limpets to the steep banks of the mainly dry Oued Edjariou. It's hard to say whether the houses are growing out of the rocks or the rocks from the houses. Palm groves straggle along the valley and water from springs and little streams trickles through them, nourishing vegetable gardens in the shade beneath the trees. The 1,000-metre (3,280-ft.) altitude makes for a touch of freshness in the air on winter days, but nights are rarely freezing, as they can be up on the plateau. It doesn't have anything of the sophisticated feel of Tamanrasset, where they've "seen it all".

You'll find most of the facilities you need—and most of what Djanet has to offer—concentrated around the little arcaded central **market** on the edge of the palm grove. The ONAT and other tour agencies, a few shops including a craft store and the Air Algérie office are here, or directly opposite at the foot of the rocks. So is the office of the Tassili National Park, where you obtain your entrance permit. Agencies may be able to do this for their clients, but it's usually necessary to go personally. If there is a delay, use the time to look around the small but good **museum** in the same building. Exhibits include flint tools up to 300,000 years old—and stone axes up to 80,000 years old. Notice, too, the delicate "microliths", tiny blades that were mounted in rows to make a deadly arrowhead. You'll also want to have a look at reproductions of some of the engraved and painted pictures that you're going to see.

There's basic (very basic) accommodation nearby in the form of traditional reed huts *(zeriba)*. They're to be found under palm trees right next to the market square.

Short Excursions from Djanet

Not all the Tassili N'Ajjer rock paintings are on the plateau itself. Some, as well as fine engravings, lie closer to Djanet. If you have a free afternoon, you could take an hour's walk to the **Ghar Es Safir** (Ambassadors' Cave). Not really a cave, but a sheltered overhang, it was where distinguished people used to lodge when visiting the chiefs of the Kel Djanet tribe of Tuareg. You'll find engraved elephants and long-horned cattle, as well as paintings of many periods. The styles represented include the "little horned devils", the "two-triangle" figures, a delightful speckled giraffe and less artistically rendered camels and goats (see pp. 183–185). The paintings date roughly from 8,000 to 1,500 years ago, though because of their easy accessibility they've been damaged and subjected to graffiti.

Out beyond the airport south of Djanet, there's a site that you won't find without a guide and a four-wheel-drive vehicle. It's hidden among huge rocky outcrops alternating with the sand dunes that mark the start of the Erg Admer. At **Tegharghart** (or Terarart) one of the rock faces was deeply engraved with wonderfully sympathetic pictures of long-horned cattle, perhaps 6,000 or 7,000 years ago (the period of the cattle herders). The tear falling from the eye of one animal in the main picture has led it to be called **"the crying cow"**. Look closely and you'll see that all the cows have the beginnings of a teardrop in their eyes.

Whoever created these engravings certainly meant them to be on display, not hidden away. They are rarely found in caves or even sheltered by rocky overhangs like the typical paintings, but on prominent boulders or dramatically sited vertical cliffs. Of course, if paintings had been thus exposed, they would have suffered more from erosion, but the early artists must have known that, too. From the lack of even badly worn paintings in open sites, we can conclude that they mainly painted in sheltered spots.

THE TASSILI ROCK PAINTINGS

The Tuareg of the Ajjer knew of the thousands of pictures in this outdoor art gallery long before they were "discovered" by Lieutenant Brenans in 1933. (Tuaregs were living in the simple shelters whose walls were covered with them.) Brenans was apparently chasing fugitives—a singularly unrewarding pursuit in this sort of area—when he suddenly noticed some pictures on the side of a chasm, and then more and more.

Although later travellers published accounts, there was no systematic study until the expeditions organized by Henri Lhote in the 1950s, when thousands of the paintings were catalogued and copied. (Some copies are in the Bardo Museum in Algiers.) Lhote's book, *In Search of the Tassili Frescoes,* describes the recording process and the extraordinary difficulties of working on the plateau.

The word "fresco" really shouldn't be used: there is nothing of the true fresco technique involved here. The paints were made from the materials at hand, by grinding up coloured friable earth and rocks called schists—and mixing them with oils, fats, the gum

Photographing the Rock Paintings

There's usually not much light on the subjects, shaded as they are by overhanging rocks. You are not permitted to use a flash—but actually this is no great loss. Automatic or manual, your camera will need long exposure times so you will have to hold it especially still. Reasonably fast film will obviously help. Use any handy rocks to steady yourself or the camera. If you can adjust the aperture, open it wide. That means that only a small range of distances can be in focus, so make sure that all parts of the area to be photographed are about the same distance from the lens. Don't "angle" the camera to the rock face. Pictures including both sunlit and shaded areas are not likely to be a success.

Come in as close as you can to capture the details, while taking some panoramas as well to give an idea of the sites. Since you can't get very near to certain subjects, a zoom lens is an advantage. In the past, photographers sponged water onto the pictures to brighten the faded colours. Although the pigments seemed at first to be unaffected, eventually some running was noticeable, especially of the whites. The technique is now forbidden. So is any sort of interference with the surface, which is more delicate than it looks.

It's a day's walk from Djanet to Jabbaren, site of ancient and fascinating rock paintings.

from acacia trees or other binders. Red-brown and red predominate, but blue, blue-green, yellow-ochre and especially off-white are common.

How old are they? Some rock faces carry lots of pictures in different styles, painted over a long period. Some scenes or images are on top of earlier ones. This means that at least a *relative* chronology can be established. Unfortunately, scarcely any artefacts associated with the paintings have been found. Flash floods washing through the chasms presumably scoured out the rock shelters many times in the past. But climatic studies show when past conditions were favourable to, say, the cattle-herding that features in so many pictures. We also know that hunting came before cattle-herding as a human occupation, that horses and especially chariots arrived in the region after that, and that camels were introduced later still.

Lhote proposed a division of

the styles into four main types, with corresponding dates. There hasn't been much serious disagreement over fundamentals since, though the dates have shifted a bit.

Hunters, before 4000 B.C: wild animals—antelopes, giraffes, elephants, big-horned mountain sheep called moufflon, even hippos and rhinos—are shown. Sometimes human figures with spears, bows and arrows and tridents appear in the same scene. Earlier pictures are small and simple; the humans have little round heads and schematic bodies. Later, heads and figures grow larger. Towards the end of the period pictures are on a huge scale and images of animals are cruder. Ghostly ritual monsters appear, resembling children dressing up in white sheets.

Cattle-herders, from about 4000 B.C. to 1500 B.C.: cows, individually or in a group, usually long-horned, often piebald are the chief subject. Human figures (apparently a different group who displaced the hunting people) join them, armed with sticks or bows and in lively motion. Their bodies are often shown as decorated. Scenes of domestic life predominate, though artists continue to depict wild animals and hunting. Human figures are charming and naturalistic. It's tempting—but simplistic—to say they seem to have little religious significance.

Horsemen and chariots, from about 1200 B.C.: a new people, assumed to have come from the east, possibly Egypt, arrive, with horses at a flying gallop, pulling carts and chariots. These stylized figures have been identified with the Hyksos of Egyptian history. If this is correct we have an unusual overlap between prehistory and recorded history. (That any wheeled vehicle could have been hauled up onto the Tassili, or even made and used there, seems incredible today.) Two triangles, perhaps representing a tunic and a skirt, and a tiny head indicate the human body. There's an "ancient Egyptian" look to some of the figures.

Camels, from about A.D. 100: initially, the style is representational, with the camel's hair suggested by hatched lines, but gradually the pictures become cruder. A triangle suffices for the animal's body and straight lines, for the legs. As much interest lies in the inscriptions, written in ancient Berber characters that developed into the Tuareg script called Tifinagh.

Up to the Plateau

Two main paths make the roughly 700-metre (2,300-ft.) ascent to the Tassili N'Ajjer. The first starts at the Tafelalet pass, 15 kilometres (9 mi.) east of Djanet. The other begins at the Aghoum (or Aroum) pass, 22 kilometres (14 mi.) south-east of Djanet. Four-wheel-drive vehicles drop trekkers and their backpacks at the foot of one of the passes. The heavier baggage is loaded onto infinitely patient donkeys. There's a ratio of approximately one donkey per human trekker. At this point you'll see why organizers specify soft bags only, one per person. You set off up the rocky track, led by your Tuareg guides.

The **Tafelalet pass** is the easier of the two access routes, but it still demands a hard two hours or more of walking and scrambling over rocks. Henri Lhote describes how his party tried to use camels as pack animals here: the terrible trouble they had comes as no surprise. Even the donkeys, who usually pick their way so daintily, bells tinkling, have to struggle in places. Even so, they'll probably overtake you while you are having your hourly rest, their drivers urging them on with whoops and shouts. First you reach a valley almost enclosed by vertical cliffs. Then comes the final ascent to the bare stony desert at the top. But there are still two or three more hours of walking to your first objective, Tamrit. It just so happens that the toughest half day is the first. Not the way you want it if you are planning to work up to fitness during the trek itself.

You know you are nearing **Tamrit** when you see the first of the incredibly ancient giant cypress trees. Called *taghout* (pronounced tarout) by the Tuareg, about three dozen survive in the "valley of the cypresses" (see p. 187), and up to a hundred elsewhere on the plateau. Their great gnarled and twisted trunks can be almost 2 metres (6½ ft.) in diameter and they may be thousands of years old. It seems that these few have survived a change in the climate only because their roots reach so deep and because their wood is so hard that the Tuareg in the past had no tools able to cut it.

Tamrit has a permanent tented camp where trekkers can spend their first night. There's even a tent with a dining table and another for the ingenious cooks. Like everywhere else on the plateau, there are no sanitary facilities at all, and only the water that the donkeys have carried up in plastic jerry cans. If you prefer to sleep out under the stars, wrap up well. You are at 1,800 metres (5,900 ft.) and the wind blows icy cold in the small hours of a winter morning.

Tamrit Area

It takes about an hour to walk north through rocky defiles to the **Tamrit gorges**. On the way you may see your first Tassili paintings. Cows of the cattle herders period feature in this area, but there are also scenes of men hunting antelope and moufflon with spears and bows and arrows. You squeeze through narrow natural alleys and out onto terraces to be confronted suddenly by a vertical chasm so deep and dark you can't see the bottom. Try throwing a stone down and counting the seconds until you hear it hit. The drop is practically equal to the whole of the height you climbed, over 600 metres (2,000 ft.).

Not far from the gorges, in a place they call **Tan Zoumaïtek**, the Tuareg guides can show you one of the most complicated groups of pictures, painted over thousands of years on one long wall. Surely this must have been a place of great, probably religious, significance. Look for the round-headed figures from the hunters period, and the various animals, some recognizable, some not. One gnu or wildebeest carries a tiny man on its back. The longer you look, the more details you'll make out. Most striking: two masked figures with painted or tattooed bodies and jewellery from the cattle-herders period, and an extravagantly horned moufflon. Notice the beautiful detail in the drawing of the horns. In the rock shelters *(abris)* scattered around you'll see many figures with their arms held out in front of them, for all the world like water-skiers. It may be that they are winnowing grain. No one can be certain.

A short walk from the Tamrit camp, the **valley of the cypresses** shelters three dozen of these venerable survivors. The trees are now assured of protection from the depredations of goats and humans, but there are still no seedlings. It's as sad as Tolkien's story of the "Ents". Evidently the climate is now too parched here, but cypress trees of this species have been grown from seed in Algiers. Although the Tuareg couldn't cut them down, they did break off the smaller branches in the past, which so weakened some trees that they died.

Rock paintings are scattered around the valley walls, but as the most accessible on the plateau they were sadly subject to damage and graffiti in the past. You'll notice some in this area with a darker or shinier looking patch. That's the result of UNESCO experiments with protective varnishes. The long-term effects have yet to be established. Look out for the painting of a river full of fish. The artist was probably thinking of the very river that flowed in this valley—and still does from time to time, judging by the jetsam stranded up in the branches of bushes.

The engraved elephant at **Timenzouzine**, an hour's walk to the east, is a rarity on the plateau. What was it that made Tassili artists concentrate so much on painting instead of engraving? Even at this site, the engraving—probably from the cattle-herders period—is superimposed with paintings which cover one of the most extensive galleries of rock shelters. You'll see fish depicted here, too, as well as archers and some kind of witch doctor figure, perhaps.

Generally known as Tuareg *they call themselves* Imohagh, *"the free".*

From Tamrit to Sefar

Treks tend to make early starts after a rough and ready breakfast. (Bread, jam and coffee just like you have at the usual Algerian hotel, but the bread gets drier and harder each day.) So you do most of the long walks in the cool of the morning. The light's better then for

photography, too. Tamrit to Sefar, a major site to the east, takes about four hours, depending on how many stops you make. The path picks its way through a maze of chasms and pillars and natural bridges. Erosion has run riot.

In Itinen (*In,* like *Aïn*, means "spring"), in the middle of this tortured landscape, boasts another full range of paintings from all eras, many superimposed. Look out for scenes from late in the first period (the hunters) with enormous white spook-like figures holding their hands high. Humans riding or even apparently vaulting over cattle date from the second per-

iod, while horsedrawn chariots and uniformed warriors belong to the third. Finally come camels and crude inscriptions. Notice the low walls in front of the rock shelters. It's impossible to tell their age: this must have been the ancients' way of getting some protection from the elements, but today's trekkers add stones to the walls, too, when they use the shelters to sleep in.

Between In Itinen and Sefar the path crosses the flat, stony desert of the higher Tassili, devoid of rivers, shelter and shade. Your guide paces ahead as if timed by a metronome, maybe chanting a song to himself. The trekkers fall into single line behind him on the narrow track.

Stores of superlatives, already depleted, run out at **Sefar**. The plateau here must have been weakened by a thousand faults. Then erosion gouged out a criss-cross pattern of gorges, with flat bottoms like streets, vertical sides like buildings. Flowing water undercut the sides to form deep rock shelters where early people took up residence. A prehistoric town! Did they have addresses? It's a vast area and very confusing.

Trekkers camp for the night here, each one picking a shelter before gathering round a fire, their enormous shadows thrown on the rock face. While expedition cooks make dinner, you may see jerboas, nocturnal desert rats with exaggeratedly long back legs like kangaroos, hopping about just out of reach. After your meal, settle

The Haughty Tuareg

Slim, tall figures, made even more impressive by their massive headdresses, they still dominate the southern Saharan scene. The Arabs gave them the name "Tuareg", implying that they were people who had "turned away from the faith" because of their resistance to conversion. They call themselves "the free", and they are now devout Muslims. If you have a Targui (the singular of Tuareg) driver, he may stop the car for his five-times-a-day prayers. Once the most feared of warriors, their swords, lances and leather shields were ultimately powerless against the modern guns of the French army in the battles of the Hoggar in 1902.

The pride remains. Tuareg know that they are the equal of anybody, and better than most. They'll address you familiarly as "tu" and rarely say please or thank you. But they're tremendous comedians and mimics: you'll laugh at their

impressions of other foreigners, and all the while they'll be noting your mannerisms for a future impersonation.

Their society was—to a great extent still is—highly stratified. At the top came the few of noble birth, the camel-owners who stooped to no physical labour and who looked on settled people, especially those who grew crops, with contempt. Their vassals were next, those who herded goats and did such work as loading the camels. Then came a caste of craftsmen, especially smiths, much darker skinned and credited with almost magical powers by those who had acquired none of their skills. At the bottom of the heap were serfs of African origin. House servants, they also did any heavy work, including cultivation. The separate groups remain to this day, though divisions are blurring and the serfs have long since been legally freed.

Women have especially high status, befitting a people who claim to be descended from a matriarch, Queen Tin Hinan, who is said to have arrived in the Hoggar after a prodigious trek through the desert. In Tuareg society, it's the men who are veiled. On special occasions they bring out the famous deep indigo cloth that used to stain their faces blue. Now that the dye is so hard to get, their everyday cheche *is green, black or white. Women show their faces, and young people can decide for themselves whom to marry.*

Life has been difficult for the Tuareg in recent years. Droughts devastated their camel herds, and the structure of their society began to break down when those beneath them in the caste system went off and made money in the oil and other industries. Some Tuareg have taken jobs as tour guides leading treks in the Tassili N'Ajjer, some as drivers in the Hoggar. No one can rival their knowledge of the country.

back to watch the stars roll past between the towering cliffs.

Sefar has some of the most famous paintings, representing every period: sinuous dancers; a famous female figure in mask and loincloth, holding a gourd; battle scenes with casts of hundreds of tiny figures; and enormous antelopes, cows and speckled giraffes. An intriguing set of masks could almost have come yesterday from West Africa. You can't miss the spook-like figures, some 3 metres (10 ft.) high: one with a horned head seems to be the object of veneration for a line

Mobile desert arabesque, source of inspiration for the motifs and designs of Islamic art.

of supplicants. You can make your own guesses as to the cults involved. Six or more thousand years after, they may be as good as anyone else's. Every

picture poses unanswered questions. Many features haven't been identified at all. The guides think they know about one tall white figure with a raised stick, apparently bashing another, who is dropping whatever he or she was holding. "It's a man beating his wife", they say with relish, despite the high status women are accorded in Tuareg society.

In similar scenery near Sefar to the north, **Tin Tazarift** has especially fine dancers and archers from the cattle-herders period, and a scene where cows and humans seem to be standing in water. Further north, another hour's walk, **Tin Abou Teka** near the edge of the plateau commands views to the east over the Fezzan in Libya. The paintings here include horses and chariots.

The Tuareg know of many different routes back to Tamrit. If they take you past **Naturhami**, look not only for fight scenes between the "two-triangle" men of the horsemen and chariots period, but pictures of men hunting with dogs. One hunting scene depicts an antelope with spears in its back, like the bull in a *corrida*. A rare feature in the same area comes from the most recent period, a set of geometric designs such as were used for carpets. In places where you have to walk across sand, look for the tracks of animals, especially the "bicycle tyre" marks of vipers.

Jabbaren

Seen from south of Djanet, near the airport, the Tassili is an unbroken wall. An extra high part stands up like a castle, marking the site of Jabbaren (the Giants). You can reach it from Sefar by a two-day march which also takes in several much less visited places on the plateau. That means a minimum itinerary of seven days ending with the descent of the Aghoum pass, but it links the two most famous collections of pictures.

The other way to see Jabbaren is to climb the **Aghoum pass,** spend a day or two on the plateau and return by the same route. The ascent is steeper than at Tafelalet, and goes higher, to 1,900 metres (6,230 ft.), so you may be grateful for the tented camp that ONAT has established here. Of the hundreds of paintings, don't miss the giant round-headed figure from the end of the hunters period, jokingly dubbed the "Martian god", or the strange "little devils" with horns. The unique line of elegant dancers, three times as slim as nature intended, you may recognize from the interior decor of Air Algérie aircraft. (Your ultra-long shadows at dusk may suggest where the artist got his idea.)

Across a gorge and higher still than Jabbaren, **In Aouanrhat** stars a horned goddess from the hunters period

The Saharan night begins by the fire, with the chants and songs of this eternal land. (overleaf) *The oasis of Kerzaz.*

and hunters in a boat chasing a hippopotamus, as well as a woman with breasts oddly positioned on her back who may possibly be swimming. There are enough sites within reach of Jabbaren to make it a great base.

For those who shun any itinerary that anyone has already followed, the adventure tour operators are coming up with ever more far-flung combinations of wheels and walks, down to the borders of Niger, or linking Djanet and Tamanrasset in a great loop. Look into what they offer, but don't miss the Tassili N'Ajjer on your first trip south.

WHAT TO DO

Sightseeing, even in a country with so much to choose from and such spectacular variety, is only one objective of a balanced journey. Getting to know the people and their way of life is, or should be, another. Shopping may be a third, more important to some than to others. And during all this, leave some time for relaxing or exercizing—and just enjoying yourself.

SPORTS

Vast stretches of seashore, undiscovered rocky bays and the blue Mediterranean make water sports the obvious first choice.

Popular resorts near the big cities have safe **swimming** at sandy beaches just a few steps away from your room, bungalow or tent. Most of the seaside hotels have a pool as well, though it's not usually heated. Some public beaches with lifeguards on duty charge admission in high summer. That's when they're crowded, of course. You'll find more space just out of season, in late spring or early autumn—when the water's warmer.

Sailing boats and **windsurfing** equipment can be hired at main centres, where there is **water-skiing** too. Sidi Fredj has

Modern beach scene and holiday village of Tipasa, a step away from its Roman ruins.

a yacht marina: otherwise, sheltered anchorages are at the ports which have yacht clubs. **Snorkelling** and just admiring the abundant, brilliantly coloured fish can be dreamlike in the clear waters of deep coves.

You can go **fishing** in the sea with rod and line, but a net will make you very unpopular with local fishermen who are trying to earn a living. To go underwater spear fishing, you'll need a license from Algiers. Try to obtain one in advance, especially if you're bringing in any cumbersome equipment. To do it the easy way, join one of ONAT's special holidays

at Tipasa, Les Andalouses or Seraïdi.

If you fancy some **hunting** and want to challenge the fierce wild boar, you can join one of the groups organized by ONAT. Be sure to make arrangements long in advance so that you have all the necessary permits. The season runs from the end of September to the end of December.

Many hotels on the coast, and some of those at the most visited oases, like Biskra and Timimoun, have **tennis** courts, so bring your rackets (balls, too) if you're keen. It wouldn't, on the other hand, be worth carrying your **golf** clubs. There is only one course in the whole country so far.

The national passion is **football** (soccer), especially now that Algeria has done so well in international competition. The newspapers are full of the exploits of the teams, and every spare piece of ground or backstreet is liable to be taken up by boys emulating them. Look as if you want to join in and they may invite you, and then run rings around you.

It's the same with **volleyball** on the beach in summer: unless you have had plenty of practice, you won't be in the same league as the locals.

There are **horse riding** centres *(club hippique)* near a few of the coastal resorts. Bloodstock specialists will want to visit the Arab horse breeding centre near Tiaret.

Spring in the mountains can be idyllic for **hiking,** especially for wildflower enthusiasts. Orchids abound, so take a close-up attachment or "macro" lens for your camera. Autumn brings delicate, gorgeously scented wild narcissi, shooting in little bunches of silver stars following the first of the rains. It's fascinating to see the miniature antecedents of our garden species, and to find masses of wild cyclamen very like the domestic variety.

Bring your binoculars for **bird-watching.** You'll spot everything from humming-birds and woodpeckers in the coastal forests to vultures and a dozen other birds of prey over the desert fringes.

Surprised that Algeria has **skiing**? You shouldn't be: the Atlas climbs high and has a hard winter. The nearest ski resort to Algiers is Chrea, a mere 60 kilometres (37 mi.) away, and Tikdja in Kabylia is only 150 kilometres (93 mi.) distant. As yet, facilities are limited, and there are only a few chalet-style hotels at each. But this is one way to enjoy Algeria in the winter.

You can't resist buying some pottery from this pint-sized seller by the roadside.

SHOPPING

The artificially high exchange rate of the dinar means that Algeria is more expensive than its neighbours. That applies to service and to nearly everything you might wish to buy, whether essentials, luxuries or handicrafts. Nevertheless, you'll be tempted by the attractive and unusual articles produced by the country's artisans—from textiles to silver jewellery. State craft shops, SNAT *(Société Nationale d'Artisanat Traditionnel)*—in all the large towns, the most popular oases, some big hotels and airports—carry a selection of handicrafts. There are a few private traders, too, and some roadside stands. Best of all, you can visit workshops and buy on the spot.

Bargaining is not much in favour in most of Algeria,

Painstaking work by a Tlemcen brassmaker; intricate silver Kabylian jewellery.

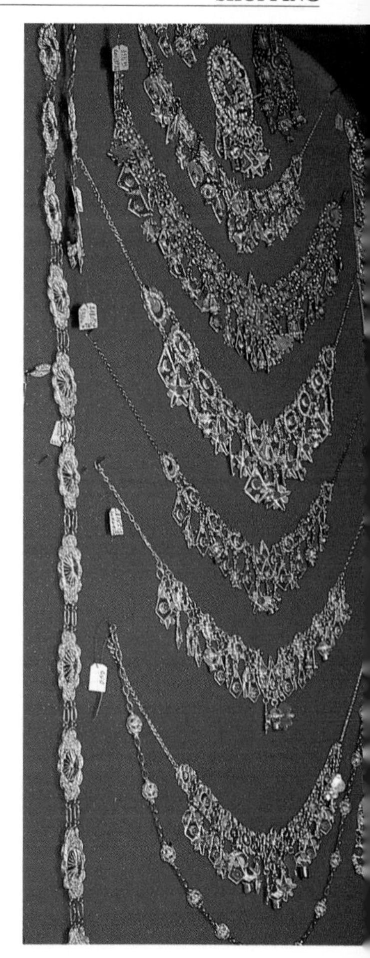

where it's thought to be mean and impolite. Naturally, it does not cut any ice at all in the state-operated shops. Only further south, in places such as Ghardaïa where there are many merchants with eclectic stocks of antiques, carpets, jewellery, clothing and souvenirs, does it come into its own. If you are forearmed with a knowledge of the prices in the fixed-price stores, you can enjoy a friendly joust, probably over a glass (or two) of delicious mint tea.

Carpets are made almost everywhere in Algeria, and you can watch them being woven in many places. The designs, traditional and geometric, vary from region to region. The close-weave type predominates, but there are thick-pile ones too. You may want to add a carpet to your baggage: the smaller ones serve as prayer mats, though nowadays the weavers probably have travellers just as much in mind.

Embroidery in metal thread on leather or fabric, or decorated clothing may appeal to you, but everyone will exclaim over the finest pieces of

jewellery. Traditional silver Berber (especially Kabyle) pieces with enamel, semi-precious stones and coral can be magnificent. Some antiques have prices to match, but craftsmen are still making fine pendants and brooches: you can visit their workshops in several Kabyle towns and villages. In the far south, Tuareg silversmiths have come up with strangely shaped pendant crosses, as well as traditional bangles and earrings. Try to find out what the silver content is: a lot of jewellery is made with nickel silver instead of purer grades.

Baskets made of palm leaves are economically priced, but don't buy them if you are going on to other countries in the region. They will be confiscated as possible carriers of a destructive parasite.

Something you will see everywhere south of the Atlas, at roadside stands and in souvenir shops, and specially characteristic of the desert, are the delicate crystal clusters called **desert roses** or sand roses. Revealed when wind and water shift the sands, they grow infinitely slowly underground. Desert roses are heavy and fragile, but they don't cost much. You'll hardly be able to resist taking one home.

You are certain to be offered **coins**, ostensibly from the Roman era. You should be deeply suspicious of their authenticity, as only an expert could tell whether they are facsimiles freshly made. Something as common as a small copper coin with the head of Constantine the Great probably *is* what it purports to be, just because examples are too numerous to be worth faking. It's a funny thing that the coins you are expected to buy are always Roman, never Arab or Turkish! Supposedly "Roman" oil lamps and statuettes are highly suspect, too.

Even more intriguing are the **flint arrowheads** and **tools** of Stone Age man, easier to find lying around here than in most places and on sale, too. How evocative to handle the sharp little weapon that may have brought down a bird or game animal 8,000 years ago.

If you have an eye for the bizarre, the stuffed desert foxes are a sad sight, but sadder still are live fennecs, tiny huge-eared foxes that little boys have trapped and hold up for you to photograph or even to buy. Don't get too near them—some are rabies carriers. Happier souvenirs of the oases, **dates** are something not to miss—and you can find special fibrous twigs to clean your teeth.

Fairs and Festivals

It's a lucky dip. Not all of the following events take place every year, and the dates are only rough indications. Oasis festivals are likely to be especially colourful. The problem is, of course, accommodation at peak times.

March/April	*Adrar:* Tomato Festival, and not only tomatoes. *El Goléa:* Festival of the Old Ksar.
April	*Biskra:* Spring Fair, folk dancing, horse races. *Djanet:* Tassili Spring Festival, folk dances and songs, camel races. *El Oued:* Carpet Festival, crafts, folklore. *Ghardaïa:* Artisans' Fair, crafts of the whole of Algeria. *Laghouat:* Spring Fair, horse races. *Touggourt:* Date Festival, camel racing.
April/May	*Boufarik:* Orange Festival, agricultural fair. *Bou-Saada:* Festival of the City of Happiness, songs and dances of the Ouled Naïl, races. *Timimoun:* Gourara Spring Festival, crafts, music, dance. *Tizi Ouzou:* Spring Fair, crafts of Kabylia.
May	*Miliana:* Cherry Festival. *Timgad* (some years): Mediterranean Culture. *Tlemcen:* Cherry Festival, traditions of the north-west. *Tizi Ouzou* (every two years): Folklore Festival.
June	*Oran* (every two years): Modern Algerian Music Festival.
June/July	*Tlemcen:* Traditional Music Festival (every two years).
August	*Tipasa:* Annual fair, beach festival.
September	*Algiers:* Book Fair. *Tiaret:* Horse Fair, bloodstock sales, races.
December/January	*Tamanrasset:* Trade fair and folk festival.

ENTERTAINMENT

Only in Algiers at the large and expensive hotels—and at the holiday resorts in high summer—is there anything in the nature of a **night club**. The featured attraction will probably be a more or less authentic "oriental" show. At the better oasis hotels you may be lucky enough to see one of the occasional displays of folk dancing. Otherwise, organized entertainment is restricted to the **cinema**. Every town has at least one, with films in French or dubbed into French.

Increasingly familiar beyond its borders, Algeria's own brand of popular **music** soon

Traditional Algerian music is definitely alive and well.

appeals to foreigners because of its vivacity and the way it reminds them of so much other music—with its blend of African and Arab, Spanish and even Indian sounds and rhythms. Called *rai*, it derives from the chants and songs of 19th-century western Algeria, Oran and Tlemcen in particular.

Enthusiasm for the genre swept through the rest of the country in the 1970s and has never waned since. Stars such as Cheb Khaled ("the King of *rai*"), Chaba Fadela, Cheb Sahraoui and "the Prince", Cheb Mami, are national idols whose cassettes sell by the million. They don't all have the same first names—"Cheb" or "Chaba" just means "young person", masculine and feminine. The first and still one of the greatest *rai* hits was Fadela's "Ana mahlali noum" (Sleep doesn't interest me any more) which she recorded in 1979. At about the same time she met Sahraoui, now her husband, who had studied at the Oran Conservatoire. Their 1985 duet "N'el fik" (You are mine) was another smash hit and helped to spearhead a *rai* invasion of Europe that led to concerts in Paris and London. You'll be lucky indeed if you can get a ticket to a performance by any of the big names, but some of the up-and-coming singers still appear at clubs and weddings—the way the top stars started.

EATING OUT

Hotels feature safe, international cuisine, perhaps with one or two bland versions of local dishes on the menu. And the price will be high for the standard offered. The same is true of the restaurants in the big cities. You'll find some acceptable fish restaurants in places near the coast, the catch being typically Mediterranean, and plain grilling the usual mode of cooking.

To sample authentic Algerian cooking, you'll have to experiment by visiting more modest eating places. In smaller, even medium-sized, towns you won't have a choice. That will be all there is.

Menus and prices in Algerian eating houses look surprisingly similar, no matter what part of the country you're in.

What to Eat

The standard simple **breakfast** comprises coffee and croissants with, perhaps, butter and jam. The coffee is often notably good. Local people add at least as much milk as coffee, and in the cafés it may come pre-mixed and even sugared. It's safer to ask for black coffee *(café noir)* and then for a little milk, if you like.

At **lunch and dinner,** service begins with the delivery of a basket of excellent bread, the long, thin French-type baguette which is the universal Algerian staple. There will be some sort of salad, tomatoes or cucumber, for example, with soup for a starter.

Chorba means soup, and what you get depends on the cook's whim. (The best versions are kept for the breaking of the Ramadan fast at sundown.) Spicy or mild, made with chicken, lamb or beef, scattered with fresh coriander or thickened with couscous, you won't know what it is until it arrives in front of you. Typically that's only a matter of minutes. There should be a pot of *harissa*, a red—and red-hot—paste of chili peppers which you can use to boost anything too bland. Experiment with tiny amounts at first.

Algerians can make a pretty good *soupe de poissons* in the *provençale* style, with the required croutons and garlic mayonnaise and several cloves of garlic on the side. Low-priced eating places often offer a simpler version.

Next you're likely to be offered *brik:* flaky pastry folded into a square flat "box" around a filling and deep-fried in oil until golden brown and crisp. In its plainest form, *brik* may contain scrambled egg, or a whole fried egg that will run out over your chin if you're not alert. *Brik tunisien* can be plain or filled with minced meat, onion, herbs and spices, olives and a soft cheese or yogurt. *Bourak* is rather similar, though it can be baked in the oven instead of fried. *Brik* and *bourak*—both words came from the same Turkish source—are often eaten as a snack, as well.

Next comes the main course. *Tadjin* signifies a meat stew slowly simmered until tender. There are as many varieties as there are cooks. Restaurant versions usually prove reliable but ordinary. The best kinds of *tadjin* are classic combinations of meat and fruit, but you may only find them in private houses these days. Sweet and sour, fiery and mild, they probably developed in Spain where the cooking of Arabia and Andalusia cross-fertilized. Traditional recipes team lamb with prunes, chicken with raisins and almonds, duck with figs and fish with hot peppers—all laced with garlic, coriander, cumin, ginger and a dozen other spices.

Then, of course, there is couscous, and very good it can be. Translating it as "semolina", with memories of the sweetened milk puddings of childhood that this word may bring, is misleading. Although couscous is made from the same coarse-grained wheat flour, it's most commonly the basis of savoury dishes—either lamb, beef or chicken. The best couscous is light and fluffy, but like the other world staples—rice, potatoes and pasta—it's only as good as the dishes served with it. Try to discover what alternatives are on offer: untutored palates usually prefer something with a good measure of liquid content. By way of accompaniments there are chick peas and a spicy sauce made with chili peppers *(marga)*.

Look out for cafés with a functioning charcoal grill—just follow your nose, for they tend to be found outdoors if the weather is right. The cook may show you the meats he has prepared: lamb chops, veal cutlets, steak and kebabs. *Merguez,* a spicy lamb sausage, can be excellent when grilled. Simply point to what you want. Various egg and chicken dishes complete the typical menu.

Expedition cooks can be surprisingly creative at producing

You can almost smell it cooking!
The familiar sight and aroma of sizzling roast lamb or mutton...
a favourite meal or snack, at any time.

a meal from soups to couscous. If you're lucky, the traditional dish of the *meharists* (Tuareg irregular troops) might be on the menu. First a loaf of semolina bread is baked in the ashes of the fire. This is then broken into small pieces and soaked in hot water to make a kind of dumpling, which is finally in-

corporated into a hot meaty and spicy stew. Delicious after a hard day on the dunes or the *piste*.

Should you be present at a special occasion, perhaps with a local family or as an honoured guest, you may feast on *mechoui*, whole roast lamb from the spit which has been

Couscous

The 600-year-old cookery book of Ibn Razin El Tudjibi laid down the right way to prepare couscous: "Take the best semolina flour and place it in a kneading trough. Sprinkle it with salted water. Knead until it begins to stick together. Then roll it between your palms until it forms small pellets the size of ants' heads. Cover and put it aside. Put the best fat meat and some bones in a large pot with salt, oil, pepper, dried coriander and chopped onion. Cover with water, put on the fire and when it begins to boil, add whatever vegetables are in season. When the meat and vegetables are done, take the special couscous dish with holes pierced in the bottom and fill it with couscous. Place it on top of the big pot of meat and vegetables and cover the couscous dish with a napkin to contain the steam. You can tell when it is done by striking the side of the dish with your hand; if it rings, it is done. Put stock from the meat in a serving dish and pour couscous into the middle and around the edges. Cover it until the couscous has drunk the broth. Test with your finger to see if it needs more. Put marrow bones in the middle, then the meat and vegetables. Sprinkle with cinnamon, pepper and ginger, and eat with delight, if God so wills".

turning for hours over a pit full of charcoal. But if you see the same thing on a restaurant menu, it will be conventionally roast lamb or mutton of unpredictable quality.

Dessert choices might be sweet pastries (some very sweet) made from sugar or honey, nuts or dates and semolina. One favourite, *kab al ghazal* (gazelle's horn), resembles a croissant with the addition of almonds and a dusting of sugar. Or try *baklava,* a flaky pastry with honey and almonds, or *losanges,* a pastry with almonds or dates. Yogurts with fruit flavourings are widely available. But the range of fresh fruits is surprisingly limited, very localized and seasonal.

Drinks

Algeria remains a major wine producer, though the area of vineyards is not as great as it once was. But it is also an Islamic nation, so alcoholic drinks are not widely available and are high-priced when you can find them. Where does it all go? The answer is that it is exported, as most of it always was, now largely to Eastern European countries.

The big hotels—and not all of them—plus a few restaurants, especially in the port cities, offer small selections of wine. They can be excellent. Look for *Mascara, Coteaux de Mascara, Coteaux de Tlemcen, Cuvée du Président* and *Miliana* among the reds. *Trappe* is reasonably smooth and *Khayyam* is a basic table red. The whites are curiously hard to find: there is rarely a choice.

Music and gastronomy go merrily hand-in-hand in Biskra.

Montagne des Lions is an ordinary rosé. Don't expect all bottles with the same label to be of the same quality.

The drinking of beer is almost as restricted as that of wine, beer being mostly available only with meals in certain hotels and restaurants. There is only one brand, but it is good. Spirits, available in hotel bars only, are very expensive. Aficionados of the apéritif can find locally made editions of famous French brands such as Ricard and Byrrh.

Algerians drink lots of tea made with fresh mint. It's an addiction most visitors acquire too. Mint tea always comes sweetened, and even if you normally hate sugar in tea, you'll probably agree that this kind seems to need it. The version made with mint-flavoured syrup is much less refreshing, so try to specify that you want *"thé à la menthe fraîche"*.

Bottled water of one kind or another is universal. *Saïda* is still (non-carbonated), and *Mouzaïa* is fizzy (carbonated). Various, mostly anonymous, soft drinks are found just about everywhere, as are canned and, much more expensive, fresh juices.

To Help You Order...

Do you have a table?		**Avez-vous une table?**	
Do you have a set-price menu?		**Avez-vous un menu à prix fixe?**	
I'd like a/an/some ...		**J'aimerais ...**	
beer	**une bière**	*pepper*	**du poivre**
bread	**du pain**	*potatoes*	**des pommes de terre**
coffee	**un café**	*rice*	**du riz**
dessert	**un dessert**	*salad*	**de la salade**
fish	**du poisson**	*salt*	**du sel**
fork	**une fourchette**	*sandwich*	**un sandwich**
fruit	**un fruit**	*soup*	**de la soupe**
glass	**un verre**	*spoon*	**une cuiller**
ice-cream	**une glace**	*sugar*	**du sucre**
knife	**un couteau**	*tea (mint)*	**un thé (à la menthe)**
meat	**de la viande**	*water (iced)*	**de l'eau (glacée)**
menu	**la carte**	*wine*	**du vin**
milk	**du lait**		
mineral water	**de l'eau minérale**		

... and Read the Menu

agneau	*lamb*
ail	*garlic*
ananas	*pineapple*
anchois	*anchovies*
artichaut	*artichoke*
asperges	*asparagus*
aubergine	*aubergine, eggplant*
banane	*banana*
beurre	*butter*
biftek	*beefsteak*
bœuf	*beef*
boulettes	*meatballs*
brochette	*skewered meat or fish*
calmar	*squid*
carottes	*carrots*
champignons	*mushrooms*
chorba	*soup*
chou	*cabbage*
chou-fleur	*cauliflower*
citron	*lemon*
clémentine	*tangerine orange*
concombre	*cucumber*
confiture	*jam*
côtelettes d'agneau	*lamb chops*
courge, courgette	*marrow, zucchini (squash)*
couscous	*steamed semolina*
crevettes	*shrimp*
dattes	*dates*
daurade	*dorado, sea bream*
entrecôte	*rib eye steak*
épinards	*spinach*
escalope	*scallop*
figues	*figs*
foie	*liver*
fraises	*strawberries*
fromage (de chèvre)	*cheese (goat's)*
gâteau	*cake*
homard	*lobster*
huile	*oil*
huîtres	*oysters*
langouste	*spiny lobster*
légumes	*vegetables*
merguez	*spicy sausage*
moules	*mussels*
moutarde	*mustard*
mouton	*mutton*
noix	*nuts*
nouilles	*noodles*
œufs	*eggs*
oignons	*onions*
pamplemousse	*grapefruit*
pêche	*peach*
persil	*parsley*
poire	*pear*
pois chiches	*chick-peas*
poisson	*fish*
pomme	*apple*
poulet	*chicken*
poulpe	*octopus*
raisins	*grapes*
rognons	*kidneys*
saucisse	*sausage*
saumon	*salmon*
tarte	*tart, pie*
thon	*tunny, tuna fish*
tomate	*tomato*
veau	*veal*
viande	*meat*

BERLITZ-INFO

CONTENTS

A ACCOMMODATION (See also CAMPING.)

Hotels. Hotels in Algeria are classified officially by stars from one to five, but this mainly gives an idea of the price, rather than the facilities or standards. There was a programme of new building in the early 1970s, notably of a chain of state-run hotels in the bigger oases. The designs, many by the architect Pouillon, can be startlingly imaginative, but the level of maintenance in these, as in older hotels, varies widely. Privately run hotels tend to be better than the state establishments in this respect. The best hotels in Algiers and Oran offer a standard of accommodation and facilities that is superior to the norm. Most places that a visitor is likely to want to stay do have at least one hotel of an acceptable standard.

Establishments in Algiers are notorious for being always full. During the summer season, hotels along the coast are often fully booked, while in winter, better hotels in the most popular oases rarely have vacancies. To counter this problem, make reservations well in advance or book through ONAT, the national tourist organization. Arrive early in the day at big-city hotels.

Rates are posted at reception desks and in rooms. A simple breakfast of coffee, bread and jam is almost always included. Only a handful of the largest establishments accept credit cards, but most of the better hotels can change foreign currency or traveller's cheques.

Don't be surprised if no one offers to carry your suitcase. This shouldn't be mistaken for a lack of hospitality, it is just the local custom: service is often on a do-it-yourself basis.

Water shortages in hotels can be a nuisance. Enquire on arrival if there is any difficulty with the water supply, and if so, when it will be (a) on, and (b) hot. Most hotel bathrooms have large plastic containers full of water (which you would be wise to keep filled whenever possible). Water shortage also often means that the swimming pool—where there is one—is often left empty. And if it is full, the water may not be changed frequently enough to be really clean.

Hammam. Literally public baths—often built on the site of hot springs in use since Roman times—*hammamat* may also have hotel accommodation attached. They are classified, like hotels, by a star system and are mostly frequented by local people taking a cure. At least a *hammam* is less likely to suffer from water shortages.

Youth hostels—for young men only—have been established in more than 20 towns as part of youth clubs. They are inexpensive, but the facilities rudimentary. For information, contact:

Fédération Algérienne des Auberges de Jeunesse, 18, rue Mouzaoui Abdelaziz, Algiers; tel. (02) 64 87 41

Do you have any vacancies?	**Avez-vous des chambres disponibles?**
a single/double room	**une chambre pour une personne/deux personnes**
with bath/shower	**avec bains/douche**
What's the rate per night/ week?	**Quel est le prix par nuit/ par semaine?**

AIRPORTS *(aéroport)*

Algeria's main gateway airport is Houari Boumedienne (ALG), some 20 km. (12 mi.) south-east of Algiers. There are also international airports at Annaba, Constantine, Oran and Tlemcen. All are equipped with snack bars, shops (including duty-free for departing passengers), city-link buses and taxi ranks. They also have currency-exchange counters, but these can only buy, not sell, foreign currency.

A couple of dozen cities and oases are connected by internal flights (see also under TRANSPORT). The smaller airports are very basic, as they may only handle one or two flights a day, if that.

Passengers on a group tour generally arrive by normal scheduled flight. If you are expecting to be met and are not, check at the ONAT desk after immigration and customs.

When departing, passengers are usually asked to identify their checked baggage as they board the aircraft. Only then is it loaded. This ensures that no one sends bags unaccompanied and reassures you that your case is indeed going on the right flight. It should be a foolproof system, but bags still go astray.

Check-in time is two hours ahead for international flights and one hour for domestic flights. Don't arrive less than 30 minutes before departure or the plane may well go without you. Assigned seats are rare.

Where's the bus for...?	**D'où part le bus pour...?**

CAMPING

Permanent, recognized campsites are limited in number. The Touring Club of Algeria has some well-equipped sites along the coast and at a couple of oases. In summer, many temporary sites near the beach resorts become very busy. Water can be a problem: there may be only one tap. Few campsites have a café or restaurant.

In some towns, camping can be arranged through the local *syndicat d'initiative* (information office), but it could be a time-consuming process. It is possible to camp in some national parks and forests, but permission must be obtained from the park office. In the countryside, you may be able to get permission to use the land of a friendly farmer.

Privately owned sites have sprung up at the more popular oases. Facilities vary: some have hot showers, others no water at all. Be sure to inspect the site and determine the price before deciding to stay.

In the oases, it sounds idyllic to sleep under the stars in a palm grove, but beware, they are alive with biting insects. Camping just anywhere, without permission, is unwise and may even be illegal and subject to fines in some places. The further south you go, the more relaxed things become. In the Hoggar, for example, you can choose your own spot.

For further information, contact: Touring Club d'Algérie, Direction des Opérations Touristiques, 30, rue Hassen Benamame, Les Vergers Birkhadem, Algiers; tel. (02) 56 47 27

Is there a campsite nearby?	**Y a-t-il un camping près d'ici?**
May we camp on your land?	**Pouvons-nous camper sur votre terrain?**

CAR HIRE *(location de voitures)* See also DRIVING.

Hiring a car is not as convenient in Algeria as it is in countries more attuned to tourism. Few vehicles are available, and the standards of maintenance vary. ONAT offices can in principle provide cars, but you will need to reserve far in advance. Private companies also exist. Credit cards are rarely accepted; a large cash deposit is usually required. Daily and mileage charges are high, being roughly twice the average rate in other countries. You will need your passport, current driving licence (held for at least two years) and an International Driving Permit (unless you have a local licence). The minimum age is normally 25.

Hiring a car with a driver is more expensive, but the difference is marginal. This may be a viable solution for a day or two, or if there are three or four passengers to share the cost.

I'd like to hire a car.	**Je voudrais louer une voiture.**
for one day/a week	**pour une journée/une semaine**

CIGARETTES, CIGARS, TOBACCO *(cigarettes, cigares, tabac)*
Algerian cigarette brands include light tobacco *(blondes)*, such as Hoggar, and dark tobacco *(brunes)*, like Afras. Imported varieties are available in the cities at several times the price of local brands. You may find some Cuban cigars in the best hotels of Algiers. It would be sensible to bring a supply of your own brand of pipe tobacco, as there is little chance of finding anything like it.

CLIMATE AND CLOTHING
The best periods to visit Algeria are probably April–June and October–November. The coast is hot in summer and it can be humid; the rest of the year is unpredictable. Winters are normally mild, but may occasionally be cold and rainy. The mountains can be bitterly cold in winter and the higher peaks and passes frequently have snowfalls. The desert in summer is as blisteringly hot by day as you would expect, but spring and autumn days can be easily bearable and nights refreshingly cold. Winter is the ideal time to visit the oases and southern Sahara, but the desert night, especially at higher altitudes, is freezing, and biting winds can blow. The following chart gives average daily maximum and minimum temperatures in Algiers. In degrees Fahrenheit:

	J	F	M	A	M	J	J	A	S	O	N	D
max.	59	61	63	68	73	78	83	85	81	74	66	60
min.	49	49	52	55	59	65	70	71	69	63	56	51

And in degrees Celsius:

	J	F	M	A	M	J	J	A	S	O	N	D
max.	15	16	17	20	23	26	28	29	27	23	19	16
min.	9	9	11	13	15	18	21	22	21	17	13	11

Temperature

°C −30 −25 −20 −15 −10 −5 0 5 10 15 20 25 30 35 40 45

°F −20 −10 0 10 20 30 40 50 60 70 80 90 100 110

For trekking or motorized safaris in the south, take your older clothes, as everything becomes impregnated with dust. Beach wear should be kept for the beach and hotel pools. Revealing clothes, even shorts, are not appropriate anywhere else. Topless bathing is not acceptable. Restaurants tend to be informal.

COMMUNICATIONS

Post Offices. Identifiable by the letters PTT in red on a yellow background, post offices are usually busy, with people waiting at every counter. Stamps are not widely available elsewhere, so stock up when you do have the chance. Letters and postcards sent from Algeria seem to get through in reasonably quick time.

The main post office in Algiers is situated at the corner of Boulevard Mohamed Khemisti and Rue Larbi Ben M'Hidi.

Poste Restante (general delivery). If you don't know ahead of time where you'll be staying, you can have your mail addressed to you c/o Poste Restante in any town, and it will be kept at the main post office there. You need to allow several days leeway, especially in the smaller places. You will have to show your passport to collect letters.

Telegrams. Main post offices accept telegrams, or will direct you to a branch that does.

Telephone. Local and long-distance direct-dialling is possible from coin-operated phones. There are too few for the demand, however, so you may have to wait. Pay phones accept 1- and 5-dinar coins and return unused ones.

In principle international calls can also be dialled direct. In practice you almost always have to go through the operator. There's generally a delay of a few minutes, but it can take much longer. Hotel reception desks will book calls with the operator and ring you back when the connection is made. The most economical method is to go to the main telephone bureau of a town and phone from there. Write down the number you want and hand it to the desk staff. When your call goes through, they will wave you to one of the cabins. You pay at the desk when you've finished.

Telex. Most of the better hotels have a functioning telex machine, which can be a great help to business visitors in particular.

express (special delivery)	**exprès**
airmail/registered	**par avion/recommandé**
A stamp for this letter/ postcard, please.	**Une timbre pour cette lettre/ carte, s'il vous plaît.**
Have you any mail for...?	**Avez-vous du courrier pour...?**
Can you get me this number in...?	**Pouvez-vous me donner ce numéro à...?**

COMPLAINTS

At all costs, keep calm and stay pleasant. Algerians take even less kindly than most people to being ordered about. Smile if you can, and put your complaint in the form of a friendly request. Demands to see a higher authority can be fruitless: there may not be any such person available. If there is, you can become entangled in official discussions and reports, so unless you think the matter crucial, pursuing this route can be time-wasting and unproductive.

CRIME AND THEFT

Take the same sensible precautions that you would in your own home country and you are unlikely to run into any problems of security. In fact, you will be as safe in Algeria as you will anywhere. There are a number of reasons why this should be so: people are basically honest and kind; there are few tourists, so the practice of exploiting them has not developed; "early to bed, early to rise" is the rule, so few people will be walking the streets late at night; and, with little or no drinking of alcohol, the crimes generated by drunkenness elsewhere are happily absent in Algeria.

As on any journey, keep separate records of your traveller's cheques, photocopies of your tickets and other personal documents and a note of useful and emergency telephone numbers. Don't carry large amounts of cash and keep an eye on your valuables.

If you are driving, it is wise to look for guarded overnight parking places for your car, or small items may disappear from the exterior. And it would be foolish here, as anywhere, to leave attractive items visible in the car, especially in the big cities.

If you lose something or have something stolen from your hotel, report it at once to the hotel management. In other cases, contact the police.

My ticket/wallet/passport has been stolen.	**On m'a volé mon billet/porte-feuille/passeport.**

CUSTOMS *(douane)*, **ENTRY AND EXIT REGULATIONS**
Holders of British passports (U.K. citizens) or of the passport of a number of other European and Arab countries do not need a visa for Algeria. All others, including U.S., Canadian, New Zealand and Australian citizens, must obtain a visa.

Visas are issued by Algeria's diplomatic and consular representatives. A fee is charged. Nationals of countries where Algeria is not represented can obtain a visa at the offices of the Air and Frontier Police at the border, port or airport of arrival. If your visa expires while in Algeria, you can get an extension at the nearest *wilaya* or *daira* office.

No visa will be granted, or entry allowed, to those whose passports show that they have been to Israel, South Africa, Malawi, Republic of Korea (i.e., South) or Taiwan (Republic of China).

No certificates of vaccination are required, unless you are arriving from a yellow fever or cholera contaminated zone.

The following chart shows what main items you may take into Algeria duty-free and, on returning, into your home country:

Into:	Cigarettes		Cigars		Tobacco	Spirits		Wines
Algeria	200	or	50	or	250 g.	1 l.	or	1 l.
Australia	200	or	250 g.	or	250 g.	1 l.	or	1 l.
Canada	200	and	50	and	900 g.	1.1 l.	or	1.1 l.
Eire	200	or	50	or	250 g.	1 l.	and	2 l.
N. Zealand	200	or	50	or	250 g.	1.1 l.	and	4.5 l.
U.K.	200	or	50	or	250 g.	1 l.	and	2 l.
U.S.A.	200	and	100	and	*	1 l.	or	1 l.

* a reasonable quantity

No more than the prescribed alcohol allowance may be imported into Algeria, duty or no duty. In addition, precious jewellery and items such as sophisticated cameras and radios must be declared on entry. Customs procedures on arrival may be very thorough and time-consuming, so be prepared to be patient.

Currency restrictions. Import and export of Algerian dinars is not permitted. On arrival, you must change at least the equivalent of 1,000 dinars (500 dinars for persons under 18), which must be spent in the country. You have to declare all your foreign currency, cash and traveller's cheques on a special form. All further transactions must be recorded on the form, but you should keep the receipts as well. Members of official delegations and organized tour groups are exempt from the compulsory exchange requirements. It is illegal to change foreign currency anywhere except at a bank or other official exchange counter, such as those at some larger hotels.

If you have dinars left over at the end of your stay, it may be possible to change them back—if you have all the receipts, if the bank at the border is open, and if it has sufficient foreign exchange. Otherwise, you will have to hand over your Algerian money in return for a receipt, in the hope of being reimbursed should you visit the country again. It's far better to plan your expenditure, changing no more cash than you need. Algiers airport in particular has some craft shops to soak up your last dinars, not to mention delicious dates to take home, except to the U.S.A.

I've nothing to declare.	**Je n'ai rien à déclarer.**
It's for my personal use.	**C'est pour mon usage personnel.**

DRIVING (See also CUSTOMS, ENTRY AND EXIT REGULATIONS.) **D**

To take your car into Algeria you will need:

- an International Driving Permit and your national driving licence
- car registration papers
- insurance coverage (The green card is not recognized and you must buy local insurance against third-party risks on arrival. It is obviously advisable to arrange insurance against damage or loss of the vehicle before leaving your home country.)
- nationality sticker

Drivers and passengers of cars fitted with seat belts are required by law to wear them. It is highly desirable to have more than one person who can drive, in case of illness or injury, and in view of the great distances.

Driving regulations. Drive on the right, overtake (pass) on the left; yield right of way to vehicles coming from your right except at roundabouts (traffic circles) and where otherwise indicated.

Speed limits. 110 kph (69 mph) on the few sections of motorway (expressway), 100 kph (62 mph) on other main roads, 40, 50 or 60 kph (25, 31 or 37 mph) in built-up areas, as indicated. The signs are not in Arabic. The word *rappel* means that a restriction is continued.

Road conditions. Algeria's roads are in general remarkably good. They have been, and are still being, improved at a rapid rate. Most N (national) and W (*wilaya* or regional) roads are well surfaced, though some are so narrow that you may be compelled to leave the paved surface in the face of determined and fast oncoming traffic. The edges can be rough. The main oases of the northern Sahara are linked by excellent roads, and the road from El Goléa to Tamanrasset is surfaced, though narrow and with patches that are breaking up. Beware of encroaching sand dunes on one side or other. If you hit a sand drift at high speed the result could be disastrous.

Piste driving. The word *piste* refers to a more or less hard-hammered unpaved road, whether earth, sand or rock. This type of surface is the norm in remoter areas and in the southern Sahara. On some *piste* surfaces it may be possible to drive safely and comfortably at 80 kph (50 mph), on others 20 kph (12 mph) is too fast. The main problems are dust, which will penetrate almost anything in time, and corrugations, which will shake almost anything loose. Beware of ruts *(ornières)* so deep that the bottom of your vehicle touches the ground between them, soft sand in which you can become stuck and, occasionally, mud and floods.

Piste driving in the south is a hazardous sport. If driving yourself, you'll need to make elaborate preparations. Do a lot of research into the routes and consider whether you'll need a four-wheel-drive vehicle. In no case should you lose sight of the *balises* (route markers). The car should be equipped with "Special Sahara" tyres fitted for desert driving, an oil-bath filter for the engine, equipment for getting out of soft sand (spades with short handles, perforated metal plates and heavy-duty jacks) and have a strong suspension. It is obligatory to carry spare parts, oil-bath bobbins, driving belts, sparking plugs, leaf springs, a toolbox for mechanical repairs, lubricants and a reserve of water. You should bring:

- spare cans of fuel
- a water reserve of 10 litres per person
- a first-aid kit containing: a band for interrupting blood circulation, a surgical knife, a pair of scissors, sterile adhesive plaster, a disinfectant, hydrogen peroxide, an antibiotic salve, tetanus syringes, a scorpion anti-venom and snake-bite serum, an analgesic, three compresses, two elastic braces, four ordinary dressings, aspirin, ampoules with haemostatics and antibiotics, a 5 c.c. syringe

- a mirror or white sheet and two smoke bombs (red and black) for signalling
- a compass
- an air pump for the tyres (To prevent the vehicle from sticking in the sand, it is advisable to ease the tyre pressure. Don't forget to pump the tyres up again afterwards.)

In the event of a sandstorm, place the vehicle with the motor away from the wind and turn off the engine.

Owing to heat and frequent sandstorms, tourists are advised not to traverse the Sahara between June 1 and September 15.

Night driving is best avoided everywhere (and on some roads in the south it is illegal). Hazards include unlit vehicles, agricultural equipment and wandering animals, which, owing to the bright lights of oncoming traffic, you may not see in time. Algerian drivers seem to have a theory that switching lights on before it is really dark ruins their night vision. They may have a point, but the effect can be alarming to a newcomer.

Parking. In city centres it is practically impossible to find a space. Even clearly illegal spots are often taken. There are some metered places but they never seem to be vacant. Wheel clamps are sporadically used, and the practice is spreading; towing away is not unknown. In any case, driving in city centres is made difficult by heavy traffic and the absence in most places of any but Arabic-script street names. In smaller towns, parking is apparently unregulated and simple.

Breakdowns. Switch on flashing warning lights and put a warning triangle 50 metres/yards behind your car. Algerians typically wave down a passing vehicle to ask for help. Because official assistance may be long in arriving, there is a good deal of camaraderie on the road in Algeria.

The Touring Club of Algeria (TCA) can be called at (02) 56 90 16, but they are difficult to reach and do not operate 24 hours. It may be necessary in the end to rely on the considerable ingenuity of a local mechanic. Try to get an estimate for any repairs in advance. It would be wise to take only a vehicle in excellent shape to begin with, and preferably one of a type widely used in Algeria: Peugeot, Renault, Citroën, Fiat, VW, Toyota, Mazda or Lada, in roughly that order. Land Rovers are common, too. Your national motoring organization may be able to supply you with a returnable parts kit. You'll have a job persuading the customs officers not to open it, though, thereby entailing an extra charge when you do return it, even unused.

Fuel and oil. Petrol (gasoline) and diesel fuel are a state monopoly and sold at Naftal stations. These are found in every town and many villages of the north and are well distributed along the main roads, including those of the northern Sahara. In the southern Sahara it is advisable to fill up wherever possible. Carry a large reserve and enquire about supplies on your proposed route (travellers coming the other way are a good source of information). Always be ready for the worst. Deliveries may not arrive, or the electricity that enables petrol pumps to work may be "off" for a while.

Petrol is sold in super (98 octane) and normal (90 octane, also called *essence*). Lead-free is not available. Naftal stations stock good 40-grade and occasionally multigrade motor oil. Attendants are happy with a small tip, but do not seem to expect one as a matter of course.

Fluid measures

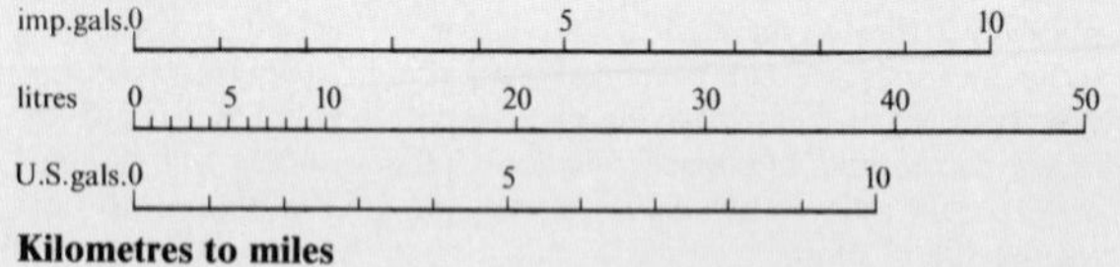

Kilometres to miles

km 0 1 2 3 4 5 6 8 10 12 14 16
miles 0 ½ 1 1½ 2 3 4 5 6 7 8 9 10

Distances (approximate). Algiers to Annaba 600 km. (370 mi.), to Biskra 420 km. (260 mi.), to Constantine 420 km. (260 mi.), to Ghardaïa 600 km. (370 mi.), to Oran 435 km. (270 mi.), to Ouargla 790 km. (490 mi.), to Setif 310 km. (190 mi.), to Tamanrasset 1,975 km. (1,225 mi.), to Tlemcen 545 km. (340 mi.).

Road signs. In addition to the usual international pictographs, you'll encounter some local variations such as the sign of a haughty camel, or warnings of "monotonous road—danger". Direction signs are in French and Arabic, except where some linguistic purist has defaced the former.

International Driving Permit	**permis de conduire international**
car registration papers	**carte grise**
Where's the nearest service station?	**Où est la station d'essence la plus proche?**
Full tank, please.	**Le plein, s'il vous plaît.**
Check the oil/tyres/ battery, please.	**Veuillez contrôler l'huile/ les pneus/la batterie.**
My car has broken down.	**Ma voiture est en panne.**

ELECTRIC CURRENT

Algeria operates on 220 volts, 50 cycles AC (in a few remote places, 127 volts). The better hotels generally provide 110/220-volt outlets. At other establishments, travellers from countries with 110 volts, who are not in possession of dual-voltage appliances, will need a transformer and adaptor plug for their shavers, hair dryers and travel irons. Visitors from the U.K. should bring a "continental" adaptor for round pins.

EMBASSIES AND CONSULATES *(ambassade; consulat)*

Contact the embassy or consulate of your home country when in trouble (loss of passport, problems with the police, serious accidents). Some 90 countries maintain embassies in Algiers, among them:

Australia 12, avenue Emile Marquis, Djenane El-Malik, Hydra; tel. (02) 60 19 65 or 60 28 46

Canada 27 bis, rue des Frères Benhafid (rue d'Anjou), Hydra; tel. (02) 60 66 11

United Kingdom 7, chemin Capitaine Hocine Slimane (chemin des Glycines); tel. (02) 60 50 38 or 60 54 11

United States 4, chemin Cheikh Bachir Ibrahimi, El Biar; tel. (02) 60 11 86 or 60 14 25

EMERGENCIES

In an emergency dial 17 for the police, 14 for the fire brigade. See also separate entries under EMBASSIES AND CONSULATES and HEALTH AND MEDICAL CARE.

G

GETTING TO ALGERIA

Consult a good travel agent well before departure for help with timetables, budget and personal requirements.

Most package holidays to Algeria come under the wing of ONAT, Algeria's national tourist organization which is represented abroad by certain officially appointed travel agencies. Ask for the agent nearest you at the Algerian Embassy in your home country or from the local office of Air Algérie.

Other operators also organize tours to Algeria, treks and expeditions in particular. You can find out about them from the destination reference books kept by travel agents.

By Air (See also AIRPORTS.)

Algiers is the main gateway to Algeria, with flights from major European, North African and Middle Eastern cities. Travellers from further afield generally fly to a European destination from where there are connections to Algeria. There are also international airports at Annaba, Constantine, Oran and Tlemcen, which mainly handle flights to or from neighbouring countries and France.

The average flight time between London and Algiers is 2½ hours, between Paris and Algiers, 2 hours.

Package tourists usually travel by normal scheduled flights, though at a reduced price as part of a deal that includes bed and full board (or most meals) within Algeria.

By Sea

Ferries operate from Marseille to Algiers almost daily in summer, and frequently at other times. There are also regular services from Marseille to Annaba, Bejaïa, Oran and Skikda; from Sète in southern France to Oran; and from Alicante (Spain) to Oran/Algiers. The crossing from France takes about 20 to 30 hours; Alicante–Oran about 12 hours, Alicante–Algiers about 14–17 hours. In cabin class, adequate meals are included in the rather expensive fare. If you travel without a cabin, which is not much cheaper, meals may be bought at a cafeteria on board. Other ferries operate from ports in Spain, France and Italy to ports in Morocco and Tunisia, from which you can continue to Algeria by land.

By Road

The boat services listed above all carry cars. In summer, it is necessary to reserve space well in advance. It is quite expensive to take a vehicle on these ferries, but car hire in Algeria is costly, too.

By Rail

There are daily train connections from Tunis and Ghardimaou to Algiers, as well as from Tunis to Annaba and Souk Ahras, and from Ghardimaou to Annaba. The journey from Tunis to Algiers takes a day and a night.

GUIDES AND INTERPRETERS *(guide; interprète)*

If given advance notice, ONAT can supply guides and arrange guided tours. At certain mosques and holy places, you have to be accompanied by a local guide, but in general no official guides conduct tours at historic sites. Unofficial ones, including young boys, may offer their services. Don't automatically reject them, for they may show you something remarkable that you might otherwise have missed, in exchange for a small sum or gift.

HAIRDRESSERS, BARBERS *(coiffeur)*

Prices are quite reasonable and are displayed at or near the doorway. Barbers, usually at street level and visible, are frequently clustered together so that you can make a choice. Women's hairdressers are not in view, but are easily found.

HEALTH and MEDICAL CARE (See also EMERGENCIES.)

Make sure that you are covered for illness or accident on your holiday, by extending an existing policy or by taking out a special travel insurance. Your insurance company, travel agent or automobile association will have details of various policies.

If you take medicine on a regular basis, be sure to bring an adequate supply with you, as well as a small general-purpose first-aid kit.

Algerian cities and large towns have hospitals, and clinics are widely distributed. In Algiers, embassies will be able to recommend a doctor; elsewhere, ask at your hotel reception. Pharmacies are indicated by a green sign marked "Pharmacie". In main centres, there will be one open 24 hours.

Risk of malaria exists in some Saharan oases. If visiting these areas, preventive drugs should be taken before leaving home and continued for a period after departure from the risk area, according to the instructions. Inoculations against polio, tetanus and typhoid should be up to date. Your doctor may also advise a gamma globulin shot to give you some protection against hepatitis.

Rivers, lakes and ponds in remote areas may be infested by bilharzia-carrying organisms, and should be avoided.

Most organized expeditions off the beaten track take scorpion anti-venom (though few scorpion stings are fatal) and snake-bite serum. You should follow suit if you plan to travel on your own steam in very remote areas. Both products can be purchased in your home country. For tours to the desert, you should also take a moisturizing cream for the face and a lip salve, sunglasses, a broad-brimmed hat and a cloth to protect your face from the biting winds.

In hot, dry conditions beware of becoming dehydrated. If you don't consume the large quantity of water that you need every day, headaches, irritability and poor judgment soon result. Their onset can be insidious and may hardly be noticed. If your urine is strongly coloured and of greatly reduced volume, you are not drinking enough.

All in all, Algeria is a healthy country, and by observing reasonable precautions, you will stay well. Minor intestinal upsets may be caused by unfamiliar food and too much sun (see also WATER).

HITCH-HIKING *(autostop)*

You'll see a lot of hitch-hikers, most of them Algerians. If you are going to try to hitch a ride yourself, you will need a lot of patience, for most local vehicles have no spare seats. Drivers that do stop for you might expect some help with the costs. It is not accepted for women to hitch-hike in Algeria.

HOURS *(heures d'ouverture)*

Banks. Generally, 9 a.m.–3 or 4 p.m., Sunday to Thursday (some close between noon and 2 p.m.).

Museums. Mostly 9 a.m.–3 p.m., Sunday to Friday.

Post offices. Main post offices open from 8 a.m. to around 6 p.m., Saturday to Thursday.

Shops. Larger stores are usually open from 9 a.m. to 6.30 p.m., Saturday to Thursday, and some open on Friday morning. Smaller shops open from 7 or 8 a.m., close at midday and reopen till 6 or 7 p.m. or later, closing Thursday afternoons and on Fridays. Shorter hours are in operation during Ramadan.

LANGUAGE (See also pp. 42–43 and 241.) **L**

The national language is Arabic, but for many people, their own first language is one of the dialects of Berber (e.g. Kabyle), which is quite different. The Tuareg of the far south use Tamahak, which is different again, though related to Berber. If you learn some Arabic and try to use it, the reply is most likely to be in French!

French is still widely studied and used. Many Algerians have been to France, lived and worked there. Although many children and students are learning English, they are hesitant about using it. Some, usually more senior, officials do speak English. People in general will expect to communicate with you, as a foreigner, in French. It is not impossible to get around without a word of it, but it is certainly easier if you understand some.

The Berlitz phrase books *Arabic for Travellers* and *French for Travellers* cover almost all the situations you're likely to encounter in your travels in Algeria.

Good morning/Good afternoon.	**Bonjour.**
Good afternoon/Good evening.	**Bonsoir.**
Goodbye.	**Au revoir.**
Speak slowly, please.	**Doucement, s'il vous plaît.**

LAUNDRY AND DRY-CLEANING *(blanchissage; nettoyage à sec)*

The better hotels will arrange for your clothes to be washed and, less frequently, to be dry-cleaned. Laundry may take 24 hours, or, in periods of water shortage, a little longer. You can find dry-cleaning shops in the main cities. Most convenient, if you are travelling around, is to have some detergent with you, wash your own clothes and hang them up to dry overnight.

LOST PROPERTY

Hotel, restaurant and other staff keep lost items until the owner reclaims them. Valuable items and personal documents might be locked up by the management or handed in to the police.

I've lost my wallet/handbag/ passport.	**J'ai perdu mon portefeuille/ sac/passeport.**

MAPS **M**

Street maps of the cities and towns are very hard to find. It is a good idea to buy a road map of Algeria from an international publisher before arriving there, as they are difficult to obtain on the spot. The maps in this guide were prepared by Falk-Verlag, Hamburg.

MONEY MATTERS (For currency restrictions, see CUSTOMS, ENTRY AND EXIT REGULATIONS.)

Currency. Algeria's monetary unit is the *dinar* (abbreviated DA or ALD), divided into 100 *centimes*.

Coins: 5, 10, 20 and 50 centimes, 1, 5 and 10 dinars.

Banknotes: 10, 20, 50, 100 and 200 dinars.

The 100-dinar notes are of various designs; 500-dinar notes are no longer valid.

Banks and currency-exchange offices *(banque; bureau de change)* See also HOURS. Many of the better hotels have a currency-exchange counter, where transactions are likely to be quicker than at banks. You do not in principle have to be staying in the hotel to use its exchange facilities, but you may have to insist—pleasantly—on your rights. You need your passport and currency-declaration form, and should retain all receipts.

Credit cards are so rarely accepted that it is unwise to expect to be able to use them at all. Major hotels in the big cities and a few beach resorts are the exceptions.

Traveller's cheques can be cashed at any official currency-exchange office. The rate is often slightly better than for cash.

Could you give me some change?	**Pouvez-vous me donner de la monnaie?**
I want to change some pounds/dollars.	**Je voudrais changer des livres sterling/des dollars.**
Do you accept traveller's cheques?	**Acceptez-vous les chèques de voyage?**
Can I pay with this credit card?	**Puis-je payer avec cette carte de crédit?**

N

NEWSPAPERS AND MAGAZINES *(journal; revue/magazine)* The *International Herald Tribune* reaches Algiers on the day of publication, but usually sells out quickly. The London papers arrive the following day. *Horizons*, a locally published French-language daily, includes some articles in English. Another French-language daily is *El Moudjahid*. Both have some international news and a great deal of sport, especially local football (soccer) reports. English-language magazines are rarely seen. *Algérie-Actualité* is a news and political weekly in French.

Have you any English-language newspapers?	**Avez-vous des journaux en anglais?**

PHOTOGRAPHY

P

Fresh film of any kind is hard to find, and your preferred brand is likely to be unobtainable. Take plenty with you, ideally in an insulated bag or box to protect it from the heat.

Do not photograph any airfield or military installation, or anything that might be interpreted as one. Some Algerians, especially women, strongly dislike being photographed. Try to avoid giving offence. Some mosques and other holy places forbid photography. So do most museums.

Experienced photographers know that in sunny countries, the light is ideal for colour pictures only in the early morning and the hour before sunset. Make the most of those times by getting up early and being out in the late afternoon. If you can, time your visits to historic places, markets, etc., accordingly. The bonus is that it will be cooler, too, and more local people will be about in the markets and streets.

May I take a picture?	**Puis-je prendre une photo?**

POLICE

Don't hesitate to ask a policeman or policewoman for assistance or directions, though you will probably need to use French. They are remarkably helpful, and quite forgiving of minor traffic transgressions committed by an obvious stranger—if you smile apologetically. The police emergency number is 17.

PRICES

To give you an idea of what to expect, here are some average prices in Algerian dinars. These are only approximate, as they will be affected by inflation and can vary seasonally and from region to region.

Airport transfers. Bus from Houari Boumedienne to Algiers centre 10 DA, taxi 80–100 DA.

Car hire. 600 DA per day.

Cigarettes. 6 DA for a packet of 20.

Hairdressers. Man's haircut 20–40 DA, woman's haircut 40 DA and up.

Hotels (double room with continental breakfast). ***** 600 DA, **** 300 DA, *** 200 DA, ** 150 DA, * 100 DA.

Meals and drinks. Set lunch/dinner in hotels 100–150 DA, ordinary restaurant on street 50–60 DA, coffee 5 DA, soft drinks 2–5 DA, alcoholic drinks where available: spirits 25–40 DA, beer 15–20 DA, bottle of wine 45 DA and up.

Museums. 1, 2 or (rarely) 5 DA.

PUBLIC HOLIDAYS *(fête nationale/religieuse)*
Some fall on the same day each year by the Western calendar, and some are fixed by the Islamic lunar calendar, the Hegira, and indeed may depend on the moon being sighted.

Fixed Holidays	
January 1	New Year's Day
May 1	Labour Day
June 19	Commemoration Day
July 5	Independence Day
November 1	Anniversary of the Revolution
Movable Dates	
Hegira (Sept. 21, in 1990)	Muslim New Year's Day
El-Achoura	New Year Festival
El-Moulid Ennaboui (in Oct.)	Birthday of the Prophet
Id El-Fitr (April/May)	End of Ramadan (two days)
Id El-Adha or *Aid El-Kebir*	Festival of Sacrifices (two days)

R **RADIO AND TV** *(radio; télévision)*
The government-run service broadcasts TV and radio programmes in Arabic, French and Kabyle. Television transmissions begin in the late afternoon, continuing into the evening. Some of the more expensive hotel rooms have sets. It is possible to pick up many short-wave radio programmes from Europe, including the BBC World Service in English, and the Voice of America, even on a pocket-sized radio.

RELIGIOUS SERVICES

Algeria is an Islamic country. There are mosques in every town and many small villages. Calls to prayer from the minarets are made five times a day, and because these may not be synchronized they can seem to be almost continuous in some places. On Friday, the Muslim holy day, mosques are closed to non-believers.

Only the largest cities have any sort of functioning church. Many former churches have been closed, turned into mosques or public buildings. Your country's embassy or consulate might be able to advise if and where there are services.

RESTAURANTS (See also pp. 208–215.)

Eating out in the evening is not, it has to be said, a way of life for Algerians. In public at least, they eat to live and expect to get it over with quickly. Only in a handful of main cities are there any but the most modest restaurants, and even these close early. So except in Algiers, Oran and Bejaïa, for example, don't leave it later than about 7.30 p.m. to go out for dinner. Hotel dining rooms operate later, dinner being served from about 7.30 until 9.30 p.m., but the fare is rarely exciting.

At lunchtime the picture is brighter. There are many simple little cafés offering tasty soups, stews or grilled meats—from a charcoal barbecue if you are lucky.

You will notice how few women are to be seen, again with the exception of big-city hotels. Men, mostly young, do the cooking, serve (quickly, as a rule) and constitute the vast majority of the customers.

Only in some hotels and the exceptional city restaurant can you buy wine or any other alcoholic drink.

TIME DIFFERENCES

The clocks in Algeria are set at GMT + 1. The following chart shows the time in some selected cities, both in winter and summer.

New York	London	**Algiers**	Sydney	Auckland
6 a.m.	11 a.m.	**noon**	8 p.m.	10 p.m.

What time is it?	**Quelle heure est-il?**

TIPPING

In hotels and restaurants, service charges are included in the bill. Extra tips are optional. Tipping is not widespread in Algeria and no one will rush to help with, for example, luggage, in expectation of a tip. For taxi drivers, round up the fare by about 10 per cent, for airport porters, 5 dinars per case.

TOILETS *(toilettes)*

Public conveniences are not easy to find, and may not be at all hygienic-looking. Even in hotels, standards of cleanliness and maintenance can be low, and the variability of water supplies does not help. It pays to carry a supply of toilet tissue in case of need.

Where are the toilets?	**Où sont les toilettes?**

TOURIST INFORMATION

The national tourist organization, ONAT, organizes tours and publishes brochures. To get information on Algeria prior to departure, you should ask at the Algerian embassy in your home country or, if there is one, the office of Air Algérie, for addresses of any ONAT-appointed travel agents.

Tourism is not highly developed in Algeria, so you will often be on your own at even the most celebrated sites, which is a wonderful feeling after being part of a herd at, say, Pompeii or the Pyramids. The other side of the coin is that information is hard to come by. Maps, guide books and even postcards are few and far between. The ONAT offices in each large town are mainly there to organize Algerians going somewhere else, though they may be able to help you as well. A few towns have information offices *(syndicat d'initiative)*. The rule is to ask—at hotels, a police officer, other travellers, people in the street. You may even get into some interesting conversations.

Office National Algérien de l'Animation, de la Promotion et de l'Information Touristique (ONAT), 25–27, rue Khélifa Boukhalfa, Algiers; tel. (02) 61 29 86

TRANSPORT

Buses. Within cities and towns they are crowded and it is usually a struggle, not always good-humoured, to get on and off. Enquire of fellow passengers in the waiting line (which will dissolve when a bus arrives) which bus to board.

Intercity buses, mostly run by the national company, SNTV, are not expensive and are much in demand. There may be a vigorous contest to buy tickets. Go to the terminal the previous day, if possible. In some rare instances, seat reservations can be made. In any case, arrive at the terminal again at least 30 minutes before scheduled departure, which for long-distance journeys—and especially those in the south—can be very early in the morning. The trick is to know which bus to board and when it should arrive and not be backward in the rush to get on. It is wise to work out on which side the sun will blaze in, for curtains and air-conditioning are rare.

Taxis. City taxis, painted yellow, are quite expensive, but it is not always easy to find one. To avoid arguments with the driver, make sure the meter is switched on. Where meters have not yet been set to the latest increase in rates, the driver will produce a conversion card at the destination. In the larger, more comfortable taxis that wait at the biggest hotels, the rate should be negotiated beforehand. "Taxi-Bus", yellow and green mini-buses, also operate in Algiers.

Shared taxis *(taxis collectifs).* These yellow cars, mostly battered Peugeots, are instantly recognizable. Operating between towns and cities, they gather in the centre and wait for a full load before leaving. The drivers are a mine of information on road conditions, travelling times, weather, etc. and it's an admirable way to meet local people. Rates are economic and fixed, but you should confirm before setting off.

Trains. SNTF lines connect the main cities of the north (Oran, Algiers, Constantine, Skikda, Annaba), and there are a few north-south spurs (Algiers–Djelfa, Oran–Béchar–Kenadsa, Skikda–Constantine–Touggourt, Annaba–Tebessa). Prices are similar to the buses, but the train takes longer. It is probably worth paying the small premium for first-class which is much less crowded. You could not make a comprehensive tour using trains alone, but one or two journeys would be an experience.

Planes. Air Algérie connects the major cities with Algiers several times a day, and with each other regularly. There are more or less frequent flights (anything between once a week and daily) to the oases. The aircraft are modern and comfortable, and costs, although several times the bus fare, are reasonable. Flights can be subject to weather delays because of sandstorms, for instance.

They are extremely busy at times when military personnel are going on leave and before and after national holidays.

single (one-way)	**aller simple**
return (round-trip)	**aller-retour**
first/second class	**première/seconde classe**
I'd like to make seat reservations.	**J'aimerais réserver des places.**

W

WATER *(eau)*

Tap water is safe in main centres, but because it is liable to interruption at times, and can be highly chlorinated, many people drink mineral water, most commonly the still *Saïda* which comes in sealed plastic bottles. Check that the seal is unbroken. In the oases, the tap water can be excessively brackish (salty) and though the palm trees can tolerate it, you can find it less than thirst-quenching, or worse. In some places, mineral water comes in glass bottles, which require a hefty deposit. Some vendors won't even sell you a bottle unless you have one to return.

Water-purifying tablets are useful for occasions when you don't feel able to trust the water and can't find any bottles. They're also recommended on treks, when the water dispensed from jerry cans may be of unknown origin.

Is this drinking water?	**Est-ce de l'eau potable?**
a bottle of mineral water	**une bouteille d'eau minérale**
fizzy (carbonated)	**gazeuse**
still (non-carbonated)	**non gazeuse**

WEIGHTS and MEASURES

Algeria uses the metric system. For fluid and distance measures, see p. 228.

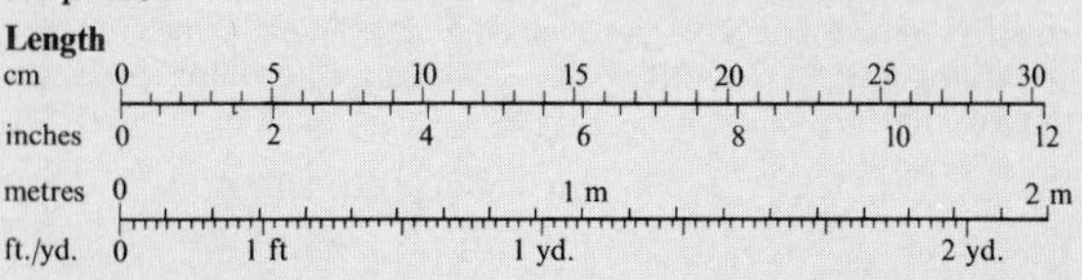

USEFUL EXPRESSIONS

yes/no	**oui/non**
please/thank you	**s'il vous plaît/merci**
excuse me	**excusez-moi**
you're welcome	**je vous en prie**
where/when/how	**où/quand/comment**
how much	**combien**
yesterday/today/tomorrow	**hier/aujourd'hui/demain**
day/week/month/year	**jour/semaine/mois/année**
left/right	**gauche/droite**
up/down	**en haut/en bas**
good/bad	**bon/mauvais**
big/small	**grand/petit**
cheap/expensive	**bon marché/cher**
hot/cold	**chaud/froid**
old/new	**vieux/neuf**
open/closed	**ouvert/fermé**
here/there	**ici/là**
free(vacant)/occupied	**libre/occupé**
early/late	**tôt/tard**
easy/difficult	**facile/difficile**
Does anyone here speak English?	**Y a-t-il quelqu'un ici qui parle anglais?**

beach	**la plage**	*path*	**le chemin**
bridge	**le pont**	*river*	**la rivière**
church	**l'église**	*road*	**la route**
cliff	**la falaise**	*sea*	**la mer**
garden	**le jardin**	*shop*	**le magasin**
hill	**la colline**	*square*	**la place**
house	**la maison**	*station*	**la gare**
lake	**le lac**	*street*	**la rue**
market	**le marché**	*town*	**la ville**
mountain	**la montagne**	*village*	**le village**
museum	**le musée**	*vineyard*	**le vignoble**

Sunday	**dimanche**	*Thursday*	**jeudi**
Monday	**lundi**	*Friday*	**vendredi**
Tuesday	**mardi**	*Saturday*	**samedi**
Wednesday	**mercredi**		

NORTHERN ALGERIA

0 50 100 km
0 50 100 miles
N

MEDITERRA

Aïn T
ALGIERS
Zéralda
Cherchell
Ténès
Tipasa
Bou
Blida
Miliana
Chré
Khemis Miliana
Ech Chlef
Bou Kadir
Mostaganem
Cap Falcon
Mers El Kebir
Arzew
Oued Rhiou
Theniet El Had
Ksar El Boukh
Les Andalouses
ORAN
Relizane
Tissemsilt
Beni Saf
Bou Hanifia
Mascara
Tiaret
Aïn Oussera
Sidi Bel Abbès
Frenda
O. Touil
Moulouya
Nedroma
Tlemcen
Télagh
Aïn Deheb
Maghnia
Saïda
Sidi Abderahmane
Djel
Oujda
Mansourah
Ras-el-Ma
El Hammam
Redjem Demouch
Chergui
Hauts Plateaux
Aflou
El Aricha
Ech
Chott
Bougtob
Brida
Djebel Amour
O. Charef
Mécheria
Aïn Madhi
Laghoua
El Bayadh
Tadjrouna
Naama
Aïn-Ben-Khelil
Brézina
Forthassa-Rharbia
Aïn Sfissifa
El-Abiodh-Sidi-Cheikh
Hassi R'M
Tiout
Aïn Sefra
Oued El Gharbi
Oued Seggueur
Grand Erg Occidental
MOROCCO
Lahmar
Beni-Ounif
Oued Namous
Boukaïs
Ben-Zireg
Oued Zousfana
Béchar
Kenadsa
Taghit

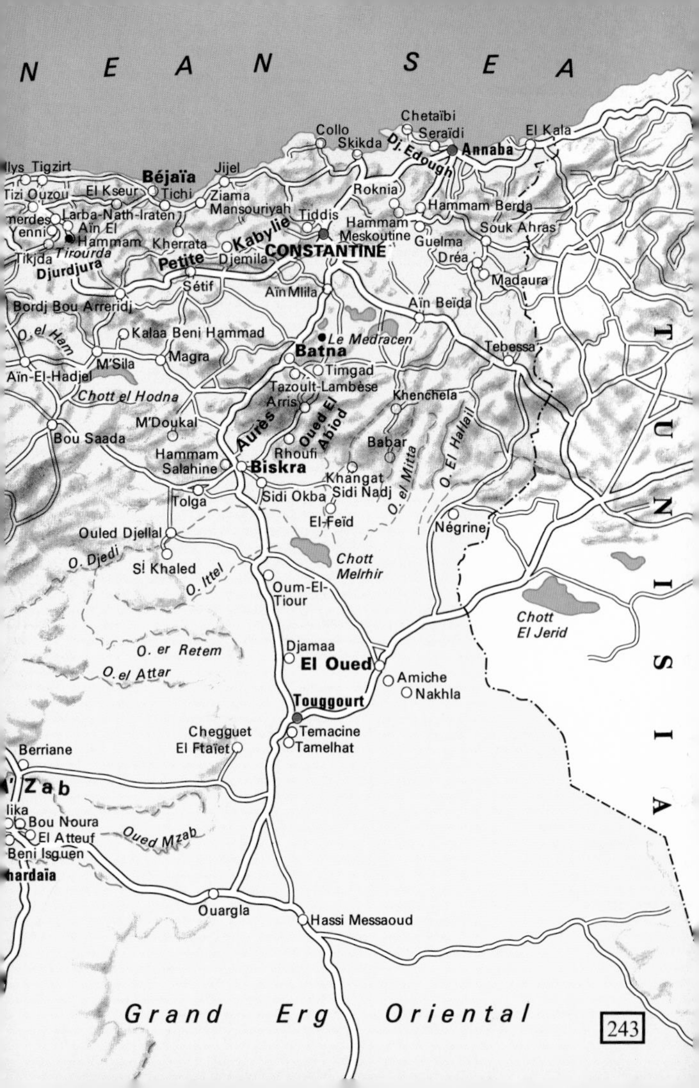
N E A N S E A
Chetaïbi
Seraïdi
Collo
Skikda
Dj. Edough
Annaba
El Kala
Tigzirt
Béjaïa
Jijel
Tizi Ouzou
El Kseur
Tichi
Ziama
Mansouriyah
Larba-Nath-Iraten
Aïn El
Hammam
Tirourda
Kherrata
Tikjda
Djurdjura
Petite
Kabylie
Djemila
Sétif
Tiddis
Roknia
Hammam
Meskoutine
CONSTANTINE
Hammam Berda
Guelma
Souk Ahras
Dréa
Madaura
Aïn Mlila
Aïn Beïda
Bordj Bou Arreridj
O. el Ham
Kalaa Beni Hammad
Le Medracen
Batna
Tebessa
M'Sila
Magra
Aïn-El-Hadjel
Timgad
Tazoult-Lambèse
Arris
Khenchela
Chott el Hodna
M'Doukal
Aurès
Oued El Abiod
Bou Saada
Babar
Hammam
Salahine
Rhoufi
Biskra
Khangat
Sidi Nadj
O. el Mitta
O. El Hallail
Tolga
Sidi Okba
El-Feïd
Négrine
Ouled Djellal
O. Djedi
Si Khaled
O. Ittel
Chott
Melrhir
Oum-El-
Tiour
Chott
El Jerid
O. er Retem
O. el Attar
Djamaa
El Oued
Amiche
Nakhla
Touggourt
Temacine
Tamelhat
Chegguet
El Ftaïet
Berriane
Zab
Bou Noura
El Atteuf
Oued Mzab
Beni Isguen
Ouargla
Hassi Messaoud
Grand Erg Oriental
T U N I S I A

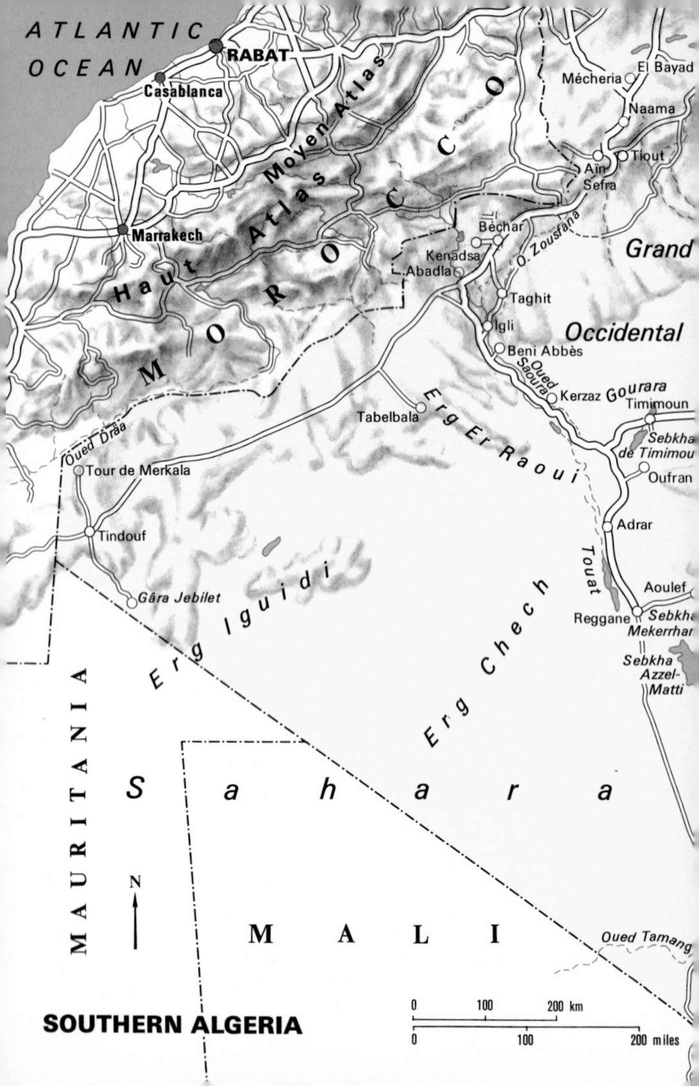

SOUTHERN ALGERIA

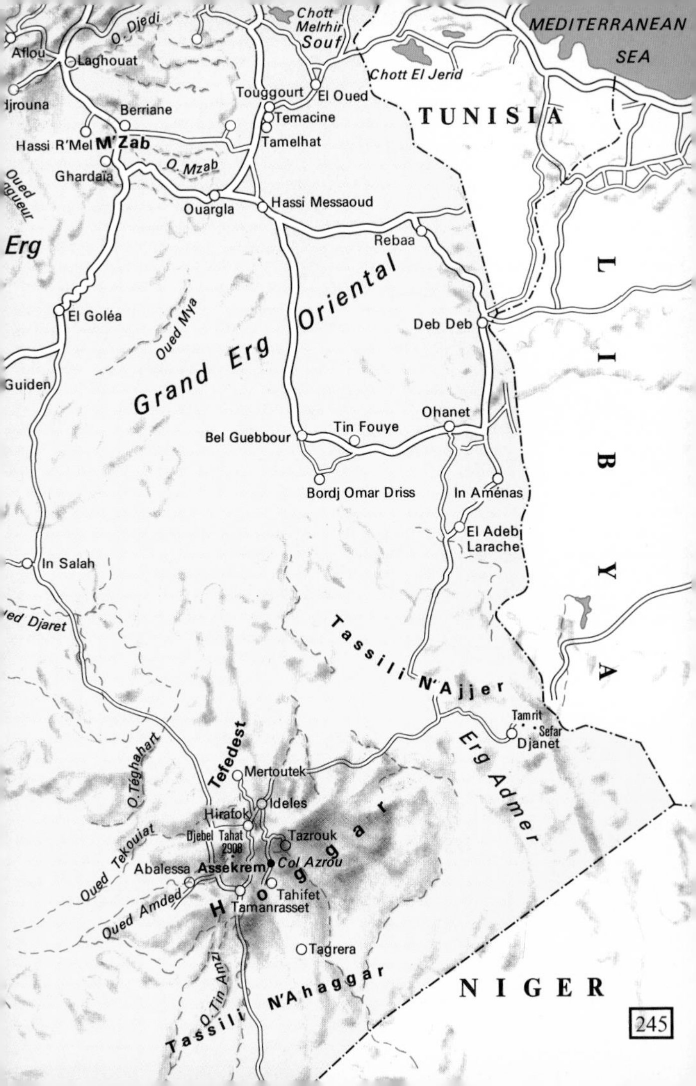
MEDITERRANEAN
SEA
Chott Melrhir
Souf
Chott El Jerid
TUNISIA
L I B Y A
Aflou
Laghouat
O. Djedi
Touggourt
El Oued
Berriane
Temacine
Tamelhat
Hassi R'Mel
M'Zab
Ghardaïa
O. Mzab
Ouargla
Hassi Messaoud
Rebaa
Erg
El Goléa
Oued Mya
Grand Erg Oriental
Deb Deb
Guiden
Ohanet
Tin Fouye
Bel Guebbour
Bordj Omar Driss
In Aménas
El Adeb Larache
In Salah
Tassili N'Ajjer
Tamrit
Sefar
Djanet
Erg Admer
Tefedest
Mertoutek
O. Téghahart
Ideles
Hirafok
Djebel Tahat 2908
Tazrouk
Hoggar
Oued Tekouiat
Abalessa
Assekrem
Col Azrou
Tahifet
Oued Amded
Tamanrasset
Tagrera
O. Tin Amzi
Tassili N'Ahaggar
NIGER

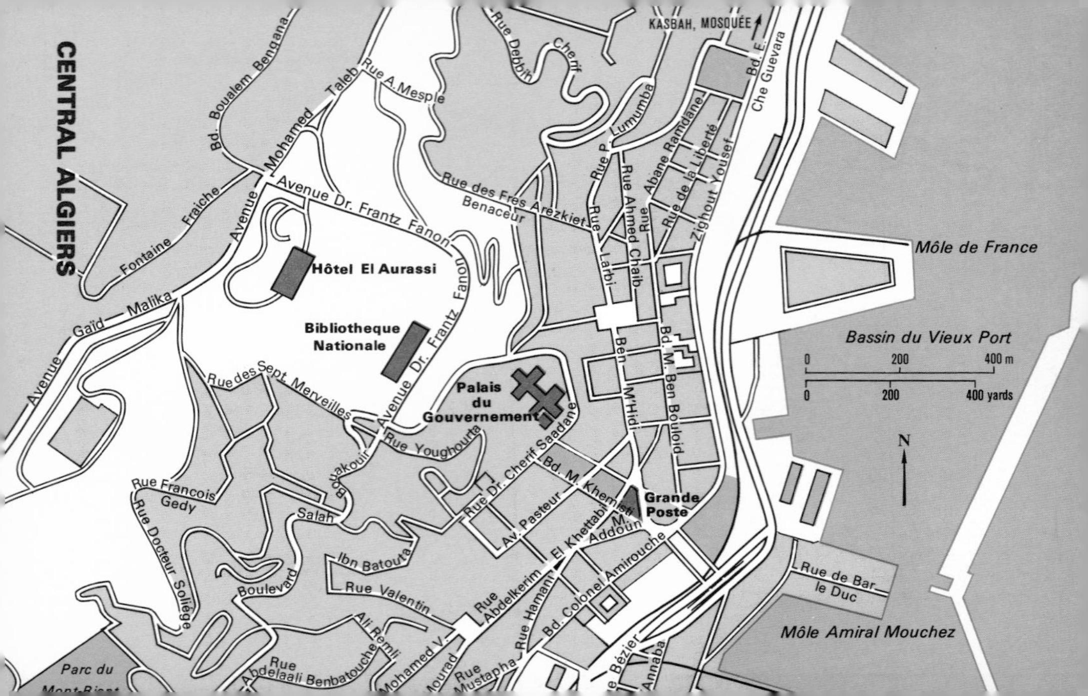

CENTRAL ALGIERS
KASBAH, MOSQUÉE
Bd. Boualem Bengana
Rue A.Mesple
Rue Debbih
Cherif
Taleb
Mohamed
Avenue Fontaine Fraiche
Avenue Gaïd Malika
Avenue Dr. Frantz Fanon
Hôtel El Aurassi
Bibliotheque Nationale
Rue des Fres Arezkiet
Benaceur
Rue P. Lumumba
Rue Larbi Ben M'Hidi
Rue Ahmed Chaib
Rue Abane Ramdane
Rue de la Liberté
Zighout Yousef
Bd. E. Che Guevara
Môle de France
Bassin du Vieux Port
0
200
400 m
0
200
400 yards
N
Bd. M. Ben Bouloid
Rue des Sept. Merveilles
Palais du Gouvernement
Rue Youghourta
Rue Dr. Cherif Saadane
Bd. M. Khemisti
Grande Poste
Av. Pasteur
Bouakouir
Rue Francois Gedy
Rue Docteur Soliége
Salah
Boulevard
Ibn Batouta
Rue Valentin
Rue Abdelkerim El Khettabi
M. Addoun
Bd. Colonel Amirouche
Rue Hamani
Ali Remli
Rue Abdelaali Benbatouche
Mohamed V.
Mourad
Rue Mustapha
Bézier
Annaba
Rue de Bar le Duc
Môle Amiral Mouchez
Parc du

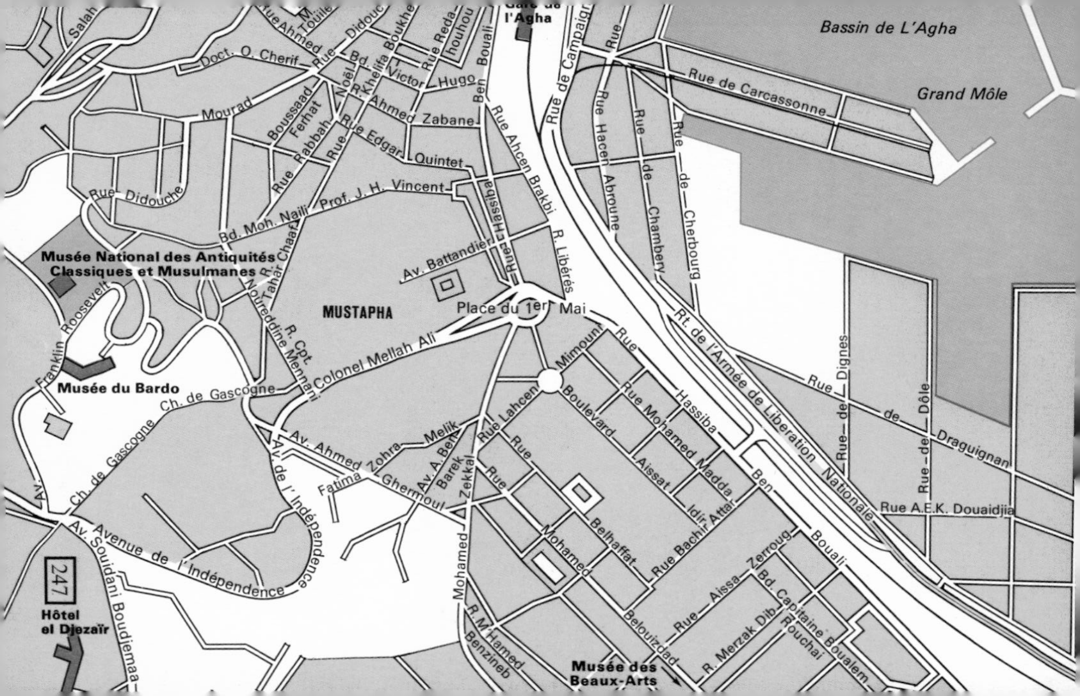

Bassin de L'Agha
Grand Môle
Gare de l'Agha
Rue de Carcassonne
Rue de Campaign
Rue Hacen Abroune
Rue de Chambery
Rue de Cherbourg
Rt. de l'Armée de Libération Nationale
Rue de Dignes
Rue de Dôle
Rue de Draguignan
Rue A.E.K. Douaidjia
Ben Bouali
Rue Ahcen Brakbi
R. Libérés
Rue Hassiba
Av. Battandier
Place du 1er Mai
MUSTAPHA
Colonel Mellah Ali
R. Cpt. Noureddine Mennani
R. Tahar Chaaf
Bd. Moh. Naili
Prof. J. H. Vincent
Rue Edgar Quintet
R. Ahmed Zabane
Victor Hugo
Rue Reda houhou
R. Kheifa Boukhe
Bd. Noël
Rue Rabbah
Boussaad Ferhat
Mourad
Doct. O. Cherif
Rue Ahmed Touile
Rue Didouche
Salah
Musée National des Antiquités Classiques et Musulmanes
Franklin Roosevelt
Musée du Bardo
Ch. de Gascogne
Av. de l'Indépendence
Avenue de l'Indépendence
Av. Souidani Boudjemaa
Av. Ahmed Zohra Fatima
Av. Ahmed Ghermoul
Melik
Av. A. Ben Barek
Rue Lahcen
Rue Mimouni
Boulevard
Rue Mohamed Madda
Hassiba Ben Bouali
Aissat Idir
Rue Bachir Attar
Belhaffat
Mohamed
Rue Zekkal
Mohamed
R. M'Hamed Benzineb
Belouizdad
Rue Aissa Zerroug
Bd. Capitaine Boualem
R. Merzak Dib
Rouchai
Musée des Beaux-Arts
Hôtel el Djezaïr
Av.

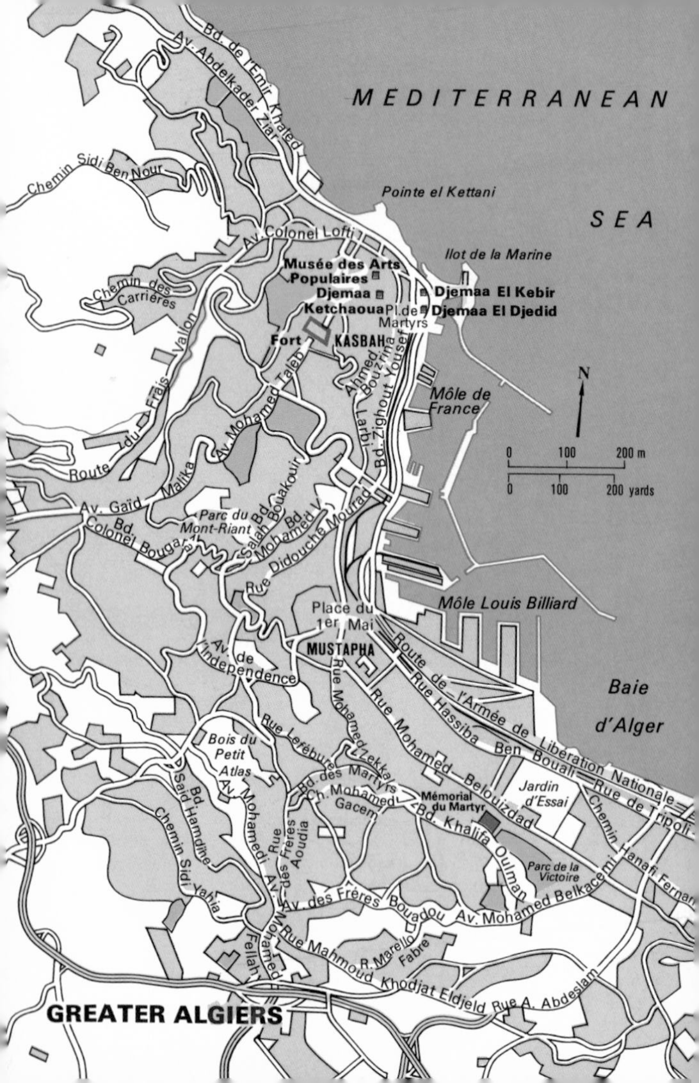
MEDITERRANEAN
SEA
Bd. de l'Emir Khaled
Av. Abdelkader Ziar
Chemin Sidi Ben Nour
Pointe el Kettani
Av. Colonel Lofti
Ilot de la Marine
Musée des Arts Populaires
Djemaa Ketchaoua
Djemaa El Kebir
Pl. de Martyrs
Djemaa El Djedid
Chemin des Carrières
Fort
KASBAH
Route du Frais Valon
Av. Mohamed Taleb
Ahmed Bouzrina
Bd. Zighout Yousef
Larbi
Môle de France
N
0 100 200 m
0 100 200 yards
Av. Gaïd Malika
Bd. Colonel Bougara
Parc du Mont-Riant
Bd. Salah Bouakouir
Bd. Mohamed V
Rue Didouche Mourad
Môle Louis Billiard
Place du 1er Mai
MUSTAPHA
Av. de l'Independence
Route de l'Armée de Libération Nationale
Rue Hassiba Ben Bouali
Baie d'Alger
Rue Mohamed Zekkal
Rue Mohamed Belouizdad
Rue Lefébure
Bois du Petit Atlas
Bd. des Martyrs
Ch. Mohamed Gacem
Mémorial du Martyr
Jardin d'Essai
Rue de Tripoli
Chemin Hanafi Fernane
Bd. Said Hamdine
Chemin Sidi Yahia
Av. Mohamedi
Rue des Frères Aoudia
Bd. Khalifa Oulman
Parc de la Victoire
Av. des Frères Bouadou
Av. Mohamed Belkacemi
Av. Mohamed Fellah
Rue Mahmoud Khodjat Eldjeld
R. Marello
Fabre
Rue A. Abdeslam
GREATER ALGIERS

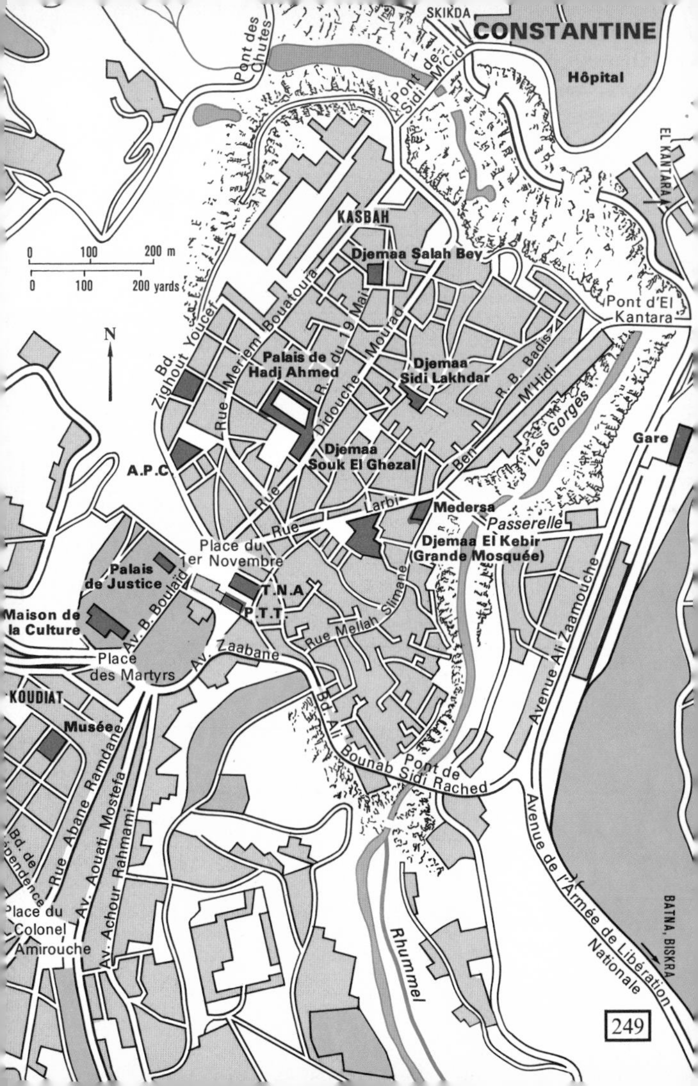
CONSTANTINE
SKIKDA
Hôpital
Pont des Chutes
Pont de Sidi M'Cid
EL KANTARA
KASBAH
Djemaa Salah Bey
Pont d'El Kantara
0 100 200 m
0 100 200 yards
N
Bd. Zighout Youcef
Rue Meriem Bouatoura
R. du 19 Mai
Didouche Mourad
Palais de Hadj Ahmed
Djemaa Sidi Lakhdar
R. B. Badis
M'Hidi
Ben
Les Gorges
Gare
Djemaa Souk El Ghezal
A.P.C.
Rue Larbi
Medersa
Passerelle
Djemaa El Kebir (Grande Mosquée)
Place du 1er Novembre
Palais de Justice
T.N.A.
P.T.T.
Maison de la Culture
Av. B. Boulaïd
Rue Mellah Slimane
Avenue Ali Zaamouche
Place des Martyrs
Av. Zaabane
KOUDIAT
Musée
Bd. Ali Bounab
Pont de Sidi Rached
Rue Abane Ramdane
Av. Aouati Mostefa
Av. Achour Rahmami
Place du Colonel Amirouche
Rhummel
Avenue de l'Armée de Libération Nationale
BATNA, BISKRA

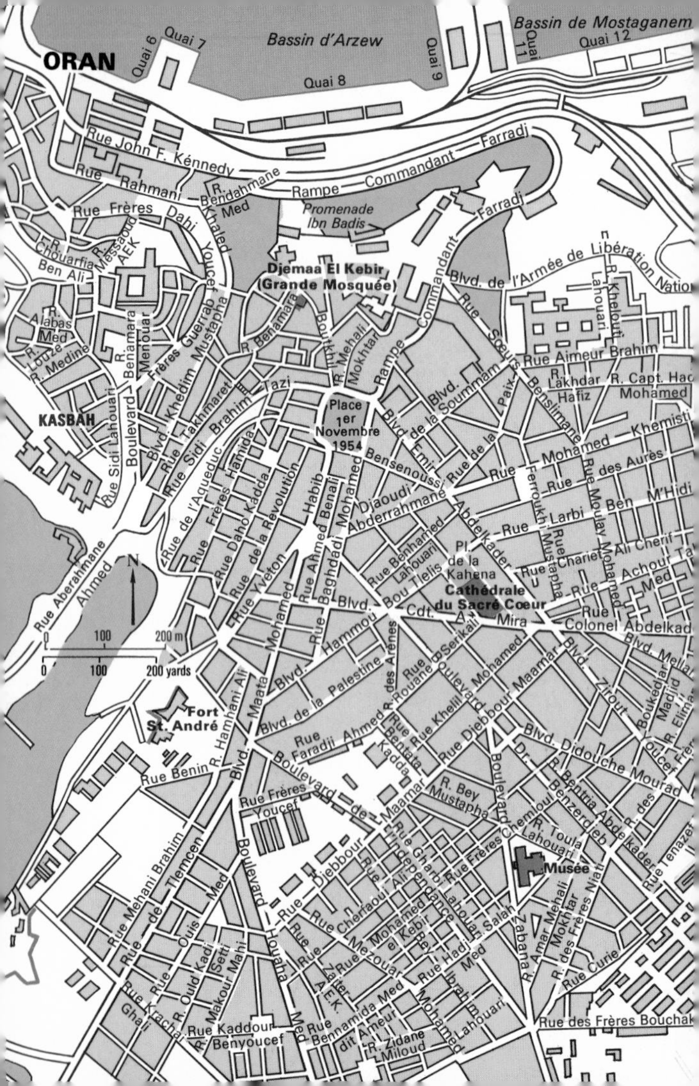
ORAN
Bassin d'Arzew
Bassin de Mostaganem
Quai 6
Quai 7
Quai 8
Quai 9
Quai 11
Quai 12
Rue John F. Kennedy
Rampe Commandant Farradj
Promenade Ibn Badis
Djemaa El Kebir (Grande Mosquée)
Blvd. de l'Armée de Libération Nation
KASBAH
Place 1er Novembre 1954
Cathédrale du Sacré Coeur
Fort St. André
Musée
Rue Aimeur Brahim
Rue Sidi Brahim
Rue de l'Aqueduc
Rue de la Revolution
Rue Larbi Ben M'Hidi
Rue des Aurès
Blvd. de la Soummam
Blvd. de la Palestine
Boulevard de l'Indépendance
Blvd. Didouche Mourad
Blvd. Zirout Youcef
Rue Aberahmane Ahmed
Rue Benin
Rue de Tlemcen
Rue Mehani Brahim
Rue Mohamed Khemisti
Boulevard Benamara
Rue Sidi Lahouari
Blvd. Hammou Mohamed
Blvd. Mohamed Benali
Blvd. Emir Abdelkader
Rue Colonel Abdelkader
Rue des Frères Bouchak
Rue Curie
Rue Zabana
Rue Ferroukhi Mustapha
Rue Moulay Mohamed
Rue Benslimane
0 100 200 m
0 100 200 yards
N

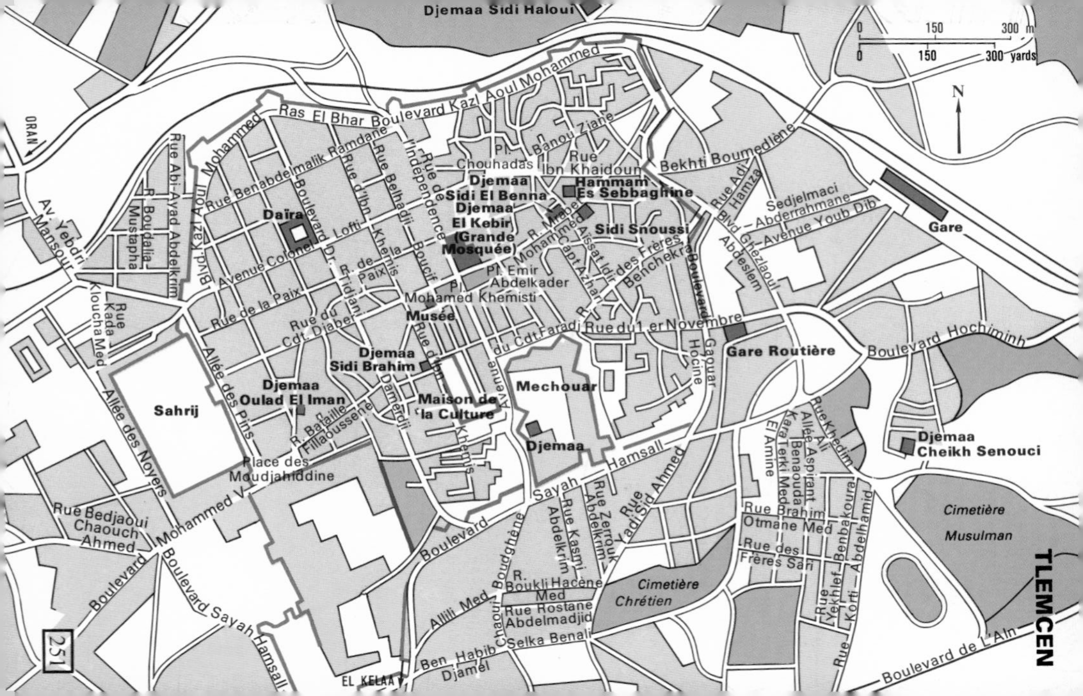
TLEMCEN
0
150
300 m
0
150
300 yards
N
Gare
Djemaa Cheikh Senouci
Cimetière Musulman
Boulevard de L'Aïn
Boulevard Hochiminh
Rue Kotti Abdelhamid
Rue Benbakoura
Rue Yekhlef
Rue Khedim Ali
Allée Aspirant Benaouda
Kara Terki Med
El Amine
Rue Brahim Otmane Med
Rue des Frères Sari
Gare Routière
Sedjelmaci Abderrahmane
Avenue Youb Dib
Blvd Ghezlaoui Abdeslem
Rue Adi Hamza
Bekhti Boumediene
Boulevard Gaouar Hocine
Rue du 1er Novembre
Frères Benchekra
Rue Lt Sid Ahmed
Cimetière Chrétien
Hammam Es Sebbaghine
Sidi Snoussi
Rue Zerrouk Abdelkrim
Rue Kasmi Abdelkrim
Mechouar
Djemaa
Rue Aïssat Idir
Capt Azhar
Rue Ibn Khaldoun
Rue Banou Ziane
Boulevard Kazi Aoul Mohammed
Djemaa Sidi Halouï
Pl. Chouhadas
Djemaa Sidi El Benna
Djemaa El Kebir (Grande Mosquée)
Pl. Emir Abdelkader
Mohamed Khemisti
Rue du Cdt. Faradj
Avenue Hamsall Sayah
R. Boukli Hacène Med
Rue Rostane Abdelmadjid
Selka Benali
Rue Boudghène
Chaouï Allili Med
Ben Habib Djamel
Boulevard
Khemis
Maison de la Culture
Musée
Rue d'Ibn
Rue de l'Indépendence
Boucif
Rue Belhadji
Rue d'Ibn Khemis
Rue Ramdane
Ras El Bhar Boulevard
Lofti
R. de la Paix
Tidjani
Djemaa Sidi Brahim
Damerdji
Dr.
Rue du Cdt. Djaber
Boulevard Benabdemalik
Colonel
Daïra
Djemaa Oulad El Iman
R. Bataille
R. Fillaoussene
Place des Moudjahiddine
Rue de la Paix
Avenue
Allée des Pins
Blvd. Kazi Aoul Mohammed
Sahrij
Mohammed V
Boulevard Sayah Hamsall
Boulevard
EL KELAA
Rue Abi-Ayad Abdelkrim
R. Boudalia Mustapha
Rue Kada Kloucha Med
Allée des Noyers
Rue Bedjaoui Chaouch Ahmed
Av. Yebdri Mansour
ORAN

INDEX

An asterisk (*) next to a page number indicates a map reference. Where there is more than one set of page references, the one in bold type refers to the main entry. For the index to Practical Information, see pp. 216–217.